The Death of Lorca

The Death of Lorca

IAN GIBSON

A Howard Greenfeld Book

J. PHILIP O'HARA, INC.
CHICAGO

lly acknowledge permission granted for the use of extracts from the following publications:

The Flowering Rifle by Roy Campbell: the Longman Group Limited.

Death in the Morning by Helen Nicholson (Baroness Zglinitski): Peter Davies Limited.

The Face of Spain by Gerald Brenan: Hamish Hamilton Limited (originally published by Turnstile Press Limited).

The Spanish Labyrinth by Gerald Brenan: Cambridge University Press.

The Origins of Modern Spain by J. B. Trend: Cambridge University Press.

The Spanish Civil War by Hugh Thomas: Eyre & Spottiswoode (Publishers) Limited; Harper & Row, Publishers, Inc.

Alfonso the Sage and Other Spanish Essays by J. B. Trend: Constable & Company Limited.

Plate No. 1, by courtesy of Don José García Carrillo.

No. 25 by courtesy of Dott. Enzo Cobelli.

Nos. 5, 7, 8, 10, 11, 15, 16, 17, 18, 19, 21, 23, 24 by Ian Gibson.

J. Philip O'Hara, Inc. 20 East Huron, Chicago 60611. Published simultaneously in Canada by Van Nostrand Reinhold Ltd., Scarborough, Ontario.

ISBN: 0-87955-306-5   LC Number: 72-95426
First Printing   E

For Carole

CONTENTS

ILLUSTRATIONS

Illustrations appearing between pages 112 and 113.

17. Víznar: the square, with the entrance to Archbishop Moscoso's palace on the right.

18. The entrance to Archbishop Moscoso's palace, district headquarters of the Falange in Víznar.

19. *La Colonia* where Lorca and other prisoners scheduled for execution were held. Ainadamar can be seen in the background.

20. *Ideal,* 16 August 1936: "Yesterday the Falange celebrated a solemn open-air mass in Víznar."

21. Víznar: the *barranco,* showing the outline of one of the graves.

22. The death certificate of Dióscoro Galindo González, who was buried in the same grave with Lorca.

23. Ainadamar or Fuente Grande.

24. Fuente Grande: the bungalows which now stand on the site of the ancient olive grove where Lorca was shot and buried.

25. Federico García Lorca's death certificate.

26. A stamp bearing Lorca's portrait issued in the Republican Zone in 1938.

Plans and Maps on pages 87 and 114.

1. Plan illustrating the principal streets and buildings mentioned in connection with Lorca's arrest.

2. Map of Víznar showing the places mentioned in connection with Lorca's execution.

ACKNOWLEDGEMENTS

This book could not have been written without the help of many people. To begin with I must thank my parents, Mr and Mrs Cecil Gibson of Dublin, whose generosity enabled me to spend a full year in Granada. Thanks are also due to The Queen's University of Belfast, which gave me a grant to return to Spain in 1967 to complete my research. Throughout the book I draw on the work of Gerald Brenan, Claude Couffon and Jean-Louis Schonberg, and am happy to acknowledge this debt here. My friend Mr Daniel de W. Rogers of Durham University made valuable, chastening criticisms of an early draft of the book, and Mr Herbert R. Southworth kindly put at my disposal his vast knowledge of the Spanish Civil War and suggested numerous improvements. Regrettably I cannot name the many people in Granada who gave me help and encouragement: to do so might be to jeopardise their safety. Three Granadine friends whose contribution to the book was fundamental have recently died, however, and I remember them here with deep affection and gratitude: Don Miguel Cerón, Don Antonio Pérez Funes and Don Rafael Jofré García. Among the many other friends and acquaintances whose assistance made my task easier it is a pleasure to thank Mme Marcelle Auclair, Dr James Dickie, Mr Bernard Adams, Dott. Enzo Cobelli, Don Manuel Angeles Ortiz, Don Rafael Martínez Nadal, M. Robert Marrast, M. Paul Werrie, Dr James Casey, Mr and Mrs S. C. B. Elliott, Mlle Marie Laffranque, Don José Luis Cano, Mr Patrick Teskey, Mr John Beattie, Dr Roger Walker, Miss S. M. Bull of the British Embassy in Mexico, Mr Leonard Downes, O.B.E., of the British Council in the same city, Dr Philip Silver, Dr E. Inman Fox, Professor and Mrs Sanford Shepard, Mr David Platt, Mr Jeffrey Simmons, Mr Howard Greenfeld and Mr Adrian Shire. Mr Neville Rigg and Mr Bertie Graham did valiant work in preparing the photographs for publication, Miss Eileen Duncan kindly drew the plan and map and my friend and colleague Professor Anthony Watson made many useful suggestions. Finally, how can I thank my wife, to whom this book is dedicated? Without her unfailing support the strain of the investigation might have proved too much.

INTRODUCTION

In the summer of 1965 my wife and I settled down to live in Granada for a year. My intention was to write a doctoral thesis on the great Granadine poet Federico García Lorca, whose work had influenced me deeply as an undergraduate.

One evening that autumn we were invited to a party at a friend's house, during which Gerardo Rosales, a poet and painter who has since died, came up to me and exclaimed: 'You foreigners, you're all the same! You come here to find out about Federico's death, yet you don't know a damn thing about what really happened in Granada in 1936. Do you realise, for example, that there weren't even fifty Fascists in the town before the war broke out?' My embarrassment was intense, and I tried to explain that my interest lay in Lorca's poetry. But Gerardo insisted. I had come to investigate the poet's death, and that was that.

Over the following months similar situations arose until, one day, I decided to accept the inevitable. I would shelve the thesis and write the book that I was already assumed to be writing.

Before we arrived in Granada I had reached the conclusion that much remained to be said about Lorca's death. Several accounts of it had come to my attention, notably those by Gerald Brenan, Claude Couffon and Jean-Louis Schonberg, and I had been struck by the frequent inconsistencies and contradictions which a comparison of their narratives revealed. Clearly a serious reconsideration of the whole question was required.

Huge estimates for the number of *granadinos* executed by the Nationalists on the outbreak of the Civil War were constantly being suggested to me; other extraordinary claims were being put forward on all sides; dozens of versions describing how Lorca had died were circulating, and one wondered where to begin. I was convinced of only one thing: that Lorca's death would have to be studied in the general context of the repression, and not as an isolated event.

I was aware that my researches, to be successful, would have to be carried out on two levels. First, starting with the indispensable pieces by Brenan, Couffon and Schonberg, I would have to read every article, book, newspaper or other document that could throw light, however dim, on Lorca's death and the Granada repression. Accordingly I drew up as complete a preliminary bibliography as I could, and sent off for

material that had appeared all over the world, often in the most in-
accessible places. It was a slow business, but little by little photo-copies,
books and cuttings began to trickle in, leading me in turn to other
publications whose existence I could not have suspected.

Secondly, I would have to track down those people who might be
able to furnish me with first-hand accounts of the repression and
Lorca's last days.

This, I well knew, would be more difficult, not only because of the
Andalusians' vivid imaginations and gift for spontaneous elaborations
of the truth, but also because I sensed that people were still afraid to talk
openly with strangers about the war, and that the police were keeping
a close eye on what was going on in the town.

Gradually some of these problems were overcome. Through a small
group of friends who had known Lorca intimately, I met an increasing
number of *granadinos* who had experienced the early months of the
rising in their home town and could give me detailed, verifiable
information on the period. Without a car it would have been impossible
to follow up the clues that came out of these discussions: often, on
being given a lead, I would drive to some village in the province in
search of a vaguely remembered witness who might be willing to talk,
only to discover that he or she had moved to Málaga, Madrid, South
America—or the local cemetery. On other occasions I was luckier.

My investigation is introduced by an account of the political situation obtaining in Spain in the years that led up to the Civil War, for I
believe that without this background knowledge the reader un-
acquainted with the period would be at a loss to understand fully what
happened in Granada in 1936.

I have taken the opportunity here to correct the many deficiencies
of the original Spanish-language edition of my book,* and have
incorporated a considerable amount of new information which has
come to light since 1971.

Ian Gibson
London
1973

---

* Ian Gibson, *La represión nacionalista de Granada en 1936 y la muerte de Federico
García Lorca* (Paris, Ruedo ibérico, 1971).

Que fue en Granada el crimen
sabed—pobre ¡Granada!—en su Granada . . .

AntoniMo achado, *El crimen fue en Granada,* 1936.

The amazing amount of paper wasted over this almost unique
stain on Nationalist arms is typical of the Anglo-Saxon Press.
When the Nationalists entered Granada the unbelievable baboon-
eries perpetrated by the Reds made them trigger-happy as they
rounded up and shot all corrupters of children, known perverts
and sexual cranks. A natural reaction, considering that the week
before the Reds had slaughtered and tortured anyone who was
under suspicion of any sort of decency at all. Maeztu, Calvo Sotelo,
Muñoz Seca, Padre Eusebio (about to be canonised) and Antonio
[sic] Primo de Rivera were all killed, not for their vices but for
their virtues. They were intellectuals on a higher scale, and died
better than the cowardly Lorca. If the author of this poem, a
better poet than Lorca, so Borges the leading South American
critic points out, had not been resourceful, he would have died,
like Lorca, but at the hands of the Reds.

Roy Campbell, footnote to his *Flowering Rifle. A poem from the
Battlefield of Spain,* 1939 (1957 edition).

Despedida

Si muero,
dejad el balcón abierto.

El niño come naranjas.
(Desde mi balcón lo veo.)

El segador siega el trigo.
(Desde mi balcón lo siento.)

¡Si muero,
dejad el balcón abierto!

Federico García Lorca, *Canciones,* 1927.

ONE

Granada and Federico

'Give him alms, woman, for nothing in
life can equal the agony of being
blind in Granada.'

F. A. DE ICAZA

Westwards from the historic Andalusian town of Granada there
stretches a fertile plain, the *vega*,* which is nourished by the rivers
Darro and Genil that descend from the snows of the Sierra Nevada,
the highest mountain range in the peninsula. The *vega* is one of the
most intensively cultivated regions in Spain, and was described
long ago by an Arab author as being 'superior in extent and
fertility to the Ghauttah, or the valley of Damascus'.[1]

With the fall of Granada to Ferdinand and Isabella in 1492 and
the expulsion of the Moors from this last Islamic enclave in Spain,
the agriculture of the plain declined and it was only at the end
of the nineteenth century, with the discovery that sugar-beet could
be grown there easily and profitably, that its exploitation began
again in earnest.

Among the tracts of land in the *vega* that benefited most from
the new activity was the Soto de Roma, a huge estate along the
banks of the Genil which had been granted by the Spanish
Government to the Duke of Wellington in recognition of his

* *Vega*, a watered valley between hills.

services in driving the French from the country. Throughout the nineteenth century the Soto, which the Duke himself never deigned to visit, had lain abandoned and untilled, but now it suddenly revived as its English administrators became aware of its economic potential. Villages started to spring up all over the estate, and after a few years it held a population of several thousand people.

In one of these villages, Fuente Vaqueros, Federico García Lorca was born on 5 June 1898. In that same year there took place the 'Disaster' in which Spain was deprived of her last overseas colonies—Cuba, Puerto Rico and the Philippines—in a humiliatingly brief and decisive encounter with the United States Navy.

Lorca's grandparents were all natives of the province of Granada and his father, Federico García Rodríguez, a successful farmer, was one of a family of eight or nine children who grew up in the *vega* and were deeply influenced by its way of life. The poet's paternal grandfather, Enrique García Rodríguez, and his three brothers, were renowned for their artistic improvisations, pranks and somewhat extravagant personalities. Enrique is reputed to have composed a sonnet in which he warned the reader against bad translations of Victor Hugo, whom he idolised; Federico played the guitar and died in obscure circumstances in Paris; Narciso drew well and travelled among the villages of the plain teaching the peasants to read; while Baldomero, the most original character of the four brothers, had a superb voice and sang *jaberas*, accompanying himself on the *bandurria*, better than anyone in the province.* It was small wonder that the young Federico adored his 'Uncle' Baldomero and wanted to resemble him.

Of the poet's numerous aunts and uncles on his father's side, only Luis, who attended a seminary, received a college education. The Garcías were all 'naturals' and their musical and artistic abilities, which Federico inherited, derived not from formal instruction but from their assimilation of the rich traditions and rhythms of the *vega*. Before he was four Federico knew dozens of folk songs by heart (many of them would later reappear, trans-

---

* *Jabera*, a flamenco song similar to a *malagueña*. The *bandurria* (from which the English 'bandore' derives) is a form of lute.

formed, in his poetry and plays) and had been given his first guitar lessons by his Aunt Isabel.

Unlike the ebullient Garcías, Lorca's mother, Vicenta Lorca Romero, was quiet and serious. She was born in Granada in 1870[2] and had been a teacher before becoming Don Federico's second wife in 1897. The poet was very fond of his mother, and later claimed that he inherited his intelligence from her and his passionate temperament from his father.*

The human and natural environment of these early years made an indelible impression on the future poet's sensibility. Later he would say:

I love the countryside. I feel myself linked to it in all my emotions. My oldest childhood memories have the flavour of the earth. The meadows, the fields, have done wonders for me. The wild animals of the countryside, the livestock, the people living on the land, all these are suggestive in a way that very few people understand. I recall them now exactly as I knew them in my childhood. Were this not so I could never have written Blood Wedding. My very earliest emotional experiences are associated with the land and the work on the land. This is why there is at the basis of my life what psycho-analysts would call an 'agrarian complex'.[3]

And again:

My whole childhood was centred on the village. Shepherds, fields, sky, solitude. Total simplicity. I'm often surprised when people think that the things in my work are daring improvisations of my own, a poet's audacities. Not at all. They're authentic details, and seem strange to a lot of people because it's not often that we approach life in such a simple, straightforward fashion: looking and listening. Such an easy thing, isn't it? [. . .] I have a huge storehouse of childhood recollections in which I can hear the people speaking. This is poetic memory, and I trust it implicitly.[4]

* In Spanish surnames the father's name is followed by that of the mother. Often the mother's name is dropped, but if the patronym is more common than the mother's name, as is the case with Federico García Lorca, the tendency is to use the latter.

Unlike J. M. Synge, whose appropriation of the folk language of the west of Ireland was the result of conscious study, Federico was himself 'of the people', for in the *vega* no linguistic and few social distinctions separated wealthy and poor, peasants and land-owners. Lorca inherited all the vigour of a speech that springs from the earth and expresses itself with extraordinary spontaneity. One has only to hear the inhabitants of the Granadine *vega* talk, and observe their colourful use of imagery, to realise that the metaphorical language of Lorca's drama and poetry, which seems so strikingly original, is rooted in an ancient, collective awareness of nature in which all things—trees, mountains, horses, the moon, rivers, flowers, human beings—are closely interrelated and inter-dependent. The landscape of much of Lorca's work is anthropo-morphic and participates in the human action: the moon may suddenly materialise before a frightened child's eyes as a deathlike woman dressed in white, the leaves of an olive tree turn pale with fear, or the first light of morning become a thousand glass tambourines which 'wound' the dawn. It is a world of strange metamorphoses, a mythical world where mysterious voices whisper in the night, the world of the first kiss and 'the first dead bird on the branch'.[5]

In 1909 Lorca's family moved from the village to Granada to see to the children's education. This was to be the second crucial stage in the poet's development when his experience of the town, with its dense historical and literary associations, fused with the childhood vision of the world he had assimilated in the *vega* to form a unique synthesis of culture of the blood and culture of the intellect.

Although by 1909 the entrepreneurs were already at work in Granada, demolishing Moorish buildings, widening streets and generally trying to make the 'living ruin', as Baedeker had called it a few years earlier[6], more modern and more 'European', the old quarters crowding the Albaicín and Alhambra Hills had changed little since the early nineteenth century, when Granada had caught the imagination of the Romantics, avidly in search of the exotic.

In 1829 Victor Hugo had exclaimed:

In 1829 Victor Hugo had exclaimed:
L'Alhambra! L'Alhambra! palais que les Génies
Ont doré comme un rêve et rempli d'harmonies,
Forteresse aux créneaux festonnés et croulants,
Où l'on entend la nuit de magiques syllabes,
Quand la lune, à travers les mille arceaux arabes,
  Sème les murs de trèfles blancs![7]

and shortly afterwards Washington Irving settled down to live in the town. His *Legends of the Alhambra* (1832), much read at the time, were to establish the Moorish palace as one of the most admired monuments in Europe. Irving was followed by scores of other writers and aristocratic visitors, many of whom felt compelled to record their impressions in print. Among these were Henry Inglis, Richard Ford (whose famous *Handbook for Travellers in Spain* remains one of the best books on the country ever written)[8], Dumas *père*, George Borrow, Théophile Gautier and Prosper Mérimée. The Alhambra's attractions were widely advertised in the exquisite engravings by Gustave Doré and David Roberts, and poems evoking Granada's Moorish past (with a proliferation of Lindaraxas, Zaydas, Aixas, sultans and weeping fountains) also became fashionable.

Nor did the town escape the attentions of foreign musicians. During the winter of 1845 Glinka spent several months in Granada. He struck up a friendship with a celebrated local guitarist, Francisco Rodríguez Murciano, who took the Russian to the Albaicín* and introduced him to the *cante jondo* of the gypsies— the primitive form of the modern *flamenco*. Glinka, fascinated by the possibilities for his own work afforded by Spanish folk music, began the experiments that led to his *Jota aragonesa* (1845) and *Summer Night in Madrid* (1848), which in turn sparked off both a new interest in folk song in Russia and a spate of Spanish-inspired pieces by foreign and national composers. As Lorca said in a

---

* The old quarter of the Albaicín, through which one must climb to reach the Sacromonte, where the gypsies live, takes its name from the Moorish refugees who settled there in 1227 when the city of Baeza, in the north of Andalusia, fell to the Christians.

lecture during the Cante Jondo Festival which he and Manuel de Falla organised in Granada in 1922:

And so you see how the sad modulations and grave orientalism of our *cante* are imparted by Granada to Moscow, and how the melancholy of the Vela* is echoed by the mysterious bells of the Kremlin.[9]

But only the delicate impressionism of Claude Debussy, who had heard a group of Spaniards sing *cante jondo* at the Paris Exhibition in 1900, was adequate to transform the idiom into something genuinely original and subtle. However successful his orchestral *Iberia*, it is in his evocative piano compositions *La Puerta del Vino* (the prelude was inspired by a picture postcard sent to him by Falla) and particularly *La Soirée dans Grenade* that Debussy most perfectly captured the hidden essence of Spanish music.

Hugo had noted, with a *frisson* of delight, that the walls of the Alhambra were crumbling, and Richard Ford tells us that the palace was allowed to fall into ruins after it had been occupied by the French under Sebastiani. He complains that

Few *Granadinos* ever go there or understand the all-absorbing interest, the concentrated devotion, which it incites in the stranger. Familiarity has bred in them the contempt with which the Bedouin regards the ruins of Palmyra, insensible to present beauty as to past poetry and romance.[10]

Sixty years later, when the Garcías moved to the town, the average *granadino's* attitude to his artistic heritage had changed little.

In Granada Federico worked for the examination that would afford him entry to the University, where he eventually matriculated in 1915. But he disliked bookwork and his real passion was for music, which he studied with Don Antonio Segura, an old *maestro* who admired Verdi and had himself written an opera, *The Daughters of Jephthah*, which was never produced. Don Antonio was a sensitive teacher and under his guidance Lorca became a first-rate pianist and wrote several compositions for the piano,

---

* The massive Vela Tower stands on the projecting prow of the Alhambra's fortifications and looks out over the plain. Its bell, known as 'La Vela', is rung at intervals during the night to regulate the *vega's* complicated irrigation procedures.

which do not, unfortunately, seem to have survived. Segura died in 1916, however, and Federico's parents decided against the musical career for which their son had seemed destined.

In the same year, and again in 1917, Lorca travelled through Castile, León and Galicia with Don Martín Domínguez Berrueta, Professor of the Theory of Art at Granada University, who encouraged him to write his first book, *Impressions and Landscapes* (Granada, 1918). This work expressed in poetic prose the author's reactions to the decaying towns, monasteries and rolling *meseta* of Old Spain. There can be little doubt that Don Martín, who died in 1920, exerted a decisive influence on his pupil by coaxing his talents into a literary channel.

The atmosphere in Granada at the time, moreover, greatly favoured the development of artistic abilities, and the town was enjoying exceptional conditions that would never be repeated. Its pattern of existence remained undisturbed by a World War that, so far as it was concerned, was being fought only on the front pages of the local newspapers; living was still cheap; there were no transistor radios, no coaches full of tourists grinding up the Cuesta de Gomeres and choking the elms of the Alhambra Wood with poisonous fumes. There was time to talk, to read, to listen to the murmuring of Granada's innumerable fountains, to contemplate the most consistently marvellous sunsets in Spain. Indeed, contemplation of beauty—what Joyce once called 'the luminous, silent stasis of aesthetic pleasure'—is the attitude of mind most readily engendered by Granada. Lorca, who perceived this better than anyone, would say:

Granada is an easy-going town, made for the contemplative life, a town in which, better than anywhere else, the lover writes his sweetheart's name on the ground. The hours are longer and sweeter there than in any other Spanish town. Granada has complicated sunsets composed of extraordinary colours which you feel will never fade . . . Granada has any amount of good ideas but is incapable of acting on them. Only in such a town, with its inertia and tranquillity, can there exist those exquisite contemplators of water, temperatures and sunsets that we find in Granada. The *granadino* is surrounded by Nature's most lavish display, but he never reaches out to it.[11]

Without the added stimulus of contact with kindred spirits, Lorca's adolescence in this contemplative paradise might have been less productive, but fortunately there was in Granada at the time a group of people passionately devoted to the arts.

Chief among them was Manuel de Falla, who had fallen in love with the gardens, perspectives and fountains of Granada in 1916 and come to live here permanently three years later in a modest *carmen** just below the Alhambra.

There was Fernando de los Ríos, Professor of Political Law in the University of Granada, a great teacher, socialist, scholar and humanist, who exerted a profound influence on his students, and whose daughter later married Lorca's brother.

Other able university teachers in the town included Martín Domínguez Berrueta (with whom Federico made his trips to Castile), the historian José Palanco Romero, and Alfonso Gámir Sandoval, an anglophile who was a close friend of the British Consul, William Davenhill.†

There were the painters Manuel Ortiz and Ismael G. de la Serna, the art historian Antonio Gallego Burín (whose *Guide to Granada* is still one of the most useful), the sculptor Juan Cristóbal, Constantino Ruiz Carnero, who became editor of the liberal daily newspaper *El Defensor de Granada*, the poets Alberto A. de Cienfuegos and Manuel de Góngora, Angel Barrios the guitarist and founder of the well-known Trio Iberia, Andrés Segovia (who had come to Granada from his native Jaén), the literary critic José Fernández Montesinos, who died recently in the United States after a distinguished academic career, the engraver Hermenegildo Lanz, the brilliant aesthete Francisco Soriano Lapresa, the cultured dilettante Miguel Cerón (one of Falla's most intimate friends in Granada), the belligerent journalist José Mora Guarnido, who later wrote a vivid account of these days in his book on Lorca[12], Miguel Pizarro and many other original and often weird figures.

* The word *carmen*, from the Arabic, denotes a hillside villa with an enclosed garden hidden by high walls from inquisitive eyes, and corresponds to the Islamic notion of the inner paradise, a reflection of heaven.

† In *South from Granada* (London, Hamish Hamilton, 1957), Gerald Brenan has given us a delightful account of the eccentric English colony in Granada in the early 1920s.

The younger members of this talented group met regularly in the Café Alameda (now a farm machinery store) in the Plaza del Campillo and their *tertulia** became affectionately known as the *rinconcillo* ('little corner') because a recess at the back of the café was reserved for their use each evening. When visiting lecturers and artists arrived in Granada, the 'rinconcillistas' would take them to the Café Alameda before showing them the Alhambra, or initiating them into the delights of Granada's hidden gardens, which so few tourists ever see. Among these privileged guests were Wanda Landowska, Arthur Rubenstein, H. G. Wells, Rudyard Kipling and John Trend.

Trend, who was to become Professor of Spanish at Cambridge, met the Café Alameda confraternity in 1919 and afterwards described his introduction to Lorca. He had gone that evening with Falla to a concert at the Arts Centre, after which they were invited to a party in an Albaicín *carmen*. Late in the night a local poet was called on to recite and, to the general amusement of the guests, forgot his lines and withdrew in confusion.

Then we were hushed and a rather shy youth recited. He did not declaim, but spoke in a soft, warm, eager voice: *la obscura, cálida, turbia, inolvidable voz de Federico García Lorca*, Gerardo Diego said long afterwards. It was a simple ballad with striking but easily intelligible imagery. 'Who is it?' 'Federico García Lorca. You must meet him.' The evening ended after 4 a.m., with the poet and myself, arm in arm, helping one another down the steep streets of the Albaicín to the main street at the bottom of the Alhambra Hill.[13]

Although Trend realised that Granada was passing through a unique period in its artistic history, he never stayed long enough in the town to form a close relationship with the 'rinconcillistas', and may not have met a member of the group who had a significant influence on Lorca: Francisco ('Paquito') Soriano.

Soriano, as has been indicated, was an aesthete, a sort of Granadine Oscar Wilde who enjoyed private means and took

* A *tertulia* is a regular meeting of friends in a café, and an indispensable part of Spanish life.

pleasure in offending the town's rigid Catholics by his flamboyance and easy morals. He was undoubtedly one of the cleverest men in Granada at the time, and his house in Puentezuelas Street contained a magnificent library of books on a wide variety of esoteric subjects and in many languages, which he lent generously to Lorca and the other members of the *tertulia* in the Café Alameda. Federico and Soriano became intimate friends, and the latter was one of the few people in the town to whom the young poet confided his problems.

Whatever the precise nature of these problems, there can be no doubt that Lorca's early poetry reveals a deep sexual malaise, a feeling of being rejected and isolated, nor that his work in general is concerned with the theme of frustration in one form or another. In Granada the poet was considered to be a homosexual, and this was a particular disaster in a town noted for its aversion towards unconventional sexuality. Many people, when they realised that Lorca was not 'normal' according to the canons of standard Spanish sexuality, became uneasy and distanced themselves from the poet. Miguel Cerón, who had been one of Lorca's closest friends, declared in 1971 shortly before his death:

Round about 1920 or 1921 Federico used to come to my flat every evening when he was in Granada, and we would spend hours talking and reading together. That was when I read *Riders to the Sea* to him, translating from the English. But when I realised that people were beginning to talk, I started to get uneasy. You know, it was awkward, I didn't want people to think that I was queer![14]

Spanish males are obsessed by stereotyped concepts of virility, and homosexuals are universally treated with disdain. The uneasiness about which Miguel Cerón spoke with such honesty could have become loathing and hatred in a less enlightened Spaniard, and it is a fact that when the Civil War began in 1936 many people were persecuted as much for sexual as for political reasons. Lorca was acutely aware of being *different*, and it seems likely that his own sense of rejection lay behind his interpretation of the personality of Granada and his identification with the sufferings of the

Moors and Jews who were persecuted by the Christians when the town fell.

I believe that being from Granada gives me a sympathetic understanding of those who are persecuted—of the gypsy, the negro, the Jew, of the Moor which all *granadinos* carry inside them.[15]

Lorca felt that Granada, despite its beauty and Romantic aura, was a town that had lost its soul in 1492, and he looked upon the philistine descendants of the Castilian conquerors with distaste.

Soon after the meeting between Trend and Lorca the poet moved to Madrid, where for ten years he lived at the famous Residencia de Estudiantes, familiarly known as the 'Resi', the nearest approximation in Spain to an Oxbridge college. In the capital he published his first collection of poems, *Libro de poemas* (1921), and became involved in the ferment of ideas, movements and 'isms' which characterised Madrid at this time. Gradually his fame spread and his *Gypsy Ballads* (1928) became the most widely read book of poems to appear in Spain since the publication of Gustavo Adolfo Bécquer's *Rimas* in 1871. In 1929 he accompanied Fernando de los Ríos to New York, where he spent nine months before returning to Spain via Cuba in the summer of 1930. *The Poet in New York*, arguably his greatest book of poems, appeared in 1940, four years after his death.

On the advent of the Republic in 1931, the Ministry of Education appointed Lorca director of a travelling theatre company, La Barraca, which under his inspiration performed Spanish plays in the squares and market places of villages up and down the country. To this task Federico wholeheartedly devoted his talents and energies, and his experience with La Barraca convinced him of the educational potential of the theatre in Spain.

From October 1933 to March 1934 the poet was in South America where his play *Blood Wedding* achieved a triumphant success in Buenos Aires.

By 1934 Lorca was the most famous living Spanish poet and dramatist but, despite his celebrity, he always remained essentially *granadino* at heart. When his play *Mariana Pineda* opened in the town in 1929 he had declared:

If by the grace of God I become famous, half of that fame will belong to Granada, which formed me and made me what I am: a poet from birth and unable to help it.[16]

Granada had made him, it was true, but Lorca never subjected his work to the dictates of that facile local colour with which Granadine artists all too readily fill out their canvases. While the poets Manuel de Góngora and Alberto A. de Cienfuegos, for example, were content to express until well into this century an outmoded Romantic concern with a pseudo-oriental Granada, Federico probed deeper and perceived in the beautiful but narrowly provincial town a tragic sense of life, an existential anguish which belies the superficial appearances. And just as Joyce had felt the need to escape from a small, claustrophobic Dublin in 1902 before being able to create a meaningful art out of his experience there, so Lorca had to abandon Granada and its *vega* so that he might recreate them in his work. As he said when launching the vanguardist review *Gallo* in 1928:

We must love Granada, but in a European context. Only in this way will we be able to discover our best hidden and most splendid treasures. A Granadine review for the world outside, a review sensitive to what is going on in the world in order better to understand what's going on here. A vital, lively, anti-local and anti-provincial review, belonging to the whole world, as Granada does.[17]

It is precisely this universality, this desire to break down the barriers of communication and reach out to the world, which has made Lorca's work so popular outside Spain, and so capable of appealing to readers and audiences widely divergent in language and way of life.

Although the poet often returned to Granada during the summer months to escape from the heat of Madrid, he increasingly found the town's inhabitants apathetic and reactionary, and his visits became more sporadic when his parents moved to the capital soon after the inauguration of the Republic in 1931.

It is to the Republic and the poet's activities during these troubled years that we must now turn our attention.

TWO

The Republic

On 12 April 1931 municipal elections were held throughout Spain. The results showed that the larger cities, including Granada, were overwhelmingly anti-monarchist and pro-Republican, and two days later King Alfonso XIII left the country. From 1923 to 1930 Spain had been labouring under the yoke of an authoritarian regime imposed by the genial, erratic and philandering General Primo de Rivera, and now she wanted a change.

As is well known, the five years of the Republic's short life were marked by a turbulence in which the hatreds, passions, contradictions, hopes and fears that had been dividing Spaniards for generations came quickly to a head and exploded in a fratricidal war that killed about 600,000 people.

The parliaments of the Republic spanned three well-defined periods. From June 1931 to November 1933 the Constituent Cortes had a strongly Republican government headed by Manuel Azaña. Then from November 1933 to January 1936 power swung to a right-wing coalition government; this period is often referred to as the 'black biennium'. Finally, from February 1936 to July 1936, when the Civil War broke out, the country was run by the Popular Front.

To understand why a Republican government that had come to power on a surge of popular enthusiasm in 1931 found itself out of office two years later, it is important to realise to what extent Spanish politics have consistently been polarised between the 'traditionalists' on the one hand and the 'progressives' on the other.

Spanish traditionalists identify Spain with the Catholic Church: Spain has been chosen by God as the torchbearer of the Faith and the guardian of Christian values in a hostile world, and virtue lies in remaining faithful to the spirit of Ferdinand and Isabella, the 'Catholic Monarchs' who unified Castile and Aragon, defeated the Moors of Granada, expelled the Jews, promoted the discovery, colonisation and conversion of the New World, and imposed state Catholicism. The intensely nationalistic traditionalists have never made any secret of their distaste for the processes of democracy and have always supported authoritarian governments. For them to be a 'liberal' is to be an enemy of the true Spain, and as recently as 1927 the following exchange appeared in a catechism published by the Spanish Church:

What sin is committed by him who votes for a liberal candidate?

Generally a mortal sin.[1]

This narrow traditionalism is found only in the ruling, proper-tied class, which has a vested interest in maintaining an autocratic system. It is not, certainly, an attitude of mind that was held by the majority of Spanish Catholics in the nineteenth century, a large proportion of whom were illiterate peasants and labourers. Indeed, as a result of the Church's lack of concern for social problems and of its political rigidity, attendance at mass had started to decline during the latter half of the century, and by 1931 it appears that, for example, only about five per cent of the villagers of New Castile carried out their Easter duties, while in Andalusia male attendance was down to one per cent.[2] In the cities the position was even worse.

Thus the Church and the comfortably-off minority, which together controlled the bulk of the country's resources, constituted a relatively small numerical group.

During the nineteenth century the battle between the two factions had centred on the problem of education, the liberals wanting to free the schools and universities from clerical influence, while the traditionalists insisted that all teaching must be controlled by the clergy. Each swing of the political pendulum brought with it new violence and disorder, and the party that acceded to power inevitably dismantled almost everything that had been done by the previous government. 'Spain', complained the journalist Larra in 1836, 'is like a new Penelope. She spends all her time weaving and unweaving.' The comparison was apt, and from Larra's day to the 1920s the fabric of Spanish political life had undergone little essential modification.

In 1931 the Republic inherited not only many problems that had been bedevilling Spanish life for centuries but a host of immediate difficulties. The economy was in a disastrous condition after the seven years of General Primo de Rivera's rule, and the situation was exacerbated by the world slump; there was chronic unemployment; there was, particularly, the agrarian question, most urgently demanding the attention of the new government, which had promised to effect a more just land distribution; there was opposition from the Army and all the forces of the Right[3]; there were bitter quarrels between the various left-wing parties; and, not least, there was the lack of political experience on the part of the liberal Republicans who had now to guide the country on a democratic course through the troubled waters of extremism on both the Left and the Right.

Unable to break out of the ossified pattern of Spanish politics, Azaña's government, in its eagerness to carry out sweeping reforms, antagonised the Right to a greater extent than it need have done. But even more instrumental than the Right's hatred in hastening the government's downfall was the stubborn refusal of the left-wing parties to compromise on their individual policies and form an electoral alliance that would enable them to benefit from the provisions of the 1932 Electoral Law. Since it was this law, enacted by the Azaña government, that regulated the 1933 election from which the Right emerged victorious, it will be worth our while to consider it here briefly.

Under the new law Spain was divided into sixty constituencies, corresponding to (1) each of her fifty provinces, (2) the eight cities which had a population in excess of 150,000 inhabitants (Madrid, Barcelona, Málaga, Seville, Murcia, Valencia, Bilbao and Zaragoza) and (3) her two sovereign cities in Morocco, Ceuta and Melilla. Each constituency was to return one member for every 50,000 inhabitants resident within it (with the exception of Ceuta and Melilla, which would return one each): thus Madrid would return seventeen members while Granada (capital and province together) would return only thirteen.

Voting was to be for lists of candidates, and the Electoral Law established that, in each constituency, a fixed number of seats would be allocated to both the winning candidature (the *mayoría*, majority) and the losers (the *minoría*, minority). In Madrid, thirteen out of the total of seventeen seats would go to the majority and the remaining four be distributed among the minority; in Granada the majority would obtain ten seats, the minority three; and so on.

The law also laid down that no candidature receiving less than forty per cent of the total vote in any constituency could be elected to the Cortes. In other words it encouraged the formation of coalitions, the intention being to force political extremism of all kinds to come to terms with more moderate opinion in the interests of its own parliamentary viability. No small party standing separately could hope to win an election under the new law: only a sudden and massive increase in extremism among voters, from either the Right or the Left, could propel a hitherto minority grouping to power, and no such contingency was envisaged.[4]

The resounding success of the Right in the 1933 election was a direct result of its determination to benefit from the advantages of the Electoral Law enacted by the Azaña government, and of the Left's inability to do so.[5] The Right went to the country in a coalition that united all the various conservative parties throughout Spain, while the Left, torn by internal dissension, failed to form a unified front. The result of the election, consequently, gave the Right a large majority in the Cortes, a majority increased by the law's provision that the winning side would automatically receive a bonus of seats. In spite of this the number of votes cast for the left-wing parties together totalled more than those polled in favour of the right-wing coalition. It was the failure of the left-wing parties to stand shoulder to shoulder that cost them the election.[6]

By far the largest of the right-wing groups to emerge from the 1933 election was the new middle-class Catholic party, the CEDA (Confederación Española de Derechas Autónomas). This was a coalition of several smaller Catholic organisations built around Acción Popular, a party founded in 1931, of which Gerald Brenan has written that it

represented the reaction of the Church and especially of the Jesuits to the Republic. It was a superficial imitation of the German Catholic party and was intended by its founders to be, not simply the party of the caciques,* the Army and the aristocracy, but of the Catholic masses as well. It accepted the Republic, but not the anti-Catholic laws, and the main part of its programme consisted in a demand for the revision of the Constitution.[7]

The mind behind Acción Popular was that of Angel Herrera Oria, a Madrid lawyer who edited the Jesuit-controlled *El Debate*, the most widely read Catholic daily newspaper in Spain. Herrera (who later entered the priesthood and became a cardinal in 1965) promoted as leader of Acción Popular a young man working on the staff of *El Debate*, José María Gil Robles, who had been educated by the Salesians in Salamanca. A marriage was 'arranged' between Robles and the daughter of the Conde de Revillagigedo, one of the richest men in Spain, and the couple spent their honeymoon in Germany, where Robles found that he greatly admired Hitler. He disapproved of the Nazi persecution of the Church, however, and eventually decided that the best model for the new Spain was Dollfuss's corporate state in Austria.[8]

Although Gil Robles never became Prime Minister, he held several important ministerial posts up to the election of February

* The Indian word for the chieftains through whom the Spaniards ruled their American colonies. In Spain the word was applied to the provincial landowners whose position gave them political power over the peasants.

1936 (from which he confidently expected to emerge as Premier of the next government), and exerted considerable influence on the course of events during the 'black biennium'. He was the 'type' of the Spanish traditionalist and the CEDA demonstrated all the perennial characteristics of the Right. It was financed by rich landowners and businessmen, and as a result was both unable and unwilling to embark on any programme of reform that might benefit the working classes, to which it was openly hostile. It was the party of stolid reaction, and increasingly attracted the allegiance of the Catholic middle-class and moneyed groups throughout the country, who realised that the growing power of the proletariat was threatening their security.

Despite its success in the 1933 elections the CEDA failed to achieve an absolute majority in the new Cortes, the first government of which was extremely vicious in its dismantling of the legislation introduced by the Azaña administration and showed a determination to suppress the rights of the working classes in favour of the privileges of the Right. Larra's Penelope was still busily at work.[9]

This reversal produced a violent reaction on the Left and a series of retaliatory strikes were quickly organised by the CNT (Confederación Nacional del Trabajo, the Anarcho-Syndicalist trade union), UGT (Unión General del Trabajo, the Socialist trade union) and the Communists, of which there were very few in Spain at the time.

The biggest of these strikes took place in Asturias, the mining district of Spain in the north–west of the country, where 70,000 workers united in a common alliance that was to be a predecessor of the Popular Front, and rose, on 5 October 1934, in a carefully planned insurrection against the government. The rising was eventually crushed, with great loss of life, by troops from Spanish Morocco under the command of General Franco, and among whom were Moorish soldiers and Foreign Legionaries of many nationalities. There were 3,000 dead and 7,000 wounded among the miners and the repression—forerunner of the atrocities committed during the Civil War—was carried out with great brutality.[10] While the defeat of the 'Reds' in Asturias looked like a

victory for the Right, and inspired Gil Robles with the confidence
that he would be the next Premier, it nevertheless showed the
workers what they might expect to achieve if they stood firmly
together in a final confrontation with the enemy.

The CEDA was in reality a pretty amorphous and soft-spined
party, with no dynamic aims or decisive leadership, and one
minority group on the Right rapidly lost patience with Gil Robles's
ineffectiveness and began to look for a new approach. These men
were attracted by the rise of Fascism in Italy and Germany and by
the political activities of José Antonio Primo de Rivera, son of the
dictator, who had founded the Falange Española (Spanish Pha-
lanx) in 1932. In 1934 the Falange merged with another Fascist
group, the JONS (Juntas de Ofensiva Nacional-Sindicalista), and
the new party was named Falange Española de las JONS.

Up to the general election of February 1936 the Falange had
only a small following and the Catholic middle class gave it very
little support, infatuated as it was with the personality of Gil Robles.
Moreover the Catholics were not yet prepared to give their allegiance to a semi-military organisation that openly preached violence. It was only after the defeat of the CEDA in the 1936 election
that the Falange really became important, and we shall be looking
at its development in Granada in the next chapter. For the moment
it is sufficient to stress that the CEDA and the Falange, while positively disliking each other, were nonetheless the outward embodiment of an attitude of mind that varied only in its degree of intensity and in the lengths to which it was prepared to go in pursuit of
its aims. Although the CEDA claimed to speak for Spanish Catholics, it was the Falange that adopted as its symbols the yoke and
arrows that had been the device of Ferdinand and Isabella, the
'Catholic Monarchs'.

During the first two years of the Republic, Granada, whose fall
to Ferdinand and Isabella in 1492 has always held particular significance for the traditionalists, witnessed frequent clashes between
the rich landowners who controlled the sugar industry in the *vega*
and the peasants, now strongly organised by the Socialist UGT.
The former, seeing in the Republic a serious threat to their privileged position, quickly threw their support behind the local

branch of Acción Popular, which had founded the Granada daily newspaper *Ideal* in 1931. *Ideal* became a vital factor in the political struggle now developing in the town, and in its columns were expressed all the most deeply entrenched attitudes of the Spanish Right. Meanwhile the left-wing *El Defensor de Granada*, launched in 1879, continued its struggle against what it considered to be the obscurantist forces that were afflicting the life of the province.

These forces were powerful enough to ensure that the right-wing coalition won the elections in Granada in 1933 and 1936. As we have seen, the thirteen Granada deputies were elected over the province as a whole, and while the Socialists were strong in the capital the Right was always successful in the rural areas of the province, where the landowners could bully the peasants into electoral submission. Thus in the 1933 election the Right had an easy victory even though the Socialists topped the poll in the capital.[11] Such a situation was intolerable to the Left.

Republican bitterness became intense when, following the Asturian insurrection of October 1934, the Socialist workers' clubs and Anarchist Syndicates were closed throughout the country and left-wing councillors deposed. In Granada the corporation that had been freely elected in April 1931 was sacked and its place taken a few days later by conservative councillors appointed by the 'authorities'. Many of the left-wing councillors were imprisoned, which explains the tremendous fervour with which the Republican council was reinstated after the victory of the Popular Front in February 1936.

On 21 December 1934, shortly after these turbulent events, *El Defensor de Granada* published an article entitled 'The poet García Lorca talks about the theatre and the artistic vocation'. This reproduced the most lively part of an interview given by Lorca some weeks earlier to the Madrid daily *El Sol*, in the course of which he clarified his attitude to the problems afflicting post-Asturias Spain:

I will always be on the side of those who have nothing, of those to whom even the peace of nothingness is denied. We—and by we I mean those of us who are intellectuals, educated in well-off middle-class families—are being called to make sacrifices. Let's accept the challenge.[12]

Spoken only a few months after the massacre of the Asturian miners, at a time when the average income in Spain was pitifully low, the poet's words left little room for misunderstanding: he was for the poor against the rich, for the workers and peasants in their fight against oppressive and anti-democratic forces which were determined to maintain them in a position of economic subservience.

The Right did not miss the underlying attitudes revealed in Lorca's statement of solidarity with the ordinary people of Spain. When his rural tragedy *Yerma* was staged a week later in Madrid, the reactionary press refused without exception to acknowledge the author's talent and claimed that his work was immoral, anti-Catholic, irrelevant to Spain's problems and lacking in verisimilitude. During the opening moments of the première a group of noisy young men tried to disrupt the performance by shouting political slogans against Azaña and barracking the actors, but the angry audience quickly silenced them.[13]

Yerma was a triumph for the poet and on 30 December 1934 *El Defensor* announced with pride that the staging of the new play had met with 'fantastic success'. The newspaper described the events of the first night and ended by reaffirming its admiration and friendship for the Granadine poet who was bringing glory to the town.

García Lorca's name was by now firmly connected with liberalism in the broadest sense of the word, with Manuel Azaña and Fernando de los Ríos (who had become Minister of Education in the Azaña government) and, as far as Granada was concerned, with *El Defensor*. Over the next two years leading up to the elections of February 1936, when the Popular Front swept to power, other reports in the local press of the poet's actions and words made his passionately democratic sympathies widely known.

In the event of a right-wing revolution Lorca's love of Granada would be no guarantee of his safety in the town.

THREE

Granada Before the Terror

On Sunday, 16 February 1936, Spain went to the polls. In Granada, as elsewhere throughout the country, the day passed off quietly enough, although there was some momentary excitement in one of the polling stations when a right-wing supporter, piqued by the high spirits of the proletariat, smashed the urn in an access of electoral despair.[1] It was a different story in the rural areas of the province, however, and *El Defensor de Granada* gave detailed accounts of electoral outrages committed by the *caciques*. In the little village of Güevéjar, for example, many of the electors were forced at gunpoint to stay away from the polling station,[2] and similar events occurred in Motril, the Alpujarras and elsewhere in those districts where the population was dependent on the big landowners for its livelihood.[3]

The final results of the election gave the Popular Front a narrow majority, the figures usually accepted as the most reliable being:

Popular Front	4,700,000
National Front	3,997,000
Centre	449,000
Basque Nationalists	130,000[4]

In considering these figures it is important to remember that the distribution of seats in the Cortes, in accordance with the 1932

Electoral Law, did not correspond exactly to the proportion of votes cast and that the victorious side automatically acquired a much increased parliamentary representation. In fact the Popular Front obtained 267 seats in the new Cortes and the Right only 132; just as in November 1933 the Right had won a huge majority of seats in spite of the fact that less votes were cast for it than for the Left.[5]

On 21 February both *El Defensor de Granada* and *Ideal* published the final results of the voting in Granada (capital and province). The Right had won a resounding victory. Infuriated by this outcome, which they attributed to the bullying of the *caciques* throughout the rural districts of the province, the left-wing organisations decided to press for the annulment of the Granada election when the new Cortes met in Madrid.

Resentment about the tactics used by the Right came to a head on Sunday 8 March, when a vast protest meeting was held by the Popular Front in Granada's Cármenes sports stadium. This was attended, according to the *Defensor*'s probably exaggerated estimate, by 100,000 people. The meeting was addressed by such well-known speakers as Fernando de los Ríos, and when it ended the vast crowd moved in a demonstration along the town's main thoroughfares: the Avenue of the Republic (later renamed Calvo Sotelo by the Nationalists), Gran Vía, Reyes Católicos and the Puerta Real. They handed a protest note to the Civil Governor, demanding that the Government should call new elections in Granada, and then dispersed.[6]

It was the most gigantic left-wing demonstration that Granada had ever seen, and it is not difficult to imagine the effect it must have produced on the minds of the town's well-off Catholic bourgeoisie.

While the results of the parliamentary elections had not been satisfactory for the Left in Granada, the Popular Front could have little complaint with the state of its municipal affairs. On 20 February Torres Romero, the Civil Governor, had resigned as an automatic consequence of the change of government,* and his

---

* Each Spanish provincial capital had (and has) its Civil Governor and Civil Government Building (I refer to the latter throughout as the 'Civil Government'). Before Franco's victory the Civil Governors were the official representatives of the government in office and, as such, at the mercy of political change.

place was taken by Aurelio Matilla García del Campo, a member of Martínez Barrio's Republican Union party.[7] Similarly the hated town council was forced to resign *in toto*, and its place was immediately taken by the Republican one pushed out of office in October 1934. These were the men originally elected on 12 April 1931 on the inauguration of the Republic, and their return now in February 1936 was greeted with jubilation by Republican supporters.

The short speech pronounced on the occasion of the opening session of the reinstated town council by Constantino Ruiz Carnero, the acting mayor, and editor of the *Defensor*, expressed the elation of these moments.

Gentlemen of the Council. People of Granada. With no more authority than the fact that I hold this office in an interim capacity I want, first of all, to offer heartfelt greetings to Granada. Here we are again after the parenthesis into which we were forced. This is not a taking of office, it is a *re*taking of office, a renewal of functions. Republican legality has been restored with the triumph of the people. Sixteen months ago we councillors, who had been elected by the people of Granada, were arbitrarily stripped of our office, not for having squandered public money, but because we were Republican councillors, for which reason they threw us out, while at the same time affording us the repellent spectacle of a bunch of fake councillors playing around with the town's affairs.

At this time I only want to speak words of peace and restraint. I recommend restraint and serenity, because the Republic must stand for restraint and serenity.

At this solemn moment we say to the town that we are here to defend its interests, to occupy ourselves with its problems and to seek its aggrandisement.

And to the people of Granada we say that we return to this Chamber with more Republican fervour than ever and are ready at all times to defend the Republic.

People of Granada! Let us work together for Granada and for the Republic.[8]

But, given conditions in Granada, the idealism of Ruiz Carnero and his colleagues was to prove inadequate to deal with the realities of the situation. Conservative opinion was hardening and there were daily encounters between rival political factions.

Widespread violence flared up just two days after the mass meeting in the Cármenes stadium. The demonstration had enflamed not only left-wing passions, and on the Monday after the meeting several cases of anti Popular–Front provocation occurred in Granada. That evening a group of Falangist gunmen opened fire on a crowd of workers and their families gathered in the Plaza del Campillo, and several women and children were wounded. The trade unions decided there and then to hold an immediate twenty-four-hour strike.[9]

When the *Defensor* appeared next morning, Tuesday 10 March 1936, by special permission of the strike committee, it carried a huge notice addressed to the workers by the local heads of the CNT, UGT, the Syndicalist Party and the Communist Party, informing them of the reasons for the strike and expressing uncompromising demands for the dissolution of right-wing organisations and the dismissal from the armed services of all known subversive elements. Such a strike was bound to lead to further exacerbation of the already dangerous situation, and in fact the day turned out to be one of unparalleled violence in Granada's recent history.

On 11 March the *Defensor* printed a very detailed account of what took place. The first action of the workers was to burn down the premises of the Falange in the Cuesta del Progreso. This occurred at 9.30 in the morning. Half an hour later another group set fire to the Isabel la Católica theatre, which had played an outstanding role in Granada's cultural life for many years. At 10.15 the crowd wrecked the 'bourgeois' Café Colón, making a bonfire of its tables and chairs and then setting the building alight. Then another café, the Royal, went up in flames. When the police tried to intervene the crowd milled around and prevented them from being effective, and at this point right-wing elements took advantage of the disorder to fire on the demonstrators and the police from the surrounding rooftops and balconies. The *Defensor* states that both police and firemen were subjected throughout the day to non-stop aggression from anti-Republican gunmen, who were doubtless grateful for this opportunity for violence afforded them by the workers.

The next building to burn was the premises of the Catholic newspaper *Ideal*, so hated by the Popular Front in Granada. The printing presses were smashed to pieces, the place was soaked in petrol and, under the very eyes of the police, set on fire. The *Defensor*'s claim that the police were surrounded by women who 'prevented them from intervening' is hardly convincing and it seems that the Republican authorities may have given orders that the workers were not to be attacked.

Meanwhile other establishments were receiving the attentions of the crowd. The premises of Acción Popular were burning merrily, so too were those of Acción Obrerista (the Catholic Workers' Organisation). The chocolate factory owned by the local leader of Acción Popular, Francisco Rodríguez, had also been set alight, as had several shops owned by 'conservatives'. Even the tennis club (doubtless an offensive symbol for the workers) was wrecked. Faced with such destruction of its property, the middle class reacted with a hatred that would vent itself at the outbreak of the Nationalist rising, when the most brutal members of the assassination squads were often from well-off families.

To round off the day's work, two churches in the Albaicín were set on fire: the convent of San Gregorio el Bajo and the church of El Salvador, the latter being completely gutted. It is hard to be sure who was responsible for these two acts of destruction, and the intervention of *agents provocateurs* cannot be ruled out. The *Defensor* reports that fire brigades were prevented from reaching the blazing buildings in time by the ferocity of the gunfire directed against them as they tried to climb the steep, narrow streets of the Albaicín, and it may well be that hired gunmen were involved. It is easy to set a church on fire and such an act would be immediately ascribed to the 'Reds' by the Catholic middle class, whose fear of the Popular Front would be increased as a result. Indeed, the *Defensor* published a warning note the following day addressed to the workers by the Popular Front Committee, in which it was claimed that the parties of the Left had been infiltrated by '*agents provocateurs* in the service of reaction', who were seeking to stir up hatred and violence in order to make matters increasingly difficult for the Government. Certainly when the Nationalists gained control of Granada some months later many of the most vociferous Communists and Anarchists of the town suddenly appeared wearing their true colours: Falangist blue.

The events of 10 March made impossible any reconciliation between the Right and Left in Granada. As the ultra-reactionary Gollonet and Morales comment in their book:

The revolutionary strike of March made a profound impression on the town. For many days there was an extraordinary lack of animation in the streets. The only people circulating were the forces of law and order and groups of workers with instructions to harass anyone wearing a collar and tie. These were, apparently, the symbols of honour and probity and as such could not be tolerated by the shameless Marxists.[10]

Many arrests were made on and after 10 March, not so much in connection with the burning of the various premises as with the numerous shooting incidents which had occurred. More than three hundred people were detained and numerous weapons were discovered in house-to-house searches.[11]

It may seem odd that there was no military intervention in the events of 10 March, so it will perhaps be useful at this point to consider the garrison and its relation to the political situation in Granada at the time.

One essential fact about the constitution and organisation of the Granada garrison must be grasped: Granada was not in 1936 a Captaincy General (that is, the head of a military region) but a Military Commandery, whose Commander received his orders from the Captain General in Seville. From this it follows that a military upheaval in Seville would cause automatic confusion in Granada, which is precisely what happened when the Nationalist rising began in July 1936.

The Granada garrison was made up of the Lepanto Infantry Regiment (300 men) and the Fourth Light Artillery Regiment (180 men). To this should be added the forty officers and men of the paramilitary Civil Guard. The *Historia de la Cruzada Española*,[12] which gives these figures, states that when the war started the garrison had at its disposal only 300 rifles, two mortars 'which had not even been tested', 72,000 cartridges and four artillery batteries which were almost without shells. The same source adds that 14,000 guns and rifles allegedly collected by the Assault Guards in the aftermath of the 10 March disturbances also became available to the Nationalists when the rising started.[13] The *Cruzada* forgets to mention that the garrison also had several machine-guns, which were used in the early hours of the rebellion with great effect.

Nor does it refer to another factor of crucial military importance to the development of the war: the existence at El Fargue, a few miles outside the town on the road to Murcia, of the largest explosives factory in Andalusia. El Fargue produced large quantities of explosives for the Army, including TNT for making bombs, and its role in the war cannot be overstressed. Indeed the first train to reach Seville from Granada after the outbreak of the war (the expedition took place on 22 August 1936) carried a huge consignment of high explosives to General Queipo de Llano, whose stocks were running very low at the time.[14] El Fargue was to provide the Nationalist forces with an uninterrupted supply of these materials throughout the war, and the Republicans never succeeded in blowing it up despite several air-raids.

Finally Granada had at Armilla—a few miles outside the town on the road to Motril—a splendid airstrip which was to prove of the greatest value to Franco, assuring the easy maintenance of contact with Seville and the rest of Nationalist Spain and serving as a jumping-off place for planes attacking Republican positions.

If these factors are borne in mind it will be easier to understand not only the role of the garrison in subsequent events but also the whole course of the war in Granada.

How, then, did the military react to the 10 March disturbances? According to Gollonet and Morales, the Military Commander, General Elíseo Alvarez Arenas, highly indignant about what was happening, presented himself during the day in the Civil Government, where a meeting was in progress between the Governor and the strike committee. He stated that the garrison would intervene to re-establish order if the strike were not terminated at once.

Gollonet and Morales believe that it was this act of defiance that brought about the General's speedy transfer to another command. He was replaced by General Llanos Medina, a man of conservative opinions who was 'ready to support, at the head of the Granada garrison, any attempt to save Spain'.[15] The Civil Governor himself was dismissed shortly afterwards, doubtless for his clumsy handling of the events of 10 March, and his place was taken on 21 March by a fellow member of the Republican Union party, Ernesto Vega, who was believed to be a particularly bitter enemy of the Right.[16]

The political situation in Granada had now become very unstable and relations between the Civil Government and the garrison grew worse daily. It seems that the Government, aware of the anti-Republican feelings of many of the officers, instructed Ernesto Vega to keep a close eye on their behaviour and movements. This interference led to strong resentment. A series of confrontations occurred between the civil and military authorities of the town, the outcome of which was the eventual dismissal of both the Civil Governor, on 25 June, and the Military Commander, General Llanos, who was transferred to Valencia on 10 July. Their places were taken, respectively, by César Torres Martínez (on 26 June) and General Miguel Campins Aura, both of whom were still in office when the Nationalist rising began. Torres was a member of the Republican Left party, a lawyer and a close friend of the Prime Minister, Casares Quiroga. He proved himself a weak and ineffectual governor, a fitting counterpart to the hesitant Campins.[17]

Meanwhile the demands of the Popular Front deputies in the Cortes for the annulment of the February elections in Granada (and Cuenca) had met with success. On 1 April 1936 the *Defensor* printed full details of the previous day's debate in the Cortes which had led to the majority decision in favour of annulment. The paper noted the furious reaction of right-wing deputies (many of whom had stormed out of the Chamber before the vote was taken) and informed its readers that a new election had been arranged for 3 May 1936.

During April the National Front agreed on the composition of its list of candidates: four Falangists, five members of the CEDA and one 'Independent Nationalist'. By joining in this coalition the Granada CEDA now lost whatever scant respect it still commanded among serious-minded supporters of the Popular Front. Previously the CEDA had remained aloof from the Falange and its violent methods, preferring legally acceptable modes of procedure and protest. But things had changed and the party had shifted its ground. It was obvious to everyone that Catholic opinion in Granada was hardening fast.

As was to be expected, the National Front's electoral campaign met with constant interference. Its candidates received threats and were sometimes physically assaulted, and its propaganda was censored by the Republican authorities. According to Gil Robles, the CEDA leader (whose account of the Granada election is inadequately documented), the Civil Governor attempted to dissuade the National Front from contesting the election: Torres Martínez claimed that their insistence on doing so would cause serious disturbances throughout the province.[18] Whether this was so or not, the fact remains that the National Front soon realised that the campaign was a waste of time and that success at the polls would be impossible. When the results of the election became known it was obvious that there had been a massive abstention on the part of conservative voters. The Popular Front won a resounding victory and not a single right-wing candidate was returned. Indeed, if the *Defensor*'s report is accurate, no National Front candidate polled more than 700 votes.[19] The *Cruzada*, whose information on the election is extremely tendentious, comments:

The last legal attempt at resistance in Granada had failed. The enemy wanted only war, war with all its consequences. (p. 272).

But it would be a mistake to attribute the failure of the National Front in Granada solely to left-wing intimidation. The Popular Front was in power and it was natural that the election should favour the Left more than the Right, particularly in the rural areas, where the *caciques* could no longer bully the peasants into electoral submission without risking legal sanctions.

The *Defensor* failed to realise, in its satisfaction with the outcome of the new election, that the complete absence of right-wing representation in the Cortes (as well as on the town council) could only be damaging to Granada's best interests in these dangerous moments. Forced into the political wilderness, conservative discontent now began to express itself clandestinely and there can be no doubt that some, at least, of the Granadine right-wing deputies who lost their seats in May became involved in active plotting against the Republic. Their task was facilitated, moreover, by the dissensions rife among all sectors of the Left in the town.

Nowhere was this more obvious than in the squabbles taking place in the town council, where the representatives of the different left-wing parties were trying to decide who should be appointed mayor of Granada. A decision was finally reached on 10 July, when Dr Manuel Fernández Montesinos, a Socialist, was elected. Montesinos (who was married to Federico García Lorca's sister Concha) was to hold office for only ten days. When the Nationalist rising began in Granada on 20 July he was arrested, along with all the other left-wing councillors.

Ideal, which had reappeared on 1 July after three and a half months' enforced absence from the political scene in Granada, was scathing in its comments on the current situation. Within the limits imposed on it by the censor, the newspaper made its political aspirations quite clear. 'We have not returned too late to join the ranks of those who have undertaken the noble task of freeing the country from its present disorder', its editorial exclaimed. 'There is still time for us to unite with those who are fighting to preserve Spain's traditionalist principles, and to return to a system which will enable the Holy Spirit to dominate the social hierarchy'.

Ideal well knew that by this time the conspiracy to overthrow the Republic was in an advanced state of preparation. Gerald Brenan writes:

Both on the Right and on the Left the leading factions were tired of half-measures and were ranging themselves under revolutionary banners. The Right kept quiet about their aims: they were organising secretly, collecting arms, negotiating with foreign governments and keeping the country in a state of continual turmoil by their provocations and assassinations.[20]

It would be a mistake, though, to imagine that the Right was united in much more than a common hatred of the Left, for there was considerable friction between the various groups. The conservative CEDA and the revolutionary Falange, for instance, were constantly at loggerheads, and their respective leaders, José María Gil Robles and José Antonio Primo de Rivera, had missed no opportunity for mutual abuse in the Cortes before they both lost their seats in February 1936.

The Falange had been numerically unimportant up to the 1936 elections, and its violent tactics had alienated Catholic support. But the Popular Front victory in February terrified the Catholic middle class which, disillusioned by the CEDA's ineffectiveness, increasingly threw in its lot with the extremists (we have seen how, in Granada, the events of 10 March assisted this process). Accordingly, there was a considerable swelling of the Falangist ranks in these months and the party rapidly became the most efficient and ruthless right-wing organisation operating in Spain. The local chief of the Falange in Seville wrote:

After the elections of February, I had absolute faith in the triumph of the Falange because we considered the Right, our most difficult enemy, ruined and eliminated. Its disaster constituted for us a fabulous advance and the inheritance of its best youth. Furthermore, we held the failure of the Popular Front to be an absolute certainty, because of its internal disorganisation and its frankly anti-national position, openly opposed to the feelings of a great mass of Spaniards. Our task consisted simply in widening our base of support among the working class.[21]

The Falange, in Granada as elsewhere, attracted its members almost entirely from the well-to-do middle class, who saw in the liberated proletariat a huge threat to their own security. Before the February elections the handful of Falangists in Granada had been the laughing-stock of the Left, and nobody took them seriously. Now the position had changed, and the Popular Front's victory in February, the post-election disturbances and the banning of the Falange on 14 March, followed by the annulment of the Granada election on 31 March, all helped to shift a considerable proportion of right-wing opinion firmly behind José Antonio Primo de Rivera's party.

With Primo in gaol it became more difficult for the Granada Falange to maintain contact with the party's central organisation. Towards the end of April 1936, however, two Falangists from Granada, José Díaz Plá and José Rosales Camacho, managed to visit their leader in the Model Prison in Madrid and received instructions from him which they took back to their comrades. Primo de Rivera promised to send a delegate to help with plans, and at the end of May the architect José Luis de Arrese arrived in Granada, where the following Falange appointments were made:

Provincial Chief	Dr Antonio Robles Jiménez
Chief of Militia	José Valdés Guzmán
Provincial Secretary	Luis Gerardo Afán de Ribera
Provincial Treasurer	Antonio Rosales Camacho
Local Chief	José Díaz Plá
Local Secretary	Julio Alguacil González

Arrese returned to Granada on 25 June to make definitive arrangements for the Falange's role in the military rising that was shortly to take place. The town was divided into three sectors, each of which was to be controlled by a squadron of Falangists under the command, respectively, of Enrique de Iturriaga, Cecilio Cirre and José Rosales Camacho.

The *Cruzada*, from which these details are taken, asserts that in Granada the Falange now had 575 members.[22] Presumably this figure refers to the province as a whole, for in the capital itself the party is unlikely to have had three hundred members before the war began.

Of the Falangist officers listed above, special attention should be drawn to José Valdés Guzmán, for it was he who became Civil Governor of Granada on the outbreak of the Nationalist rising on

20 July. Valdés was born in the town of Logroño in northern Spain. His father was a General in the Civil Guard and the son inherited his military interests. Valdés joined the Army and fought in the Moroccan war during the years 1918–23. Having sustained serious injuries during an offensive, he was forced to spend seven months recuperating in a Seville hospital. He underwent an operation for a duodenal ulcer in 1929 and seems to have been unwell for the rest of his life (he died later of tuberculosis or cancer of the intestine). On the inauguration of the Republic in 1931, Valdés was sent to Granada in the capacity of War Commissioner (*Comisario de guerra*), a position he held until the outbreak of the rising.[23] His rank was that of Comandante, that is to say, four grades below the General's rank which has sometimes been ascribed to him. The fact that Valdés was an 'old shirt' member of the Falange* as well as an army officer explains the influence he exerted during the preparations for the rising and the position he assumed once it began. While Military Commanders and Civil Governors had come and gone regularly since 1931, Valdés had retained his post, and thus by 1936 must have had his finger on the political pulse of all his fellow officers in the Granada garrison. Through him the rebels could gauge pretty accurately how much support they could expect from the officers when the insurrection got under way.

José Rosales has spoken of his meetings with Valdés and the other conspirators in these last few weeks before the war. In order to avoid suspicion they met in an empty flat in San Isidro Street which Rosales was decorating in preparation for his forthcoming marriage, and on several occasions they were almost caught red-handed with incriminating papers and material.[24]

It should be clear that, while Valdés and José Rosales were close associates, the former nevertheless held a position of far greater authority within the hierarchy of the Nationalist conspiracy in Granada. To state, as Claude Couffon has done, that the Rosales brothers were 'chefs tout-puissants de la Phalange' in Granada and that José was the 'chef suprême de la Phalange'—a claim also made

* *Los camisas viejas*, the nickname by which the original, pre–Civil War members of the Falange are known.

by Schonberg—is to fail to grasp the realities of the situation.[25]
Rosales, after all, was merely one of the three Falangist sector
chiefs, while Valdés was supreme commander of the Falangist
militia in Granada, as well as being an Army officer and, once the
rising began, Civil Governor. Rosales, unlike Valdés, was a civilian, and the Falange, without the military rising, would never
have been in a position to impose itself on the community. This is
stressed here because, as we shall see, the Rosales family found itself
much involved in the circumstances surrounding the arrest of
Federico García Lorca.

Valdés had become the leading conspirator in Granada when
the Government sacked General Llanos Medina, who had been
deeply committed to the rebellion, on 10 July 1936. When General
Queipo de Llano visited Llanos Medina at the beginning of the
month to inform him of the progress of plans for the rising, Llanos
had reaffirmed his allegiance to the Cause and assured Queipo that
he could count on the support of the Granada garrison. The
Government was informed of the meeting and immediately dismissed General Llanos, thereby causing an unexpected blow to the
conspirators. 'Granada', comments the *Cruzada*, 'had lost the
brains behind the insurrection'.[26]

The new Military Commander was General Miguel Campins
Aura. Campins had a fine military record and was known to be
friendly with General Franco. He turned out to be a staunch Republican, however, and the rebel officers soon realised that they
could expect no collaboration from their new chief. Plotting continued behind the General's back and he seems to have been quite
unaware of what was happening until it was too late.

Among the conspirators, both Colonel Basilio León Maestre,
commanding officer of the Lepanto Infantry Regiment, and
Colonel Antonio Muñoz Jiménez of the Fourth Light Artillery
Regiment, were actively plotting against the Republic and were to
play a vital role in the rising.[27]

They were supported by several of their officers, among whom
Captain José María Nestares was outstanding. Nestares had attended the Military Academy in Toledo and was a handsome
young man with a liking for women and the other prescribed

pursuits of the Andalusian *señorito*. In this, as in his rabidly anti-Republican sentiments, he was out of the same stable as the Rosales brothers and, like José and Antonio, had joined the Falange in its early days. Although Nestares was a Captain of Infantry, he had been connected to the police security department until being dismissed after the events of 10 March 1936, and this experience was to prove particularly useful to him when the rising started. He was then appointed 'head of public order' and became one of the most dedicated organisers of the repression. At the end of July Nestares took command of the Falangist position in Víznar, a little village five miles to the north-west of Granada below the Sierra de Alfacar. I shall have more to say of him, and of Víznar.

One other notable conspirator against the Republic who should be mentioned here is Lieutenant Mariano Pelayo, the hated Civil Guard whose cruelty during the repression of Granada became proverbial. Under Pelayo the Civil Guard sided with the rebels from the start and vindicated the reputation for brutality by which they are known in Spain.

These, then, were some of the more prominent Nationalists who dedicated themselves during the summer of 1936 to making preparations for the rising in Granada. Before tracing the development of events in the town, however, some consideration should be given to the activities under the Popular Front of the poet who is the principal concern of this book.

FOUR

Garcia Lorca and the Popular Front

By 1936 Lorca was the most famous young poet and dramatist of his generation in Spain and his reputation had already spread far beyond the confines of his native country.

Wherever he went, whatever he wrote, success was immediate. His life was caught up in a constant whirl of social engagements, performances of his plays, lectures and poetry recitals, between all of which he nevertheless managed to find time to continue writing. In January 1936 he returned to Madrid from Barcelona, where his play *Doña Rosita the Spinster* had received acclaim from critics and public alike; he was working on several new projects; and in this first month of the year he published *Blood Wedding*—the play had enjoyed more than a hundred consecutive performances in Buenos Aires in 1933—and a small book of poems, *Primeras canciones*. It seemed that the poet led a charmed life.

In the weeks leading up to the general election of February 1936, the atmosphere in Madrid was extremely tense. Politics and the arts had become inextricably mixed, and political significance was given to the smallest word or most trivial action on the part of well-known artists and writers. Keenly aware of the threat of Fascism to Europe, the majority of these openly voiced their support for the Popular Front and used their influence as public figures to attack the Right.

It is indisputable that, in the last months before the rising, Lorca took part in gatherings of a markedly anti-Fascist and Republican character. On 9 February 1936 a banquet was offered to the Communist poet Rafael Alberti on his return from Russia. Federico delivered the speech of welcome and read an anti-Fascist manifesto drawn up by a group of Spanish writers.[1] On 14 February a celebration in memory of the playwright Valle-Inclán, who had just died, was organised in the Zarzuela Theatre by Alberti and his wife, María Teresa León. Of this gathering, in which Federico took part, reading poems in praise of Valle-Inclán composed by Rubén Darío, a Spanish critic has written: 'The occasion could not fail to have a certain political flavour which the organisers themselves made no attempt to conceal'.[2]

Shortly after the Popular Front's success at the polls, the great poet Antonio Machado and other intellectuals signed the manifesto of the Universal Union of Peace on behalf of its Spanish committee, and *El Sol* published a list of prominent men of letters, including García Lorca, who supported it.[3]

On 1 April Lorca, together with a number of fellow poets and intellectuals including Alberti, Luis Cernuda and Manuel Altolaguirre, signed another manifesto, this time demanding the release from gaol of the Brazilian revolutionary leader Carlos Prestes.[4]

Later in the month the poet again aligned himself politically, sending a message to the May Day issue of the weekly magazine *¡Ayuda!* ('Help!') which was published by the International Red Aid Organisation:

I send my affectionate greetings to all the workers of Spain, united on this May 1st by a passionate desire for a more just society.[5]

During the first weeks of May, in which the political atmosphere in Spain grew steadily worse, it seems that Federico signed a second anti-Fascist manifesto.[6] Then, on 22 May, he attended a huge banquet given in honour of three French writers who were visiting Madrid as representatives of the French Popular Front: André Malraux, Jean Cassou (a friend of Lorca) and the dramatist

Lenormand. Two hundred distinguished guests, including several
cabinet ministers, were present at this pre-eminently left-wing
gathering, during which the Marseillaise and the Internationale
were sung by the banqueters.[7] The event was widely covered by
the Madrid press the following day.

But to what extent was Federico's support for the Popular
Front based on seriously-held political opinions? Dámaso Alonso
has recalled that, in July 1936, Lorca exclaimed, on hearing that
one of their friends had become politically involved: 'I'll never be
a politician, never! Like all true poets I'm a revolutionary, but a
politician—never!'[8]

Not only had the poet no intention of becoming a politician, he
never joined a political party or identified himself with any particular left-wing group, as many of his fellow writers had done. He
was a liberal in the broadest sense of the word and had no deep
interest in politics as such. An interview published in the Madrid
daily La Voz on 1 April 1936 is indicative of the poet's approach
to the political situation in Spain at the time:

As long as there is economic injustice in the world, the world will be
unable to think clearly. I see it like this. Two men are walking along a
river bank. One of them is rich, the other poor. One has a full belly and
the other fouls the air with his yawns. And the rich man says: 'What a
lovely little boat out on the water! Look at that lily blooming on the
bank!' And the poor man wails: 'I'm hungry, I can't see anything.
I'm hungry, so hungry!' Of course. The day when hunger is eradicated
there is going to be the greatest spiritual explosion the world has ever
seen. We will never be able to picture the joy that will erupt when the
Great Revolution comes. I'm talking like a real Socialist, aren't I?[9]

In terms of the political situation in Spain at the time, Lorca was
indeed talking like a real Socialist, despite his lack of formal membership of any left-wing party. The poet sympathised with the
ordinary, economically depressed people of Spain, he disliked the
traditionalist mentality, he saw the dangers of Fascism. He was an
idealist with his heart in the right place who, like so many of those
gentle intellectuals actually holding political positions under the

Republic, wanted a more humane society in Spain, wanted a new liberalism, but could not cope with the harsh realities of political life.

In fact there can be little doubt that the poet was politically somewhat naïve, and it has recently become known that, despite his anti-Fascist declarations, he was on friendly terms with the Falangist leader José Antonio Primo de Rivera, who greatly admired his poetry. On 7 March 1936 Lorca gave a talk in San Sebastián on his *Gypsy Ballads*, which, since their publication in 1928, had become the most famous modern poems in the language. During his stay on the coast he met the young poet Gabriel Celaya, who was rabidly anti-Fascist. In 1966 Celaya published an article in which, quoting from the diary he kept during Federico's stay in San Sebastián, he revealed the contents of his discussion with the poet on that occasion. Federico had asked Celaya to meet him at the Hotel Biarritz, and when the latter arrived he found to his dismay that the poet was deep in conversation with José Manuel Aizpurua, an intelligent young architect who had founded the local branch of the Falange. During the evening Celaya stubbornly refused to speak to Aizpurua and later Lorca, angered by this behaviour, exclaimed:

José Manuel's like José Antonio Primo de Rivera. Another good chap. I have supper with him every Friday evening, you know. Honestly. We go out in a taxi with the curtains pulled down, because he doesn't want to be seen with me and I don't want to be seen with him.

Celaya comments:

Federico was laughing. He believed that it was all a bit of childish fun. He saw nothing behind it. He laughed as if it were all a big joke. But that laugh, that confidence that people are always good, that belief that a friend is a friend, Fascist or no, cost him his life. Because it was his friends, friends whom he counted among his best, who at the last moment turned out to be Fascists first and foremost. Oh no, *they* didn't shoot him. They washed their hands of him and then handed him over to those who did.[10]

Celaya's revelations prove that Lorca was not so politically committed as some left-wing propagandists would have us believe. José Antonio was a man of charm and intelligence, and he and Lorca seem to have arrived at an easy understanding of one another. But their friendship could not last, for on 14 March, a week after Federico's lecture in San Sebastián, the Falangist leader was imprisoned. Since the war Falangist apologists have made much of their acquaintance, arguing illogically that because of it the Falange could not have been responsible for the poet's death, and that Lorca was in fact veering politically towards the party when he died. As we shall see presently, the matter is very much more complicated.

Lorca had been increasingly concerned, since returning from his first trip to America, with the social mission of the theatre in Spain. The formation of the travelling company La Barraca gave him a marvellous opportunity to bring Spanish classical drama to the *pueblo*, and he devoted tremendous energy to ensuring the success of the project. This new social concern was reflected in his ideas about what modern drama should seek to achieve, and he came to feel that the playwright could no longer afford not to identify with the social realities of his own day and age. In the last interview published before his death he said:

The idea of art for art's sake is something that would be cruel if it weren't, fortunately, so ridiculous. No decent person believes any longer in all that nonsense about pure art, art for art's sake.
At this dramatic point in time, the artist should laugh and cry with the people. We must put down the bunch of lilies and bury ourselves up to the waist in mud to help those who are looking for lilies. For myself, I have a genuine need to communicate with others. This is why I knocked at the doors of the theatre and why I now devote all my talents to it.[11]

In the same interview, Lorca was asked for his opinion on the fall of Granada to Ferdinand and Isabella in 1492. His reply, which in itself could have been sufficient to endanger his life in the town, is final proof that his attitude to Spain was utterly unlike that of the Granadine conspirators who were at this very moment plotting against the Republic:

It was a disastrous event, even though they say the opposite in the schools. An admirable civilisation, and a poetry, architecture and delicacy unique in the world—all were lost, to give way to an impoverished, cowed town, a wasteland populated by the worst bourgeoisie in Spain today.

After this outburst Federico proceeded to define his feelings about being a Spaniard:

I am totally Spanish, and it would be impossible for me to live outside my geographical limits. At the same time I hate anyone who is Spanish just because he was born a Spaniard. I am a brother to all men, and I detest the person who sacrifices himself for an abstract, nationalist ideal just because he loves his country with a blindfold over his eyes. A good Chinaman is closer to me than a bad Spaniard. I express Spain in my work and feel her in the very marrow of my bones; but before this I am cosmopolitan and a brother to all. Needless to say, I don't believe in political frontiers.[12]

El Sol, where this interview appeared, was one of the most widely read newspapers in Spain and the piece did not miss the attention of that Granadine middle class characterised by the poet as 'the worst in Spain today'.

And then it was July. Federico had announced in April that he was planning a trip to Mexico, where he would see his plays performed and give a lecture on the seventeenth-century poet Quevedo[13]; it seems that he intended to take a short holiday with his parents in Granada, and then to set off on his trip. He was bubbling over with ideas and literary projects, and in an interview given at the beginning of July (but not published until 1937, several months after his death) he said that he had six books of poetry ready for the press and three new plays, one of which was to be an Andalusian drama set in the *vega* of Granada and the other 'a social play . . . in which the audience and people in the street take part; a revolution flares up and the theatre is taken by force'.[14]

On 5 July Federico's parents returned to Granada to spend the summer with their daughter Concha, wife of the Socialist town councillor Dr Manuel Fernández Montesinos (who became mayor of Granada five days later), and their children. Federico was at Madrid's South Station to see them off and it was agreed that he himself would join them on 18 July to celebrate St Frederick's Day.[15]

A few days later an ugly incident took place in Madrid. On the evening of 12 July Lieutenant José Castillo of the Assault Guards was shot dead by four Falangist gunmen in reprisal for the death of one of their members. The dead man's colleagues decided to avenge his murder by assassinating two of the political leaders of the Right, Gil Robles (the CEDA chief) and Calvo Sotelo (Monarchist). They failed to locate Robles, but Calvo Sotelo was taken from his flat in the early hours of 13 July, shot dead and dumped at the East Cemetery. As Hugh Thomas comments:

It was now natural to assume that the Government could not control even its own agents, even if it wished to do so.[16]

Everyone felt that the country was on the brink of civil war, and the huge funerals of Castillo and Calvo Sotelo on 14 July turned into frenzied political demonstrations.

Federico, always terrified by violence, had now to make a decision. Should he return to Granada or stay in Madrid? If there were civil war and the Right triumphed, where would he be safest?

One of his closest friends, Rafael Martínez Nadal, has recalled the poet's state of mind during the week before the rising began:

The unease which all we Spaniards felt took in him the form of disorientation and depression. Since the publication of the *Gypsy Ballads* I could not remember having seen him so depressed as during those last days in Madrid.[17]

Federico persistently asked his friends what he should do. It has been said that among those who recommended his return to Granada was Luis Rosales, who pointed out that there Lorca could count on the protection of both the Left and the Right and in the event of the town's falling into the hands of the Nationalists would be able to depend on the Rosales family to guarantee his safety. Lorca's friend Fulgencio Díez Pastor, a deputy in the Cortes, was insistent that the poet should remain in Madrid and his advice was repeated by the poet Agustín de Foxa, a Falangist, who tried to make Federico understand that he would be safer anywhere than in Granada.[18] But Lorca continued to vacillate.

On the evening of 13 July, following the news of Calvo Sotelo's murder, he paid a visit to his old schoolmaster, Antonio Rodríguez Espinosa.[19] Claude Couffon, who talked to the eighty-year-old Espinosa in Madrid in 1950, has evoked the friendship that existed between the two men:

It had begun one day in the autumn of the year 1902, when Don Antonio was village schoolmaster in Fuente Vaqueros. One morning the teacher had seen his former colleague, Doña Vicenta Lorca Romero, now married to the rich landowner García Rodríguez, enter the school courtyard. She was holding a timid child by the hand. 'This is Federico, Don Antonio,' she had said to him. 'He's a sensitive child and I hope that he'll satisfy you'. Don Antonio had shown Federico some mineral specimens, insects and butterflies, and the child, more confident now, had smiled at him. Classes were held in the morning. In the afternoon, during the hours when heat stifles the plain, Federico would often rejoin Don Antonio in the cool of his room and watch in silence as he worked.[20]

Since then the timid little boy had become a famous poet, and Don Antonio had taken a personal pride in his successes. When the maid opened the door, Don Homobono Picadillo, as Federico introduced himself in a squeaky voice, asked if he might be allowed to speak to Don Antonio. But the old schoolteacher was used to his favourite pupil's jokes and appeared grumbling, 'And what the devil does Don Homobono want this time?' Rodríguez Espinosa's memoirs record that Federico borrowed two hundred pesetas from him to pay the train fare that evening to

Granada. 'There's a storm brewing and I'm going home', the poet told him. 'I'll be out of danger there'.[21]

But Federico did not leave Madrid that evening, for after his visit to Don Antonio he gave a reading of his play *The House of Bernarda Alba* to a small group of friends in Dr Eusebio Oliver's flat. The poet Dámaso Alonso was there and has described Lorca's noticeable tenseness, his nervousness about the political situation and his impatience to depart for Granada.[22]

July 16 was the last day Federico spent in Madrid, and we are fortunate that Rafael Martínez Nadal, sensing the poignancy of the occasion, wrote a full account in his diary that evening of the day's events and his conversations with the poet.

Nadal describes how, after lunch, they took a taxi to the Puerta del Hierro outside Madrid. Federico was gloomy and uncommunicative. He wanted advice. Should he return to Granada? Finally, without changing the tone of his voice, he jumped to his feet and exclaimed: 'Rafael, there'll be bodies all over these fields. I've made up my mind, I'm going to Granada. God's will be done'.

On the way back to Lorca's flat in 102 Alcalá Street they stopped at Thomas Cook's, where the poet booked a sleeper on that night's Andalusian Express. Then Nadal helped him to get his things ready. Later, as they were about to leave the flat, Lorca handed him a packet of personal papers with the words: 'Take this. If anything happens to me, destroy everything. If not, you can give it back to me when I see you again'.[23] Nadal accompanied Federico to the station and went with him to the sleeping car, where the poet autographed copies of his books for friends in Scandinavia, which Nadal posted.

Then, suddenly, the poet received a nasty shock:

Somebody moved down the corridor of the sleeping car. Federico, rapidly turning his back, stretched his forefinger and little finger in the air, and waggled them.
'Lizard! Lizard! Lizard!' he exclaimed.*

---

* There is an Andalusian folk custom whereby the assistance of the harmless lizard— traditional enemy of the snake—is invoked in the presence of the dangerous reptile and, by extension, of undesirable humans.

I asked him who it was.

'One of the Granada deputies. A really nasty character.'

Obviously nervous and annoyed, Federico stood up.

'Look, Rafael,' he said, 'off you go and don't wait on the platform. I'm going to draw the curtains and get into bed so that that animal doesn't see me.'

We embraced rapidly and for the first time ever I left Federico in a train without waiting for it to leave, without horse-playing right up to the last minute.

Nadal has assured me that the Granadine deputy who produced such an adverse reaction in Lorca was Ramón Ruiz Alonso, who lost his CEDA seat in the reconvened election of May 1936. Since Ruiz Alonso will play an essential role in our narrative this is probably the best moment to provide the reader with some information about his background and personality.

An important clue to an understanding of the man's character is given by José María Gil Robles, the CEDA leader, in his prologue to Ruiz Alonso's book *Corporativism*, which was published in 1937.

Ruiz Alonso comes from the workshop, surges from the very heart of the people, whose sorrows and whose aspirations he shares. Forced by adversity to live in a social environment notably inferior to that which corresponds to him by birth, Ramón Ruiz Alonso is a living synthesis of what the harmony of social classes guided by Christian principles could be like. Far from feeling the bitter spite of those who see their security clawed from under them by the cruel talons of life, Ruiz Alonso has managed to rise above his ill fortune and to extract from his own suffering the fertile germ of a social apostolate.[24]

Ruiz Alonso was born at the turn of the century in Villaflores in the province of Salamanca and, as Gil Robles indicates, his home environment was a comfortable one. Like Robles he was educated by the Salesian brothers in Salamanca, for whom he has since retained a genuine gratitude and over whose old boys' association he has presided for many years.[25] Alonso reveals in the last chapter of his book an obsessive concern with his family's fall from its pristine social status, and a nagging preoccupation with his sufferings at the hands of fate. The chapter contains a synopsis of the principal events of his life, and furnishes us with several important details about this man that might not otherwise have come to our notice.

Ruiz Alonso begins by urging his readers never to give up hope, never to bow before adversity. To encourage them the author will set out an account of his own achievements in the face of hardship. We are made immediately aware of Ruiz Alonso's intense Catholicism, his hatred of democracy, his enormous pride and his sentimentality (seen particularly in his maudlin descriptions of the death of his small son). Before the advent of the Republic, we learn, Alonso had worked as a draughtsman for the Company of Aerial Photogrammetry in Madrid, as well as doing private work of the same kind. At this period his life was prosperous. Under the Republic, however, he found himself converted into a menial bricklayer, earning only eight pesetas a day. He does not tell us how this came about, although elsewhere in the book we learn that he was persecuted for his anti-Marxist ideas and that his dismissal was secured from six jobs because he refused to join the ranks of the left-wing trade unionists. The genuine proletariat with which Ruiz Alonso was surrounded evidently took an immense dislike to the violently anti-Republican *nouveau pauvre* who refused to participate in their class struggle.

But life, with all its hardships, could not keep Ruiz Alonso down, mainly, he tells us, because the memory of his well-off family and its subsequent impoverishment acted as a powerful stimulus to his urge for success. He, Ramón Ruiz Alonso, was not going to be pushed around by left-wing rogues and anti-Catholic atheists!

I have mentioned that Ruiz Alonso, like Gil Robles, was educated by the Salesians in Salamanca. While we do not know if the two men were contemporaries at the college, it is certain that they became close associates in Madrid, where Ruiz Alonso took a part-time job on the Jesuit-controlled daily newspaper *El Debate*, the most influential Catholic voice in Spain. Gil Robles was on the

1. Federico García Lorca and Constantino Ruiz Carnero, editor of the left-wing
El Defensor de Granada, on the terrace of the García villa.

Ruiz Alonso, el proletario "honoris causa", huésped de gran hotel y plañidero en un taxi

¡A por los trescientos... a por los trescientos kilómetros por hora hacia Madrid!

Don Ramón era un ferviente trescientista. Era y lo es. Y ahora veremos esta adoración por la cifra a través del tiempo. Don Ramón, además de este fervor, tenía otros entusiasmos. Sentía la caricia del pijama de seda en los soliloquios del hogar y amaba el traje de mahón para lucir el de obrero cuando entraba en funciones oratorias. Y lo mismo que se dejaba abrazar por estos cariños, se abandonaba al temor de los descalabros. Ejemplo al canto: don Ramón tuvo necesidad un día de acomodarse entre el terciopelo de un taxi de magnífica carrocería para marchar a Algeciras con unos discursos preconcebidos. Don Ramón realizó el viaje de ida y vuelta sin novedad. La novedad la tuvo el chófer. No le pagó. Y bastó que un día se lo recordásemos, a los tres meses del viaje, para que el temor a los cuchicheos le convenciera de que debía dar lo suyo al proletario que le trasladó a Algeciras. Pagó tarde, pero en fin, pagó. Somos justos y lo declaramos así.

Hoy hemos sabido otra cosa. Don Ramón, el mismo domingo electoral—él sabrá por qué—se trasladó a un elegante hotel de la Alhambra. El «maitre» le recibió en el «hall» con galantería estudiada para turistas:

—Caballero, el cuarto número... Hay baño, calefacción. Todo. ¿Quiere que le preparemos el baño?..

Un botones se le cuadró con amabilidad de gran hotel:

—Señorito, por aquí...

En fin, el obrero, el proletario o el jornalero de la Ceda, como ustedes quieran llamarle, era aquel día todo un caballero, todo un señorito. Cena espléndida, lecho tierno y acogedor. El hotel elegante de la Alhambra no era exactamente una posada como esas donde van a dormir los «pardillos» que le han votado—porque algunos le han votado—cuando vienen a la ciudad a que les pegue guantadas en las espaldas don Ramón.

El día del lunes amaneció esplendoroso para el Frente popular. Don Ramón paseaba con su pijama azul por los pasillos del gran hotel Entraba a su habitación, todo confort, marcaba un número del teléfono, recibía una noticia alarmante y sus chinelas zapateaban de indignación por el brillo de los baldosines.

Llegó un taxi a la puerta del hotel de lujo.

Quince minutos después don Ramón salía acompañado de unos señores. Y ya con el pie en el estribo del coche, un diálogo breve y tierno. Puños cerrados, miradas feroces. Y al fin lo conmovedor. Los señores desconocidos abrazan a don Ramón y todos lloran. Un pañuelo de despedida. Don Ramón ordena al chófer:

—¡Vamos a por los trescientos...; a por los trescientos kilómetros por hora hacia Madrid!

Y el taxi se perdió en unos minutos.

2. *El Defensor de Granada*, 19 February 1936, satirises Ruiz Alonso.

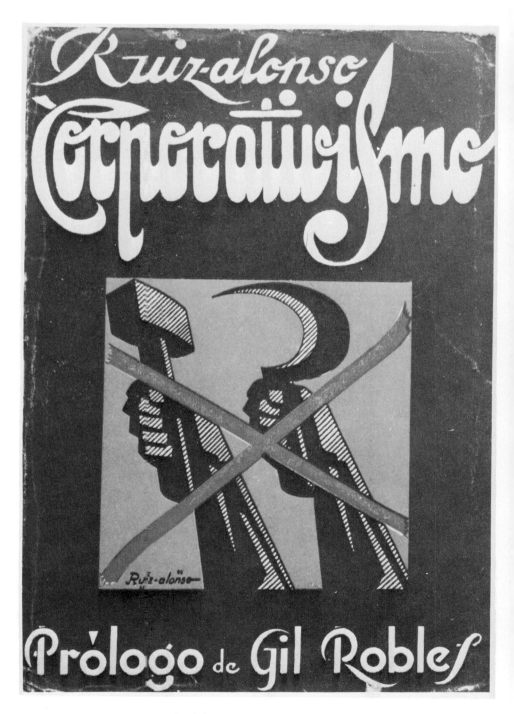

3. ¡Corporativismo!, a book by Ruiz Alonso which attempted to describe an
ideal Spanish Fascist state.

Ramón Ruiz Alonso

obrero tipógrafo

Diplomado en Ciencias sociales y exdiputado a Cortes

¡Corporativismo!

Ya sé que habrá por ahí quien diga...

que capital y trabajo serán siempre rivales irreconciliables y que jamás será salvado el abismo
insondable que les separa marcando a cada cual
su rumbo, su camino, su meta...

...También se repelen y se rechazan los colores.
El blanco es pureza, candor, júbilo, alegría; eco
triunfal de esponsal que avanza por templo en-
galanado en busca de un altar y una ilusión.
El negro es luto, pena, amargura, tristeza, llanto;
lúgubre acento de arrogante figura que fué y tan
solo espera ya una fosa en que aniden los gusanos.

Y sin embargo...
¡Ovejas negras aciertan a parir corderillos blancos!

1937
——————— **Primera edición** ———————
Composición e impresión de la Comercial Salmantina
Prior, 19 ——————— **Salamanca** ——————— **España**
——————— **Primer año triunfal** ———————

4. The title page of Ruiz Alonso's book.

5. Ruiz Alonso seen by the political cartoonist Sirio in 1933. Alonso arrested Lorca on 16 August 1936.

6. *Left*. Commandant José Valdés Guzmán, Civil Governor of Granada during the repression, gave the order for Lorca's death.

7. *Above*. Part of the outside wall of Granada cemetery, where many executions took place, as it looked in 1966.

8. The ossuary of Granada cemetery in 1966.

staff of the newspaper and it can be no coincidence that Ruiz Alonso's book was concerned with corporativism, the political system envisaged by Gil Robles as the one best suited to Spain, nor that the CEDA leader should have agreed to write an introduction to it. Robles must have become aware of the services that his colleague on *El Debate* could lend to the party, and it was probably due to his influence that Ruiz Alonso was sent to Granada in 1933 to work as a typographer for *Ideal* which, like *El Debate*, was controlled by Editorial Católica, the Jesuit publishing company.

Things were now looking up for Ruiz Alonso and his satisfaction must have been complete when the CEDA decided to include him on their list of candidates to contest the 1933 election. On 4 November 1933 *El Defensor de Granada* announced:

Last night we learned that the organising committee of the right-wing coalition has agreed to modify its list of candidates. Don Alfonso García Valdecasas has been excluded and his place taken by the typographer Ramón Ruiz Alonso.

The Right, as we know, won an overwhelming victory in the election, and Ruiz Alonso became an MP as representative of Acción Obrerista, the Catholic workers' party that formed part of the larger CEDA organisation.

During his first year in the Cortes the 'domesticated worker' (*obrero amaestrado*, as he had been nicknamed, allegedly by José Antonio Primo de Rivera), failed to distinguish himself on behalf of Acción Obrerista, over whose central committee he now presided. On 18 November 1934 he published an open letter in the Madrid daily *ABC* in which he formally dissociated himself from the party, claiming that politics were vilifying the soul of the proletariat and that the class struggle should be divorced altogether from party politics and restricted to the trade unions, where it belonged. Acción Obrerista reacted furiously to its leader's treachery and published a rejoinder in *ABC* on 20 November in which it deplored the underhand method chosen by him to announce his resignation, reminding him that he should now

relinquish the seat in the Cortes which he was occupying on its
behalf. The statement expressed its opinion of Ruiz Alonso's
parliamentary record in a pungent paragraph:

We appreciate that Ramón Ruiz Alonso should decide that he does not
want to discuss politics, even when they have to do with the workers—
with the defence of the working classes. His total failure to take part in
parliamentary proceedings during the past year has made this patently
obvious.

Far from giving up his seat, however, the 'domesticated worker'
now chose to ally himself more closely with the work of Acción
Popular, in whose ranks he militated during the two years leading
up to the elections of February 1936 and the triumph of the Popular
Front. But he lost his seat in the Cortes as a result of the annulment
of the Granada election, and his humiliating defeat in the reconvened election of May 1936 confirmed him in his already aggressive
loathing of democracy:

The Parliament was all lies, all deceit.
It was necessary to destroy it, to shake its very foundations, to leave not
a stone standing, in order to build anew, to construct, to preserve.
And a Parliament which did not want to die threw me from its midst
so that I should not be a witness to its shameful downfall nor read its
death sentence on its face. Before this it had proposed the annulment
of my election and the acceptance of its own candidates for Granada . . .
How disgusting! How disgusting! How disgusting!
And how proud I was!
By this time people were talking about a revolution. I returned to the
people, I identified with the people and became again what I had been
before.
The people!
I breathed again with expanded lungs. I learned what it was like to
conspire, because I became a conspirator . . .[26]

Ruiz Alonso's book is little more than an unoriginal Fascist
manual and, having attempted to describe what a Spanish corpora-
tive state would be like, he appends a translation of 'The Corpora-

tive Laws of Italian Fascism', headed with the words: 'The complete text of the documents necessary to study the Italian regime'. The attitude of mind revealed on every page is a Fascist one, and Ruiz Alonso shows himself to be an implacable enemy of democracy and the political freedom of the Spanish people. Between his political objectives and those of the Falangist and military conspirators in Granada, with whom he collaborated, there can have been little essential difference. Ruiz Alonso's Fascist attitudes attracted the dislike of the left-wing *Defensor de Granada*, which barracked him with unfailing zest during the months that led up the rising, and there is no doubt that the town's Republicans regarded him as one of their most unpleasant enemies (see plate 2).

This, then, was the man who returned to Granada on the same train as Federico García Lorca on the night of 16 July 1936. Did they know each other? Federico's startled reaction to seeing Ruiz Alonso suggests that they did, and that there may have existed between them some mutual antagonism whose origins we cannot trace. And was Gil Robles's disciple, now by his own admission a conspirator against the Republic, aware of the presence on the train of a poet whom, even if he did not know him personally, he must have detested?

We cannot tell, but one thing is certain: Federico's arrival in his home town did not pass unnoticed. On 16 July *Ideal*, the newspaper by which Ruiz Alonso was employed, announced in its personal column:

The Granadine poet Don Federico García Lorca is in town.*

Exactly a month later the poet whose name will always be linked with that of Granada was arrested.

The man who detained him was Ramón Ruiz Alonso.

* It seems that *Ideal* had been misled by a rumour regarding the poet's imminent arrival into the belief that he was already in Granada. Nadal insists that Federico left Madrid on the night of 16 July.

FIVE

The Fall of Granada

For well over a century the Army has been a decisive factor in Spanish politics, and the military coup or *pronunciamiento* a much abused means of effecting political change. This was so throughout the nineteenth century and in the case of Primo de Rivera's accession to power in 1923; and it was so with the Nationalist insurrection in July 1936, although Franco had to wait two and a half years for the eventual fall of Madrid.

The rebellion began on 17 July 1936 with the revolt of a small group of officers of the Melilla garrison in Spanish Morocco who, supported by troops of the Foreign Legion, soon took the city. Similar risings in Ceuta and Tetuan were equally successful and, by midnight, the insurgents had gained almost complete control throughout the area and were pushing ahead their preparations for the military offensive on the Spanish mainland.[1]

A few hours later Generals Franco and Orgaz seized control of Las Palmas in the Canary Islands, and at 5.15 a.m. on 18 July Franco's famous Manifesto announcing the Nationalist Movement* and calling on the support of loyal Spaniards was broadcast to the mainland from all Canary and Spanish-Moroccan radio stations.[2]

---

* El Movimiento (Nacional), the name by which both the Nationalist rising and the subsequent political system in Spain are commonly known.

That same morning the Madrid Government transmitted a bulletin in which it informed the Spanish people that a military rising against the Republic had taken place in Morocco but that everything was quiet on the mainland.[3] The broadcast came too late for the morning newspapers in Granada, however, and the only indication in *Ideal* on 18 July that all was not normal appeared in an announcement on the front page that 'causes beyond our control have prevented us from obtaining our customary general news'.

But everything was *not* quiet on the Spanish mainland, despite the Government's assurances, and that morning General Queipo de Llano seized command of the Sevillan garrison in a coup of the greatest audacity. Queipo, who had been sent to Seville as Director of Customs Police, arrested almost single-handed the Captain General of the region, General Villa-Abrille, and the Colonel of the Regiment, and with the help of as few as one hundred soldiers and fifteen Falangists gained control of the city centre by nightfall. Joined now by the Civil Guard and the artillery section of the garrison, Queipo's success was certain; the workers, demoralised and weaponless, could only barricade themselves into the populous quarters on the outskirts of the city and await the inevitable repression.[4]

During 18 July the Government continued to broadcast in-accurate bulletins on the course of what it refused to admit was a full-blooded military rising. At 7.20 p.m. it announced that Queipo de Llano had proclaimed martial law in Seville, adding that 'various seditious acts have been perpetrated there by rebel military elements which have now been crushed by Government forces. Cavalry reinforcements have just entered the city . . . The rest of the Peninsula remains loyal to the Government, which is in complete control of the situation'.[5]

One and a half hours later Queipo broadcast from Radio Seville the first of what was to be a long series of nightly bulletins notable for their fiery rhetoric, misrepresentations and gruesome fanaticism. The General announced that the Nationalist rising had triumphed everywhere in Spain except Madrid and Barcelona; that the transportation of troops from Africa was being effected

at that very moment; that columns would advance immediately
on Granada, Córdoba, Jaén, Extremadura, Toledo and Madrid
and that the Marxist scum (*canalla*) would be exterminated like
wild animals.[6]

Queipo's bulletin threw the people of Granada into confusion,
and both the garrison and the civilian population of the town dis-
played extreme uneasiness in the face of the disturbing, and in-
compatible, reports being broadcast from different radio stations.
The garrison, it will be remembered, was at this time subordinate
to the Captaincy-General in Seville, and Queipo's assumption of
command there inevitably challenged the loyalties of Granada's
soldiery.

The General's account of the military situation on the night of
18 July had been intentionally misleading, for in fact the rising had
so far been restricted to Andalusia, where resistance from the
Republicans had been more or less overcome in all the main cities
except Málaga, which remained in the hands of the Popular
Front.[7]

In Madrid the Government floundered in a state of extreme
confusion and seemed unable to decide what should be done or
even to grasp the significance of what was happening. Precious,
irrecuperable time was lost in prevarication and until 19 July the
Government stubbornly refused to distribute arms to the people.
Indeed the Prime Minister, Casares Quiroga, announced that anyone who did so without his permission would be shot: a warning
that was heeded by the majority of Civil Governors throughout
the country, including Granada, and that facilitated more than
anything else the easy Nationalist successes of July 18.*

We possess little trustworthy documentation on the events that
led up to the rising in Granada, particularly because no copies
seem to have survived of the left-wing *Defensor de Granada* for
July 1936, which could usefully be read against Nationalist
accounts (the newspaper was closed on the first day of the Move-

---

* Hugh Thomas, p. 135: 'But had the liberal Government of Casares Quiroga
distributed arms, and ordered the Civil Governors to do so too, thus using the
working class to defend the Republic at the earliest opportunity, it is possible
that the rising would have been crushed'.

ment in Granada and never reappeared). According to Gollonet and Morales there was constant activity in the Civil Government on 18 July, with meetings between the Governor, Torres Martínez, and the leaders of the various trade unions and left-wing political groups,[8] while *Ideal* mentions that during the afternoon Torres Martínez was visited by General Campins.[9] Since Gollonet and Morales state that no journalists were allowed to be present at these meetings it will be wise to treat with care their account of the conversations that allegedly took place. What is certain is that General Campins was determined to support the Government and that Torres Martínez flatly refused to distribute arms to the workers, despite constant and well-reasoned demands to do so from leaders of the left-wing groups. Gollonet and Morales repeatedly claim that arms were in fact allotted to the 'Marxist rabble'[10] but this seems no more than an attempt by Nationalist propagandists to justify the subsequent repression. I have been unable to find any evidence in Granada that the authorities distributed arms to the people. On the contrary, the survivors of the repression with whom I talked unanimously criticised the weak Torres Martínez for his failure to act decisively in this matter (had he in fact distributed arms he would no doubt have been executed immediately; in the event, the Nationalists spared him).[11] Moreover, there was virtually no armed resistance to the rebels when the Movement began, which speaks for itself. It is undeniable that the Republicans had only a very limited supply of pistols and rifles, and these without adequate ammunition.

The *Cruzada* provides information about the formation of various workers' groups and describes the setting-up on 18 July of a joint committee that would sit permanently in the Town Hall and try to coordinate plans to resist the Movement.[12] But despite the desperate efforts made by the Popular Front to organise a workers' militia that would allow them, first, to contain a rising by the garrison, and then to resist outside attack, nothing constructive was achieved.

During the night of 18 July few *granadinos* can have slept soundly. The local radio station continued to relay Government bulletins and to broadcast exhortations from Popular Front spokesmen, while from Radio Seville came reports of Nationalist victories all over the country. What would happen in Granada? Would the garrison rise in arms against the people? With such thoughts the citizens anxiously awaited the new day.

Next morning, Sunday 19 July, Granada received confirmation that Queipo de Llano was indeed in control of Seville. The headline on the front page of *Ideal* read THE GOVERNMENT DENIES THE EXISTENCE OF A MILITARY RISING, but the subtitle IT SAYS THAT THE RISING IS RE-STRICTED TO MOROCCO AND SEVILLE showed that things were much more serious than the Government allowed. *Ideal* had been unable to receive information from Madrid through the normal channels and had been forced to rely on official Government bulletins for news of what was happening throughout the country. It had also been subjected to censorship. No one could doubt that Spaniards were once again engaged in civil war.

Ideal had managed to obtain an early morning interview with the Civil Governor, who had declared that all the necessary steps had been taken to prevent the outbreak of any disturbance in Granada.[13] But plans for the capture of the town were already well advanced.

According to the *Cruzada*, Colonel Antonio Muñoz of the Artillery Regiment had visited his colleague Colonel Basilio León Maestre of the Infantry Regiment at 4.00 that morning to discuss tactics for the rising. They had been unable to reach a firm agreement about the final details, and meetings between the various rebel officers continued during 19 and 20 July until the Movement began.[14]

The same source states that General Campins received an urgent telephone call from the Government at 11.00 that morning. He was to organise immediately a column to relieve Córdoba, which had fallen to the insurgents. Campins summoned his two Colonels and explained the position, ordering them to prepare their men at once for the expedition. Muñoz and León were now in a quandary. If they obeyed the General's instructions the garrison, already depleted by leaves of absence, would not be strong enough to guarantee the success of the rising. So they decided to play for time, and throughout the day the General was fobbed off with one excuse after another: the officers were unhappy about leaving Granada, the equipment was being checked and so on. In the early hours of the afternoon Captain Nestares visited the Artillery and Infantry barracks to convince Muñoz and León of the necessity of assuming immediate command of the situation. His movements were noticed and reported to the Civil Governor, who rang Campins to inquire about Nestares's behaviour. Torres Martínez, who had been receiving contradictory telephone calls from the Government all day long and was mentally exhausted, was told by an equally harassed Campins that he would look into the matter. The General telephoned the Artillery barracks and was once again put off with a vague explanation. He was clearly quite out of touch with the situation.

Meanwhile the workers were becoming uneasy. They had noticed the comings and goings between the barracks, and had been listening to the radio bulletins that gave evidence of bitter fighting all over the country. They now decided to form a column of their own to relieve Córdoba, and a call for support was put through to Madrid. Shortly afterwards Lieutenant-Colonel Fernando Vidal Pagán of the Civil Guard received orders from the Government to collect weapons for the provision of the workers' column from the arsenal in the Artillery barracks. But the artillerymen under Muñoz had already decided that they would refuse to hand over the arms. More telephone calls to and from Madrid. Eventually, at 9.00 p.m., Campins decided to visit the barracks himself.

Once there he delivered a lecture to his officers and ordered them to supply the necessary arms to the Civil Guard. He returned to the Military Commandery, apparently still unaware that he no longer held effective control of the garrison and that his orders were being disregarded.

That night further instructions were received from Madrid that the firearms were to be collected from the artillery arsenal, and at this point Vidal Pagán delegated responsibility for carrying out these orders to Lieutenant Mariano Pelayo who, unknown to his commanding officer, was one of the leaders of the conspiracy.[15]

From now on events in Granada were to move rapidly against the Republic.

At 1.30 a.m. on Monday 20 July, Pelayo arrived at the Artillery barracks with a Government order demanding the provision of 3000 weapons for the Córdoba column. The decision to withhold them was ratified and Campins was informed once more that the arms were still being prepared and would be ready within a few hours. At 7.00 a.m. Commandant Rodríguez Bouzo of the Artillery Regiment was sent by Muñoz to sound out Captain Alvarez of the Assault Guards, who immediately promised his support, while a similar confirmation was received from the officers of the Civil Guard. It was now evident to the rebels that they would have complete military control when the rising began; it was equally evident that Campins could no longer be deceived and that the workers might at any moment storm the barracks. The conspirators decided that the troops would be taken into the street that afternoon.[16]

It is oppressively hot in Granada in the months of July and August, and General Campins may have been taking a fitful siesta after lunch when he was informed that the call to arms had been heard sounding from the Artillery barracks and that several civilians had been seen to enter the building. Campins immediately set off for the barracks and was dumbfounded to see the regiment, in full battle dress, drawn up in the courtyard. With the soldiers were thirty Falangists under the command of Commandant José Valdés Guzmán.[17] The inevitable confrontation between Campins and Muñoz now took place and it must have come as an unpleasant shock to the General to realise that his subordinate had been plotting behind his back. Informed that the Infantry Regiment, the Civil Guard and the Assault Guard had all thrown in their lot with the rebels, the despairing and incredulous Campins was escorted by Muñoz to the Infantry barracks. Here, too, the troops were already drawn up.

Shortly afterwards the General, now a prisoner, was driven back to the Military Commandery and forced to sign the proclamation of war which had been prepared for him by the rebel officers.

By now the troops were in the street and batteries of artillery were being placed at strategic points throughout the town: in the Plaza del Carmen, opposite the Town Hall; in the Puerta Real, the town's hub; in the Plaza de la Trinidad, behind the Civil Government. The time was 5.00 p.m. According to *Ideal* the steel-helmeted soldiers were cheered by the public as they marched through Granada[18], although the *Cruzada* notes that there was considerable confusion as to the political significance of what was happening:

Even the Reds, tricked into believing that the troops have left their barracks to 'fraternise with the people', applaud the march past. They soon learn their mistake. The troops open fire on them and the Reds, battered and in disarray, run in panic up the Carrera del Darro . . .[19]

As the various artillery positions were being set up throughout the town another detachment of soldiers drove to the airport at Armilla, taking it without opposition, while resistance at the vital explosives factory in El Fargue on the Murcia road was quickly crushed.

At about the same time Captain Nestares arrived at the Police Commissary in Duquesa Street, across the road from the Civil Government. The police had decided that morning to support the Movement and all day had persistently refused to distribute arms to the workers. Shortly after Nestares entered the building a group of Assault Guards left to take up positions around the town.

At 6.00 p.m. an artillery section commanded by Captain García Moreno and supported by Valdés and his Falangists arrived in front of the Civil Government. They were joined by Nestares, who had been waiting in the Police Commissary. The few Assault Guards at the entrance to the Civil Government, realising that opposition would be futile, stood aside. The rebels met no resistance as they ran into the building. The Civil Governor was arrested in his office and Rus Romero, secretary of the Popular Front Committee, and Virgilio Castilla, head of the Granada County Council, who had been in discussion with him, were taken across the road to the Police Commissary (and shot a few days later). Lieutenant-Colonel Vidal Pagán, head of the Civil Guard and a loyal Republican, was also taken into custody.

Valdés now assumed the post of Civil Governor. The first thing he did was to instal a machine-gun at the entrance to the building, a weapon whose use in such a narrow street would have been devastating. Then he telephoned all mayors throughout the province and ordered them to hand over their authority to the local Civil Guard. About this time hundreds of middle-class *granadinos* started to arrive at the Civil Government to declare their loyalty to the Nationalist Cause and offer their services to the new Governor.

Meanwhile the rebels entered the Town Hall. They met with no resistance here either and the municipal guards and other personnel who happened to be in the building had little option but to throw in their lot with the troops. Manuel Fernández Montesinos, like Torres Martínez, was arrested in his office, and Lieutenant-Colonel Miguel del Campo of the Infantry Regiment took his place as mayor.[20]

By nightfall the whole centre of Granada had fallen to the rebels. Hundreds of 'undesirables' were already in gaol. Virtually no resistance had been offered to the troops and *Ideal*, referring to the large numbers of civilians who flocked to put themselves at the disposal of the Military Commander, observed:

People commented on the complete ease with which all the official centres had been taken, without there having been the least resistance and without any violence at all having been necessitated . . .

Indeed, *Ideal* insists on the facility with which the centre of the town was occupied, and comments later in the same report:

Not a single person wounded by the troops has entered any charitable establishment, in spite of the fact that some shots were fired in different parts of the capital, either at suspicious individuals who ignored the order to raise their arms as they walked down the street or in answer to the very occasional pistol shots fired at the troops . . .[21]

The *Cruzada* is even more explicit:

By the afternoon of 20 July the town was almost completely sub-
jugated, and with such small loss of life that it was necessary to regret
only the death of a Security Guard, killed as he accompanied Captain
Nestares along the Carrera del Genil . . .[22]

At 6.30 p.m., and subsequently at half-hourly intervals, the
proclamation of war drawn up for Campins by the insurgents was
read over Radio Granada:

PROCLAMATION

I, DON MIGUEL CAMPINS AURA, Brigadier-General and
Military Commander of this Region, ANNOUNCE:
First article. Given the state of disorder prevailing throughout the
country for the past three days and the lack of initiative on the part of
the central Government, and with the purpose of saving Spain and the
Republic from the present chaos, a STATE OF WAR is hereby
proclaimed from this moment throughout the province.

Second article. All officials who fail to use every means at their disposal
to maintain the public peace will be automatically dismissed from their
positions and held personally responsible for their actions.

Third article. Anyone who, in order to disturb the public peace, to
intimidate the inhabitants of a town or to carry out any retaliation of a
social character, uses explosives or inflammable material or any other
means or appliance adequate and sufficient to cause serious damage, or
accidents to trains or other terrestrial or aerial modes of locomotion,
will be punished with the maximum penalties prescribed under present
laws.

Fourth article. Anyone who, without the necessary authorisation,
fabricates, has in his possession or transports explosives or inflammable
material, or possessing these legitimately, delivers or facilitates them
without previous guarantees to persons who proceed to use them to
commit the crimes defined in the previous articles, will be punished
with a sentence ranging from 4 months to 12 years.

5th article. Anyone who, while not directly inducing others to commit
the offences punishable under the first article, should publicly encourage
others to commit it, or justify the same infraction or anyone committing
it, will be punished with a sentence ranging from 4 months to 6 years.

Sixth article. Robbery with violence or intimidation carried out by two or more malefactors, when one of these is in the possession of arms and when murder or injuries listed in the first article of this law result, will be punished with death.

Seventh article. Anyone possessing arms of whatever sort, or explosives, must deliver these before eight o'clock this evening to the nearest Civil Guard post.

Eighth article. Groups of more than three persons will be dissolved with maximum energy by the troops.
CITIZENS OF GRANADA: For the sake of the peace that has been disrupted, for order, love of Spain and the Republic, for the re-establishment of the labour laws, I expect your collaboration in the cause of order.

Long live Spain. Long live the Republic.[23]

The *Cruzada*, published two years after the end of the Civil War, states that this document reflected the confusion in which Campins now found himself.[24] Doubtless this is true but it must also have reflected the confusion of the rebel officers who had drawn it up and who can have had no clear ideas about the political system envisaged by the insurrectionary generals.

Campins's declaration to *Ideal* on the night of 20 July also had the flavour of a document prepared for him by the rebels:

I have sought consistently to remain within the bounds of legality; but faced with the manifest state of abandon in which the Government was leaving us, and the lack of attention from the Civil Governor, with whom I have tried at all times to maintain contact, I have deemed it expedient to proclaim a state of war throughout the province.

Moreover, the extremist elements in the town were actively engaged in inciting the soldiers by distributing leaflets in which they urged them to rebel against their officers, and other things: this in spite of the Army's gentlemanly behaviour.

I informed the Governor of what was happening but he did nothing to prevent these disgraceful incidents from taking place.

As a result the Army was showing signs of great uneasiness. The extremist elements had also asked the Civil Governor to allow the arms in the Artillery barracks to be handed over to them. This is what really decided me to take the solution adopted, since I could not allow these arms to fall into the hands of such elements, even though the Governor had assured me that they would not be used against us but against military units from other capitals. As you will appreciate, I could not hand over weapons to be employed against our brothers-in-arms. Another very alarming rumour circulating in the town was that there was a plan afoot to attack the Infantry barracks . . .[25]

Only in the old quarter of the Albaicín, with its labyrinth of steep and easily-barricaded streets, had there been any opposition to the Nationalists, and it was here that the Republicans, almost without arms, now prepared as best they might to resist the inevitable rebel onslaught. Later that night another bulletin, allegedly from Campins, assured citizens listening to Radio Granada that the garrison was determined to serve the best interests of Spain and of the Republic ('the faithful expression of the will of the Spanish people') and went on to warn of the penalties awaiting those who failed to comply with the wishes of the authorities:

The maximum rigours of martial law will fall on any misguided individual who fails to do everything in his power to prevent disturbances to the normal life of this town. Likewise, I demand that every attempted disturbance be denounced to me personally, and I assure you that I have taken every precaution to see that martial law, which is not to interfere in any way with the life of the town, means inflexibility with those who disregard my orders.[26]

For the people of the Albaicín the meaning of what was happening had become abundantly clear. Everyone knew that an offensive against the quarter was imminent, and feverish attempts were now made to prepare its defences.

The main access to the Albaicín from the centre of Granada runs along the narrow Carrera del Darro to the Paseo de los Tristes and then up the sharply-angled Cuesta del Chapiz. It was essential that this entrance to the Albaicín should be barricaded and accordingly a deep trench was cut across the bottom of the

Cuesta del Chapiz to prevent vehicles from climbing the hill. Similar trenches and makeshift barriers quickly sealed off the many other, narrower streets.

Seeing these preparations the Nationalists made plans to crush the workers' opposition. First two artillery batteries were placed in strategic positions overlooking the quarter: one just below the Church of Saint Christopher above the Albaicín on the road to Murcia, and the other on top of a bastion of the Alhambra directly facing the Republicans across the gorge of the river Darro. Night had by now fallen and the rebels decided to take no action till the following morning. There was some sporadic shooting, however, which claimed two Nationalist deaths and probably many more Republican ones.[27]

On 21 July both batteries opened fire on the Albaicín and violent shooting took place between the rebels (Infantry, Assault Guards and Falangists) and the scantily-armed workers who, from the windows and balconies of their tightly-packed houses, were in an advantageous position to attack the troops with the few pistols and rifles at their disposal. But the Nationalists soon managed to penetrate the Albaicín at several points and many arrests were made. No accurate figures for casualties are available. Radio Granada, meanwhile, continued to broadcast appeals from the rebel authorities to the 'loyalty' and 'good sense' of the people, and made it quite clear that as much force as was necessary would be used to crush all resistance in the Albaicín:

The criminal conduct of a band of outlaws who, in the last death-rattle of their attempt to devour our country, have been disturbing the life of Granada from the Albaicín, is about to come to an end; following the norms of the last decree, with which Granada is already familiar, our valiant troops of Assault Guards, Infantry and Artillery have now gone to attack the wild beasts in their lairs. I rely on the serenity of the citizens of Granada not to be alarmed by our resolution that the town shall be able, at last, to enjoy again the calm of its incomparable nights.

Your Military Commander joins with you in a vibrant 'Long Live Spain! Long Live the Republic! Long Live Granada!'[28]

The new military decree to which this note refers had been issued earlier that evening, when León Maestre had officially taken over from General Campins as Military Commander of Granada.* Maestre was now the supreme military authority in the province, and his decree reflected the ruthless intransigence with which enemies of the Nationalists could henceforth expect to be treated:

I call on all those Granadine patriots who love the one, noble and glorious Spain, and ask them to give their whole hearts and serene self-discipline to the carrying out of my orders.

1. The capital and province are now under martial law and every offence will be dealt with by military tribunals.

2. Anyone committing aggressive acts and hostilities against the Army and the forces of law and order will be given a summary trial and executed.

3. Anyone caught carrying arms, or who within three hours has not handed over any arms in his possession to the Civil Guard, Assault Guard or Police, will be given a summary trial and executed.

4. Groups of more than three people are strictly forbidden and will be dissolved by the troops without previous warning.

5. From the moment this decree is promulgated the driving of all vehicles of whatever kind by civilians is strictly forbidden.

6. The right to strike has been abolished and strike committees will be executed.

7. Anyone committing sabotage of whatever kind, and especially against communications, will be given a summary trial and executed.

Given in Granada on this 21 July 1936, to be scrupulously obeyed.

LONG LIVE SPAIN. LONG LIVE THE REPUBLIC. LONG LIVE GRANADA.[29]

---

* The unfortunate General Campins was flown to Seville and executed by firing squad on 16 August 1936 on the orders of Queipo de Llano. His death was announced by *Ideal* on 18 August.

In the early hours of the following morning, 22 July, an ulti-
matum clarifying the implications of the previous night's bulletin
was read over Radio Granada to the inhabitants of the Albaicín.
Within three hours the women and children were to leave the
quarter and assemble at places designated by the authorities; the
men were to stand in the doorways of their homes with their arms
up, having first thrown their weapons into the centre of the street,
and white flags were to be hung on the balconies of all the houses
that surrendered. In the event of non-compliance with these
orders the Albaicín would be bombarded at 2.30 p.m. that day
from the artillery emplacements and also from the air.[30]

Shortly after the announcement, long lines of frightened
women and children started to wind their way down the narrow
streets and make for the assembly points. There they were
questioned and searched by female rebel supporters, and taken to a
provisional concentration camp outside the town. The men of the
Albaicín refused to capitulate. Shooting soon broke out again
between them and the rebels, who then retired to allow the
artillery the freedom to bombard the quarter in earnest. This it did,
supported by three fighter planes captured that morning at
Armilla[31], which now flew low over the Albaicín and opened fire
with machine-guns on the pockets of resistance. Hand-grenades
were also dropped.[32] Many buildings were badly damaged in the
bombardment, but in spite of this the workers had still not been
dislodged from their 'lairs' when night fell.[33]

On the following morning, 23 July, the artillery bombardment
was intensified, and this time it met with success. Improvised
white flags began to appear at windows and balconies and the
firing dwindled to occasional outbursts. The little ammunition the
workers possessed had run out and it was clear that further resistance was impossible.

At this moment waiting bands of soldiers and Falangists
invaded the Albaicín, and soon it was all over.[34] Those workers
who were lucky managed to escape from the back of the town
across-country to the Republican lines near Guadix; others less
fortunate were caught trying to get away, while many were
cornered in their own homes. All of these were led away for

interrogation at official centres and the majority were shot soon afterwards. As the *Cruzada* comments: 'The last hope of the Reds in Granada had vanished.'[35]

On 22 July *Ideal* exultantly announced the extinction of resistance in the Albaicín and published a piece by one of its reporters who had visited the quarter after the surrender. 'The power of modern weaponry has left evidence of its irresistible efficacy', he comments. 'The walls of many houses are pitted with fire from rifles, pistols, machine-guns and artillery'. Several buildings had been completely gutted, and the journalist sneers at the pathetic efforts of the workers to defend themselves behind makeshift barricades against the superior equipment of the troops. *Ideal* was now showing its true colours.

Resistance had ended. Other small pockets of opposition in the town had also been crushed and on the night of 23 July the rebels could congratulate themselves on having so easily gained complete control of Granada. They had lost no more than half a dozen men.

As was mentioned earlier, the workers in Granada were almost without arms. Nationalist documentation itself proves this. A handful of pistols and rifles without ammunition is no answer, as the *Ideal* reporter reminds us, to modern artillery, aeroplanes, grenades and machine-guns. Granada fell to the rebels because, quite simply, they had the weapons and the training to use them effectively. One cannot forget, either, the vacillations of the Civil Governor, Torres Martínez, or the ineptitude of General Campins, nor the lack of decisive leadership on the part of the Popular Front organisations. If arms had been distributed to those members of the left-wing groups capable of using them, or if the workers had had the enterprise to seize them by force, the rising in Granada might have been averted and the course of the war altered in favour of the Republic. But none of this happened. The 'resistance' which the Nationalists crushed with such facility was, in reality, no resistance at all, and it is this fact, continually stressed by *Ideal*, that made the subsequent repression of Granada one of the outstanding crimes of the war.

SIX

The Repression

Granada had fallen, but the rebels knew that their position was far from secure. The town was almost completely surrounded by Republican territory and a counter-attack might be launched at any moment. It was essential, therefore, that the Nationalists should immediately consolidate their supremacy in the capital by strengthening its defences and eliminating all possibility of renewed resistance from within the town itself.

To achieve these ends new civilian militia were clearly needed to supplement the forces already in action, and it was for this purpose that on 25 July—Saint James' Day, Spain's national holiday—General Orgaz Yoldi arrived in Granada from Tetuan, touching down at Armilla airport in a German Junkers.[1] He had come with direct orders from General Franco to supervise plans for the defence of Granada, and a few days after his arrival the formation of the civilian militia began. It may now be found useful to detail the principal military groups, civilian organisations and other bodies active in Granada during the war, always bearing in mind that these tended to overlap in practice.

1. *The Military Commandery*. As has been explained, the garrison was made up of an artillery and an infantry regiment. The acting Military Commander after General Campins's arrest, Colonel Basilio León Maestre, was replaced on 29 July 1936 by General

Antonio González Espinosa, who arrived by aeroplane from Seville.[2] Lists of those to be tracked down and shot were drawn up daily in the Commandery. A local judge, Francisco Angulo Montes, was put in charge of these activities. He was assisted by Sergeant Romacho of the Civil Guard, and both men are remembered for their brutality during the repression.

2. *The Civil Government.* Commandant Valdés was surrounded by a mixed group of Falangists, policemen, officers and thugs who devoted themselves to organising the Granada repression. Prominent among these men were the Jiménez de Parga brothers, Julio Romero Funes (the hated policeman who was responsible for the deaths of hundreds of people and who was later killed by the notorious Queros brothers in a gunfight in Granada), a brutal lout nicknamed Italobalbo for his likeness to the Italian Fascist leader, Antonio Godoy Abellán (a rich landowner and old guard Falangist who regularly participated in the shootings in the cemetery) and a certain Captain Fernández. During the interrogations in the Civil Government torture was often used. An instrument known as the 'aeroplane' had been set up in one of the rooms. On this, victims with their arms tied behind their backs were hoisted to the ceiling by their wrists. The screams of men being tortured were often heard by the concierges (with whom I have spoken) and on several occasions prisoners threw themselves from top windows in an effort to kill themselves.

3. *The Falange.* I have noted earlier that the Falange had very few members in Granada before the rising. According to a note published in *Ideal* on 22 July 1936, the organisation was now prepared to enlist anyone who could be vouched for by an 'old shirt' member of the party.[3] The recruitment office in the Civil Government was soon inundated with requests for membership: the *Cruzada* claims that 900 recruits were enlisted in a few days, while Gollonet and Morales put the figure much higher and state that 2000 were enrolled in twenty-four hours.[4] The new recruits were organised, according to Falangist practice, into two 'lines': the first line would fight along the combat fronts with the Army, while the second would be based in the capital and help with the running of essential services. An article on the Granada Falange

published in *Ideal* on 1 September 1936 states that the second line 'is obliged to denounce all those cases which it knows of that are contrary to the Fatherland and to the Spanish Falange'. The Falange was directly responsible for the deaths of many hundreds of *granadinos*.

4. *The 'Españoles Patriotas'.* This was the first civil militia formed by Orgaz, and within a few days it numbered 5175 men under the command of 29 officers and 150 NCOs.[5] Its quarters were established in the bull ring. The Españoles Patriotas first served as a kind of municipal police but later several of its sections fought in the field.

5. *The Requetés (Carlists).* In *Ideal* on 22 July the Carlists pledged their full support for the Movement: 'Our Communion offers its services to the Army, that is to say to Spain herself, asking God and His Holy Mother to protect our forces.' All members were ordered to report immediately to the organisation's HQ, where they would 'make out lists and help in the most useful way possible'. While there were few *requetés* in Granada before the rising (the organisation was strongest in the north of Spain), it was nevertheless soon possible to form a complete battalion.

6. *The Spanish Foreign Legion.* General Orgaz had become aware during his short visit that Granada, even with the aid of the newly formed militia, would not be sufficiently protected to withstand a concerted Republican attack. He decided, therefore, that the garrison should be quickly strengthened with trained military reinforcements. Accordingly at 10.30 a.m. on 3 August 1936 a three-engined Junkers transport landed at Armilla from Tetuan with the first twenty men of Sixth Battalion of the Foreign Legion.[6] Their arrival in Granada was greeted with immense relief by Nationalist supporters, and their presence meant that a Republican recovery of the town would now prove very much more difficult. The Legionaires were employed in the offensives against Republican pockets throughout the province, notably in the taking of Loja on the road to Málaga, and the Moorish soldiers particularly became famous for their savagery.

7. *The Pérez del Pulgar Battalion.* During the siege of Granada by Ferdinand and Isabella in 1491 a Spanish nobleman, Hernán

Pérez del Pulgar, distinguished himself one night by scaling the walls of the town and fixing a scroll bearing the words 'Ave Maria' to the front door of the chief mosque. The battalion named after him was formed at the end of August 1936[7] by Ramón Ruiz Alonso, who spoke to me of it in these terms: 'The battalion was formed to give political prisoners, who would otherwise have been shot, a chance either to redeem themselves on the field or else die with honour before enemy fire. In this way their children would not suffer the stigma of having had Red fathers'.[8] The battalion, which played no part at all in the repression, recruited about 500 men, and Ruiz Alonso has shown me a photograph of himself proudly leading them out of Granada to the front at Alcalá. He forgot to mention, however, that the battalion's behaviour on the field lacked enthusiasm and that one night, perhaps in emulation of the original Pérez del Pulgar, many of the men slipped across the lines to join their Republican brothers. The battalion was disbanded shortly afterwards.

8. *Defensa Armada de Granada.* Formed in September 1936, *Defensa Armada*—its members were popularly known as the 'mangas verdes' ('green-sleeves') because of their green armbands —was composed of civilians unfit for military service through age, infirmity or other causes. Its men were ordered to spy on their neighbours and to denounce any suspicious activities which came to their notice. *Defensa Armada* divided Granada into three sectors, each with its own head who in turn appointed area chiefs and street chiefs within his sector. Each house in Granada was expected to have at least one member, and it was planned that the organisation should eventually assume the municipal functions of the *Españoles Patriotas*, thereby freeing these for military action. By 6 September 1936 *Defensa Armada* had 2086 members, plus 4000 applications which were being carefully screened in order to eliminate all those with even a suggestion of leftish inclinations or past history.[9] In this atmosphere worthy of Orwell's *1984, Defensa Armada* was responsible for the deaths of a huge number of innocent people, often for reasons of personal animosity, jealousy and other non-political factors.

9. *The Civil Guard.* During the repression the Civil Guard

vindicated its reputation for brutality and, with the Falange, took part regularly in the executions in the cemetery. It was a small garrison and, unlike the other right-wing groupings in the town, did not take on new recruits. It was commanded by Lieutenant Mariano Pelayo, who still lives in Granada.

10. *The Assault Guards.* The *asaltos* were at first hesitant to throw in their lot with the rebels, for they were a special constabulary formed by the Republic for its own protection. In Granada many of them were executed, and those who remained did as they were told.

11. *The Police.* The Police HQ was just across the road from the Civil Government (situated in Duquesa Street) and there was constant coming and going between the two buildings. Julio Romero Funes, the police chief, has already been mentioned. One of his most brutal accomplices was a Falangist named Arenas, who joined the police when the rising began.

12. *The 'Black Squads'.* We come finally to the notorious 'Black Squads' about which so much has been said in books on Lorca. It is important to understand that these squads of killers did not constitute a tightly-knit organisation such as, for example, the Falange or the *requetés*. The 'Black Squads' were little more than a loose collection of individuals who enjoyed killing for the sake of killing and to whom Valdés, in order to reduce the population of Granada to the greatest possible state of panic, had given *carte blanche* to carry out assassinations. They worked in close collaboration with the Civil Government, and many of those who operated with the squads were thugs who had joined the Falange in the first days of the Movement, often middle-class thugs. Others saw in the squads an opportunity for working off long-standing grudges against society. All took positive pleasure in killing. Men such as Francisco Jiménez Callejas (known familiarly as 'El pajarero'), an expert throat-slitter who today runs a thriving timber business in Granada; José Vico Escamilla, who owned a small shop in San Juan de Dios Street and is now a rich man; Perico Morales, a night-watchman who had been a member of the Anarchist CNT before the rising; the López Peralta brothers, one of whom, Fernando, later committed suicide; Miguel Fenech, one of the

most active members of the squads, who later became a university professor; the brothers Pedro and Antonio Embíz, Cristóbal Fernández Amigo, Antonio Godoy Abellán (already mentioned in connection with the Civil Government), Miguel Cañadas, Manuel García Ruiz, Miguel Hórques, Carlos Jiménez Vílchez (who still works in the Town Hall in Granada) and the individuals nicknamed 'El Chato de la Plaza Nueva', 'El cuchillero del Pie de la Torre', 'El afilaor' and 'Paco el motrileño'. Few members of these gangs are alive today: many of them later met violent deaths, and those who survive are shunned by the local populace.

The 'Black Squads', as befitted their office, functioned mainly by night and Claude Couffon has graphically described their methods:

The mopping-up operations practised by the Black Squad have an evocative name: *el paseo*. They are carried out to such a characteristic pattern that one can talk of a method. For the men singled out by the killers the first thing (usually in the small hours of the night) is the noise of a car pulling up outside the front door. There are shouts, laughter and curses; if the victim inhabits one of the lower-class districts where families live crammed on all the floors, this is followed by steps on the staircase. And then the terrible scene: the mother clinging to her son, pleading with the killers, who push her away with their rifle-butts; the children and weeping wife at whom the guns are now pointed; the husband, dressing hurriedly, is jostled and bundled out into the stairs. An engine starts up and the car speeds away. Behind the closed shutters the neighbours, waiting, wonder if it will be their turn tomorrow . . . Sometimes the reports ring out at the corner of the street or, still nearer, on the pavement. And the mother or wife goes downstairs, knowing that she'll find a corpse. But she must be careful not to go out into the street too quickly or else more shots might ring out, tumbling her on top of the body she had gone to recover.[10]

Every morning the bodies of the dead and dying were collected in lorries and taken to the San Juan de Dios Hospital. Before he died in 1971, Dr Rafael Jofré (a close friend of Lorca and an expert on *cante jondo*), who was on duty in the hospital during the repression, told me about his sickening experiences there. He was in charge of the ward where wounded prisoners were brought. Often members of the murder squads would arrive and drag dying men out into the street to shoot them. In particular he remembered the visits of a brutal sergeant of the Civil Guard who on one occasion shot a father and son who had been admitted to the hospital months before the rising began. He also recalled the arrival of a batch of foreign prisoners wounded in the famous Barranco de Buco offensive: these were removed and shot almost immediately, as was a boy of fourteen who was arrested while defending the Albaicín.

These, then, were the principal groups and organisations responsible for the military affairs of the province and the repression of the civil population. No information at all about the Granada killings is provided by *Ideal*, Gollonet and Morales, the *Cruzada* or any other Nationalist publication on the war. It is as though they never took place.

As soon as the town fell to the rebels, lists began to be drawn up of those 'undesirables' considered, for whatever reason, to be enemies of the Movement. Before long the provincial gaol, situated on the road to Jaén on the outskirts of the town and originally designed to accommodate a maximum of four hundred men, contained two thousand prisoners in the most deplorable conditions. Those who survived this imprisonment speak with horror of their experiences in the gaol. Nobody knew when it might be his turn to die, for every evening the lists came from the Civil Government and Military Commandery and the names were read out of the men to be shot before sunrise. And frequently members of the 'Black Squads' would arrive and drag someone away, or batter their victims senseless in the cells. The condemned men were herded into the prison chapel and more or less forced to make their last confession. There they spent the night and then, an hour or two before dawn, the scene was always the same: the prisoners were taken from the chapel, roped or wired together and bundled into the lorries waiting to drive them to the slaughter.

The place of execution was the municipal cemetery. This stands behind the Alhambra to the south-west and dominates one of the most beautiful mountainscapes imaginable. Beyond the deep valley of the Genil the Sierra Nevada looms mistily in the last moments before dawn and an expectant silence veils the hills and olive groves. It was to the outside wall of the cemetery that faces the Cerro del Sol that the victims were taken; here that they had their last glimpse of Granada.

Before the lorries reached the cemetery they had first to climb the steep Cuesta de Gomeres. Every morning the British Consul, William Davenhill, and his sister Maravillas, would hear them labouring up the hill, and try not to listen. One morning Maravillas looked out of the window as two lorries turned past the Consulate. 'It was ghastly,' she told me, 'in each lorry there must have been twenty or thirty men and women piled on top of each other, trussed like pigs being taken to market. Ten minutes later we heard shooting from the cemetery and knew that it was all over. It was terrible'.

Spanish military law stipulated that prisoners should be shot blindfolded and facing the firing squad, but in the cemetery such niceties were not observed. The normal procedure was to stand the victims against the wall and shoot them in the back. The firing squad was composed of two lines, the first kneeling, and the signal to shoot was given when the officer commanding the operation dropped his raised sabre. The *coup de grâce* was then administered to each man to ensure that death had taken place (a necessary measure since it often happened that some of the prisoners were not instantly killed by the volley).[11]

The echoes of the fusillades could be heard all round Granada in the silence of the dawn. Helen Nicholson, the American author, who was staying at her son-in-law's house near the Alhambra at the time, has described in a little-known book her experiences in Granada during the first month and a half of the war. Referring to these early-morning executions in the cemetery, she writes:

On Sunday, August the second, we had our early [air-]raid at half-past four, and the second one at eight o'clock, after which we breakfasted downstairs in dressing-gowns. I remember that we were all feeling rather grumpy, for four and a half hours' sleep is an insufficient ration in war-time, when one is under a constant nervous strain. After break-fast we all dragged ourselves rather wearily upstairs, and my daughter and her husband said they were going to Mass. Not being a Catholic myself, I went to my room hoping to snatch another hour's sleep, but there seemed to be an unusual number of soldiers' lorries rattling past our house, and what with the noise they made, sounding their horns every other minute, and the clatter from the servants' *patio*, it was difficult to doze for more than a few minutes at a time. Also I was haunted by an uneasy memory of the night before. About two o'clock I had been awakened by the sound of a lorry and several cars going up the hill towards the cemetery, and shortly afterwards I had heard a fusillade of shots, and then the same vehicles returning. Later I became all too familiar with these sounds, and learned to dread the early morn-ing, not only because it was the enemy's favourite time for bombing us, but also on account of the executions that took place then.[12]

During August Miss Nicholson was to witness the growing intensity of the Nationalist repression of Granada, and the fact that her own right-wing sympathies are evident on every page of her narrative makes her testimony doubly convincing. One final quotation from her account illustrates the horror of the shootings:

For some time the executions had been increasing, at a rate that alarmed and sickened all thinking people. The concierge of the cemetery, who had a modest little family of twenty-three children, begged my son-in-law to find him some place where his wife and his twelve younger children, who were still at home, might live. Their home in the lodge at the cemetery gates had become unbearable to them. They could not help hearing the shots, and sometimes other sounds—the cries and screams of the dying—that made their lives a nightmare, and he feared the effect they might have upon his younger children.[13]

How many people were liquidated by the firing-squads in the cemetery? One of the grave-diggers told Gerald Brenan in 1949 that 'the list of those officially shot shows some eight thousand names'[14], but this figure, which has been widely repeated, is in-accurate. The interment records for 1936–39, which are kept in the cemetery office (no one is allowed to see them without official authorisation), list the names of 2137 men and women shot between 26 July 1936 and 1 March 1939. In the 'cause of death' column for the early victims one finds the euphemistic phrase 'killed by detonation of firearm', but almost immediately the formula 'order of military tribunal' is substituted for it. This figure, it must be stressed, is that given in the official burial records of the cemetery and as such must be taken as a completely accurate *minimum* total of people executed there. It is almost certain that other killings took place in the cemetery which were not recorded officially, but these would probably not constitute a large addition to the sum total. The figure takes no account of the shootings in Víznar nor of the hundreds of assassinations committed by the 'Black Squads' and other killers in the villages of the *vega*. At a conservative estimate it is unlikely that the number of people shot in Granada and the nearby villages including Víznar could be less than 4000. Over the province as a whole the total was very much higher.

Even if the figure of 2137 were to be taken as the sum of all the killings in the capital, however, it would still be an appalling one. The greatest number of executions took place in August 1936, for which month the burial records list no less than 572 names. One appreciates Miss Nicholson's alarm. The figure for September 1936 is 499, for October 190, for November 88. Apart from 143 executions in February 1937, 96 in March and 90 in April, the figures decrease month by month with only occasional sharp rises, as when a batch of prisoners was shot in reprisal for a Republican air-raid or, as was the case on 4 October 1938, for the injury caused to the hated Civil Guard Mariano Pelayo by a letter-bomb meant for someone else.[15]

The daily executions created serious problems for the staff of the cemetery. Bodies were interred in twos and threes wherever room could be found, and eventually the cemetery had to be extended. Brenan writes:

Every morning the wives and mothers of the people who had been arrested would climb the hill to search for the bodies of their menfolk.

There they lay in heaps as they had fallen, till later in the day squads of Falangists would set about burying them. Since the labour of interring so many bodies was considerable, they were bundled into shallow cavities from which their feet and hands often stuck out. An English friend of mine who, at some risk to himself, visited the place a number of times, told me that he saw the bodies of boys and girls still in their teens.[16]

Whatever the risk to Brenan's friend, Nationalist sympathisers, at least, were sometimes allowed to witness the executions. One man whom I met in 1965 at the house of the British Consul told me, with perfect equanimity and quite unaware of my reaction, that he had taken his young children several times to the cemetery to see how 'the enemies of Spain paid for their crimes'.

The flower of Granada's intellectuals, lawyers, doctors and teachers died in the cemetery, along with huge numbers of ordinary left-wing supporters. The more eminent victims, particularly the town councillors, were allowed preferential treatment in the matter of burial and their families were permitted to inter them privately. Today only the tomb of Manuel Fernández Montesinos (see plate 11) can be located with any facility.*

Some of these victims should be mentioned briefly. One of the graves seen by Brenan in 1949 belonged to a 'famous specialist in children's diseases'[17]: this was Rafael García Duarte, Professor of Paediatrics in Granada University, a much-loved man who treated his poorer patients free of charge. His crime was to have been a freemason.

Constantino Ruiz Carnero was editor of the left-wing *El Defensor de Granada*. He was an obvious target for the rebels' hatred and they arrested him on the first day of the rising. Ruiz Carnero suffered from very deficient eyesight and wore glasses with thick lenses. On the night before his execution a prison guard smashed these into his eyes with a rifle-butt. Medical assistance was refused and Ruiz Carnero lay in agony all night. Next morning he was bundled into a lorry with other victims, but when they arrived at the cemetery he was already dead.[18]

* A complete list of the executed town councillors is provided in Appendix A.

Also shot in the cemetery in these early days of the repression was the brilliant engineer Juan José de Santa Cruz, who had constructed the marvellous road to the top of the Sierra Nevada (today the pride of the Spanish Tourist Board). The night before his execution Santa Cruz was allowed to marry the gypsy girl with whom he had lived for many years. The charge against the engineer, trumped up by his enemies, was that he had mined the River Darro where it flows under the streets of Granada.[19]

Other distinguished men shot in the cemetery included the Rector of Granada University, Salvador Vila, a noted Arabist; Joaquín García Labella, who held the Chair of Political Law at the University and was once the youngest professor in Spain; Jesús Yoldi Bereau, Professor of Pharmacy at the University, who with García Labella had been forced in the first weeks of the rising to dig the graves of the victims despatched by the killers in Víznar; José Palanco Romero, Professor of History at the University; José Megías Manzano, Assistant Professor in the Faculty of Medicine; Saturnino Reyes, a well-known doctor; the lawyer José Villoslada (who had tried to kill himself in the prison by slashing his wrists); and even the gentle Protestant pastor, José García Fernández. Names of other notable victims of the firing squads would make the list interminable. Enough has been said to demonstrate that in Granada, as elsewhere throughout Nationalist Spain, the so-called 'Red' intellectuals were hunted down with fanatical zeal, accused of having subverted the masses by preaching liberalism and democracy, and eliminated.*

Little trace can now be found, thirty-seven years after the beginnings of the Civil War, of the last remains of these unfortunate people, for a few years after their death most of the bodies were disinterred and removed to the ossuary at the western edge of the cemetery, near the spot where the Moorish palace of Alixares once stood. The ossuary is a wide, uncovered pit enclosed within high walls, full of a revolting heap of bones, skulls, tattered shrouds and even complete skeletons still wearing their boots.

When Brenan visited the place in 1949 the skulls of the executed

---

* In Appendix B I attempt to estimate as carefully as possible the number of deaths attributable to the Nationalist repression of Granada (capital and province).

men, shattered by the *coup de grâce*, were pointed out to him by a helpful grave-digger. But by 1965, when I scaled the ossuary walls, the exhumed bodies of the victims had already been buried under new layers of bones and shrouds. I took my photographs (the visions of Bosch and Goya came to mind) and left.

9. Lorca's family home, the *Huerta de San Vicente,* in 1967.

10. View from the terrace of the *Huerta de San Vicente*. (See plate No. 1)

11. Manuel Fernández Montesinos, who was married to Lorca's sister, served briefly as mayor of Granada and was executed early in the repression at the Granada cemetery.

IDEAL

Granada, sábado 22 de agosto de 1936   NUM. 1.2

Tendillas de Santa Paula, 6

de Castejón se aproxir

aca ha dado una noticia viste indudable impor-Asegura que las fuer-la Guardia civil y de-tar y están en sus cuar-se dirigen hacia la ciu-la que la que le presta is columnas que operan arse sobre la capital o son objetivos militares t. Es muy probable que tas posiciones debe pre-

por tierra del resto de España, parece que, por Una emisora extranjera stián, a la vista de los marxistas, han decidido o tendría nada de ex-vascos padecen la triste icia de Vasconia—y eso ina—, en todo lo demás s.

táctica que se ha ope-mejores resultados, pero ta confesión de fracaso. Guerra, hizo una incur-idalucía. El empeño era Madrid. Ahora aparece aquella plaza. Allí es-cito considere oportuno iarxismo.

con caracteres bien vi-l Norte el cerco que pa-uertos y el material que prender que la resisten-fuerzas de Mola están vencer sin grandes es-

Don Jacinto Benavente, el mundial-mente conocido comediógrafo, que ha sido asesinado en Madrid por las tur-bas marxistas, que por destruir ya no vacilan ni ante el genio. Benavente nunca se había significado en política y sin embargo ha bastado que sea una personalidad de relieve para supri-mirlo. ¡Después dicen que en Madrid no están mandando los comunistas!

Ya ha pasad
de Yagüe

Se asegura que
San Seba:

—

Fuerzas marxistas
fren una derrota
gran

En los tres últimos
do destruida:
e

ENTRE LOS ASES

TETUAN. Castalan au

12. *Above.* The front page of *Ideal*, 22 August 1936: the "assassination" of Jacinto Benavente.

13. *Right.* The front page of *Ideal*, 23 August 1936: the "assassination" of "José" Zuloaga and Pedro Muñoz Seca.

e de las columnas del Sur

ue cantar para ahuyen-
miedo. Y a Madrid se le
acabando ya hasta los
s. A la Puerta del Sol
cistas. Iban a Gobernación
ovimiento militar. A na-
el hecho tiene contra los
nas a sus gentes. Y estas
nta de su situación. Los
que ellos estaban en la
ocho ningunas fuerzas de
. Y sin embargo, los mi-
r sido derrotados por el
) organizaron la manifes-
la agencia Havas, cuya
s.

., en su resumen oficial
) confirma. Confirmación
era una arenga a las mi-
a los Regulares. Llegó a
demostrar que «de hom-
puede hablar sin mentir
a ȵtecedentes, decía que
en Madrid, en Extrema-
habían presentado. Con
seguir llevando a los po-
ede más que los engaños.
nos cuando oficialmente
en vez de patrullar por
no haya deserciones. Por
e del Guadarrama es sa-
ni salir de la ciudad. En
ayona a la Agencia Havas
natural que eso ocurra.
ble que cada uno hubie-
lo para que no le rogie-
no olvidemos que eso lo
preparados para la fuga.
das en todas partes. No
.rxistas supervivientes del
lupe había pocas muni-
a columna de Castejón y
que hablar de que fueron
nuertos. Y un periodista
desbandada de los pocos
allés de ella. El material
ches, días y sus ametra-
que no queremos repetir
da libre para el avance.
a Madrid. Pero pasando
aviación les ha comuni-
ayer a Salamanca para
ativos del ataque.
Oviedo ha comunicado a
do Zarauz. No se puede
) de las gestiones de los

para ver por encima de
ntir. El marxismo es un
s solo cuestión de días.

VICTIMAS DE LA BARBARIE ROJA

Otro eximio artista ha caído bajo la
mano criminal marxista. José Zuloaga, el ceramista admirado en el
mundo, que sucumbe bajo la barba-
rie roja infiltrada en hombres españoles que han olvidado su patria
y han perdido hasta el sentimiento
artístico, innato en la raza hispana.

Don Pedro Muñoz Seca, el más popular y fecundo de los comediógrafos
nacionales, asesinado, según parece,
por las hordas marxistas que tienen
puesto especial interés, por lo visto,
en suprimir a todos los hombres que
representan nuestra intelectualidad y
nuestra arte.

Triunfo rotundo

Atacó por retag

do estaban comb

de Guadalupe

UN PERIODISTA PRESE
QUE

ZARAUZ HA S
QUEDA AIS

MOLA Y YAGÜE

De Gibraltar comu
Málag

BURGOS.—La emisor
dió cuenta anoche de la c
frida por las fuerzas
mandadas por el capitá
en el pueblo de Guadalu
En Guadalupe se hacía
destacamento de fuerza
listas en espera de la lle
columna del comandante
El jefe de dicho destac:
uzó la imprudencia d
car a Sevilla la escasez
ciones. El aviso telefón
tervenido por la column
que se dispuso a atacar t
ta a las fuerzas situad:
dalupe. Estas se habían
en el Monasterio para
mejor.

Los marxistas se arroj
que, pero inopinadamer
las fuerzas del comand
jón, que hicieron un
un estrago enorme. Seg
posteriores, se sabe qu
unas dos mil bajas. La
zación fué absoluta. L
y jefes huyeron a la
camino de Talavera de

Cesa en el Gobierno Civil el señor Valdés, por reintegrarse a su cargo militar

D. JOSE VALDES GUZMAN

SE HA POSESIONADO INTERINAMENTE DEL MANDO DE LA PROVINCIA EL CORONEL SEÑOR TAMAYO ORELLANA

D. LORENZO TAMAYO ORELLANA

Por reintegrarse a su cargo militar, ayer entregó el mando de la provincia don José Valdés Guzmán al coronel de Infantería y presidente de la Diputación don Lorenzo Tamayo Orellana, quien ha sido designado, con carácter interino, gobernador civil.

La toma de posesión se verificó en la tarde de ayer y al recibir a nuestro redactor político las autoridades entrante y saliente le facilitaron las siguientes notas:

El nuevo gobernador

«Cumpliendo lo ordenado por necesidades militares me he encargado interinamente del cargo de gobernador civil de esta provincia, en sustitución de mi buen amigo el señor Valdés, cuya labor patriótica en momentos difíciles para la Patria todos conocéis.

Durante el tiempo que desempeñe este cargo me ofrezco incondicionalmente al pueblo de Granada para todo cuanto redunde en bien de nuestra querida España y de esta provincia.

¡Viva España! y ¡Arriba España!

¡Viva siempre el generalísimo Franco!—Lorenzo Tamayo Orellana.»

Despedida del señor Valdés

«Estimo un deber ineludible, al cesar en el cargo de gobernador civil de esta provincia, el despedirme del pueblo de Granada, a quien tanto quiero y en el que puse todos mis desvelos, todos mis entusiasmos y sacrificios, para con mi ejemplo cooperar con vuestro indiscutible apoyo a salvarlo de la tiranía roja, en lo que nuestra gloriosa guarnición supo poner el principal jalón para la salvación de nuestra España.

El mando ha estimado más necesarios mis servicios, dada mi cualidad militar, en otro puesto, en el que me ofrezco a vosotros y en el que con toda mi alma seguiré, como hasta ahora, luchando por la Patria. Dios quiera iluminarme y que de él salga con la misma tranquilidad de conciencia con que abandono éste y con la íntima satisfacción que siempre produce el deber cumplido.

Podéis tener la seguridad de que el que me sustituye, con sus relevantes cualidades, mejorará el desempeño del cargo para bien también de Granada.

¡Granadinos! Yo os pido perdón si, en el inexorable cumplimiento de las obligaciones de mi cargo, no fui con vosotros el benévolo que hubiese querido, pero no olvidar nunca que hemos vivido seis meses históricos y que las responsabilidades que en mí encarnaban ante Dios y ante mi Patria eran tremendas; cuando el tiempo haga su perspectiva más distante todos lo comprenderemos en sus justos términos.

Granada es un pueblo hidalgo, patriota y austero como pocos y como vibran en vosotros los sentimientos del patriotismo, tened la seguridad que Granada será grande como ya lo es por su historia. Dios os dé mucha felicidad; para mí sólo le pido que jamás olvidéis los días que luchamos juntos por nuestra Granada y por nuestra España.

¡Viva España! ¡Arriba España! ¡Viva siempre el generalísimo Franco!—José Valdés Guzmán.»

Despedida de amigos y funcionarios

Al conocer la noticia de haber dejado el Gobierno civil el señor Valdés acudieron a este centro numerosos amigos particulares, como así los funcionarios del Gobierno, para despedirle. El señor Valdés agradeció a todos el concurso que le habían prestado durante su actuación y les reiteró su amistad sincera.

Los funcionarios del Gobierno civil fueron presentados después al señor Tamayo por el secretario del Gobierno, don Vicente Hita.

14. *Ideal*, 22 April 1937, announces the "resignation" of Valdés from the Civil Governorship of Granada.

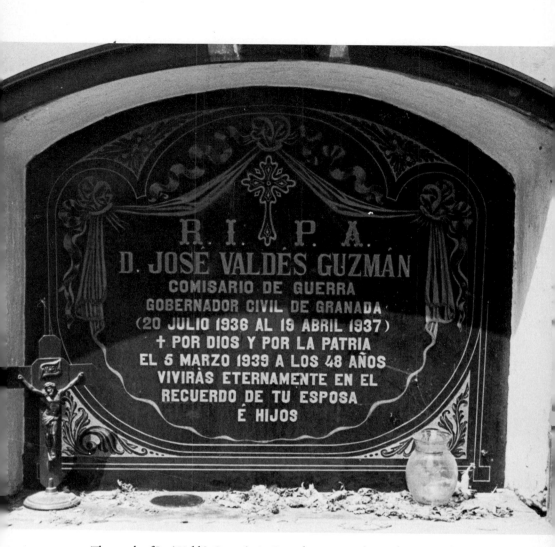

15. The tomb of José Valdés Guzmán in Granada cemetery (Patio de Santiago).

16. Angulo Street, where Lorca was arrested at the home of the poet Luis Rosales (See map, page 87). Photo from the Plaza de los Lobos, 1967.

SEVEN

The Arrest of Garcia Lorca

If one walks into the *vega* and looks back towards Granada, one observes that the town stands on a gentle slope that drops down from the base of the Albaicín and Alhambra Hills to the edge of the fertile plain. The view is spoiled, however, by a line of large, badly-proportioned buildings that stretch along at the foot of the town and stand between it and the *vega*. These blocks of flats have been thrown up along an ugly new street, the Camino de Ronda, which enables traffic coming from the south to bypass the centre of Granada and join the road to Jaén and Madrid. When the Camino de Ronda was constructed a few years ago it ran several hundred yards away from the edge of the town, but since then this area has been almost entirely filled in with a maze of new streets and buildings, leaving only occasional patches of open ground. Virtually no control has been exerted over this rapid expansion, the result of which has been to cut off the prospect of the *vega* previously enjoyed by the houses on the rising ground behind.

Before the road was built this whole countryside was a paradise of orchards, farms, villas and gardens through which little lanes picked their way out into the *vega*. Off one of these, the Calle-jones de Gracia, Federico's parents owned a charming house, the

Huerta de San Vicente*; and here the poet loved to spend his summers, away from the oppressive heat of Madrid.

The Huerta de San Vicente, which still belongs to the family, is typical of the villas that dot the *vega*, and seems to grow with a complete naturalness out of the exuberant vegetation that surrounds its white walls. Federico's bedroom was upstairs, and from his balcony he could look across the fields to the snow-covered peaks of the Sierra Nevada. 'I'm now at the Huerta de San Vicente', he wrote to the poet Jorge Guillén in 1926. 'There's so much jasmine and nightshade in the garden that we all wake up with lyrical headaches'.[1]

It was to this pleasant retreat that the poet returned on the morning of 17 July 1936 to be with his parents on Saint Frederick's Day (both Lorca and his father were named after the saint, so 18 July had special significance for the family). But news of the rising in Morocco, and of the following morning's disturbing reports of events in Seville, cast a shadow over the annual celebration.

Miguel Cerón remembered seeing Federico during these last hours before the Granada garrison rose on 20 July:

Yes, I met Federico once after he returned from Madrid just before the rising. I bumped into him in the street. Girls kept coming up to us and asking for a contribution to International Red Aid.† Federico gave them something and turned to me half joking: 'How about a trip to Russia, Miguel!' I never saw him again.[3]

On 20 July 1936, the first day of the Movement in Granada, the Socialist mayor, Dr Manuel Fernández Montesinos, Lorca's brother-in-law, was arrested in his office at the Town Hall and imprisoned in the provincial gaol along with scores of other Re-

---

* *Huerta*, a cross between a market garden and an orchard.

† In Spanish, *Socorro Rojo Internacional*. According to Thomas, p. 232, the Comintern's International Red Aid organisation 'had been active in assisting the revolutionaries of the Left in Spain since 1934.' When the Nationalist rising began, anyone who was accused of having contributed money to Socorro Rojo was liable to be shot. As noted on p. 39, Lorca sent a May-Day greeting to the workers of Spain in Socorro Rojo's periodical ¡*Ayuda!* (1 May 1936) and it is possible that the Nationalist authorities in Granada were aware of this.

publicans. His wife and three children were staying at the Huerta
de San Vicente, where the family now received news of his detention.

At least one witness of the events that took place at the Huerta
shortly afterwards was still alive in 1966—Angelina, the Montesinos's nanny, who was with them when the rising began. When I
finally located Angelina she was not at first willing to talk about
her experiences of those days, but once her understandable reluc-
tance was overcome she became intimate in her confidences.
Already an octogenarian when I met her, she retained a marvellous vitality in spite of her years and a memory astonishing in its
clarity.*

Angelina described the family's terror during the opening days
of the rising and recalled particularly the Republican air-raids
directed against the town's installations, which were carried out at
dawn. When the bombs began to fall the women and children
would hide under Federico's grand piano, and on one occasion the
poet came down the stairs in his pyjamas, trembling with fear, to
join them. 'Angelina', he muttered, 'if they killed me would you
cry a lot?' 'Go on with you', she replied, 'always on about the
same thing!'

Claude Couffon was the first to describe, in 1951, the following
incident at the Huerta:

One morning—about a week after his arrival at the Huerta—Federico
notices the unexpected presence of two individuals at the garden gate.
The two men, whom the poet does not recognise, examine the house
and garden through the grille, seem to deliberate a moment, and then
leave. Some mistake? Or is he perhaps being watched? The poet is
worried. About midday he receives an anonymous letter that confirms
his fears. In insulting but precise terms it reproaches him for what I have
already mentioned, his demagogy, his political friends, his irreligion,
his private life. The letter ends by threatening his life.

What should he do? Federico, whose anxiety is now extreme, decides
to wait till nightfall. Meanwhile he will think. But at about five o'clock
the two men reappear at the grille. As in the morning they look around
carefully, deliberate—a little longer this time—and then leave. His

* All my conversations with Angelina were tape-recorded.

position is now becoming dangerous. There can no longer be any hesitation. He must leave.[3]

In the later, definitive version of this account Couffon names as the source of his information a certain 'Isabel R, one of Federico's cousins, who was staying at the time with the family at the Huerta', and adds that the threatening letter received by the poet reproduced parts of his recent declarations to the press and termed him a 'loathsome and dangerous parasite'. Lorca's cousin told Couffon:

That afternoon Federico seemed to us to be in the grips of an insurmountable depression. Seated at the window, motionless and extremely pale, he wouldn't speak and appeared to be waiting for something which we hoped wouldn't happen but which clutched us by the throats . . . Suddenly—it must have been about five o'clock—I saw him turn towards me. Then, after murmuring my name with profound sadness, he said in a choking voice: 'Look, *this time here they come* . . .' It was they right enough. Already their footsteps were crunching on the path.[4]

Couffon goes on to explain that the two men were not in fact looking for Federico but for the brother of the caretaker at the Huerta who, it seems, had been involved in the burning of the parish church of his home village Asquerosa (later renamed Valderrubio) in the *vega*, where Federico's father also owned a house and land. The caretaker's brother was not to be found on the premises and, after searching the house from top to bottom (it adjoins the Lorcas' villa), the men demanded the identity of all those staying in both buildings. Federico tried to intervene and was struck full in the face. 'So it's you, is it! It's no good *your* trying anything!', sneered the individual who had hit him. 'We know all about you, Federico García Lorca!'[5]

Couffon's account, based as it is on the memory of the poet's cousin Isabel, may not be accurate in every detail but it does show that Lorca's presence at the Huerta was now known and that the men were distinctly hostile towards him.

Angelina agreed that the visitors were looking for the caretaker's brother and not for Federico, and remembered that, when they discovered that the person they wanted was not there, they tied his brother Gabriel to a cherry tree and beat him with a whip. Manuel Montesinos, who was about four at the time, also vividly recalls seeing the unfortunate Gabriel tied to the tree, his face pouring with blood.[6] The men then entered the caretaker's house, pitched his mother down the stairs and dragged the whole family out into the yard, apparently with the intention of shooting them. When Federico protested the aggressors hurled abuse at him, calling him a *maricón* ('queer'), and knocked him to the ground.

Angelina was sure that the men were from Asquerosa or Pinos Puente (a detail confirmed by the poet's close relatives in Granada) and remembered Gabriel's mother begging them not to shed innocent blood and reminding their leader that she had been his wet–nurse in their village years before.*

Realising that things were taking a nasty turn, Angelina now hurried the three Montesinos children across the field behind the villa to the safety of a neighbouring house. It seems that the owner, hearing her account of what was happening at the Huerta de San Vicente, telephoned Falange HQ to protest, for shortly afterwards another group arrived and prevented the killings from taking place.

These events occurred many years ago and Angelina was an old lady when I met her. It was particularly gratifying, therefore, to find documentary confirmation of her story. On 10 August 1936, *Ideal* published the following note among a list of recent arrests:

Detained on suspicion of withholding information

For being suspected of concealing the whereabouts of his brothers José, Andrés and Antonio, who have been accused of the murder of José and Daniel Linares in one of the villages of the province on 20 July, a retired sergeant of the Civil Guard yesterday arrested Gabriel Perea Ruiz at his house in Don Federico García's *huerta* in Callejones de Gracia. After interrogation he was released.[7]

---

* I have not myself followed up these clues. It ought to be possible to make enquiries in Asquerosa (now Valderrubio) and Pinos Puente which could put one on the trail of the visitors to the Huerta.

This news item proves conclusively that Federico was still at the Huerta de San Vicente on 9 August, because we know from the first-hand accounts of Lorca's cousin and Angelina that the poet protested at the brutality with which the individuals who searched the house treated Gabriel. It also confirms that the first visitors to the Huerta were not looking for the poet. While the identity of the Civil Guard remains obscure, it does not seem unreasonable to assume that it was he who now informed the rebel authorities in the Civil Government of Lorca's presence at the Huerta and his intervention in the matter of Gabriel Perea's 'interrogation'. However, we know for a fact that the Civil Guard was accompanied by several other men, and any one of them could have spread the news.

According to Couffon (above), at about noon on the day these events occurred, Federico received an abusive letter from an anonymous source, which ended with a threat to kill him. It is regrettable that the poet's family has not preserved this letter, about which we possess no trustworthy information. Was there any causal connection between it and the men who first visited the Huerta in search of Gabriel's brother? Couffon's account undoubtedly leads the reader to assume such a link between the two, but the visit and the letter might well have been quite independent of each other. Can we even be sure that the groups of men who visited the Huerta that day were the same? The likelihood is that there was in fact no connection between letter and visits for, if these men were also responsible for the letter, why did they not devote their undivided attention to the poet on their second visit that evening, which Couffon assures us took place? Unless more evidence is produced regarding the threatening letter it will be fruitless to speculate on the identity of its author.

Jean-Louis Schonberg is not of this opinion, for without having seen the letter he decides that it emanated from the homosexual source to which he is determined to trace the motivation for Lorca's death. He concludes that the letter contained threats of blackmail:

But this black, clandestine hand? It is a menacing hand, an intransigent one, imposing blackmail or, rather, *threatening revenge*.[8]

Schonberg implies that the poet's enemy demanded money in return for his life, but there is no evidence for this. On the contrary, Lorca's relatives in Granada have unanimously denied that any such blackmail was exerted, and this is confirmed by Luis Rosales.[9] Nor has any member of the poet's family come forward with proof that the letter really existed: perhaps this detail of Couffon's account, which has been appropriated by Schonberg, is the result of some misunderstanding.

Be this as it may, Federico now seems to have been subjected to

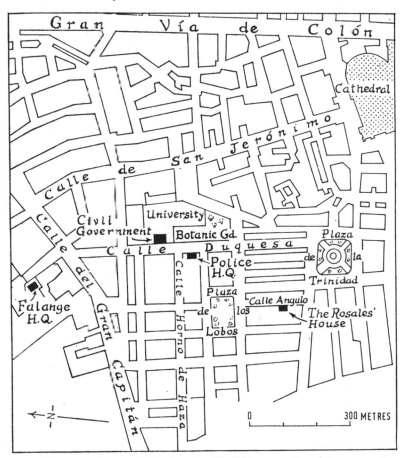

Plan illustrating the principal streets and buildings mentioned in connection with Lorca's arrest.

further intimidation by the rebels, perhaps as a consequence of the Civil Guard's visit. Angel Saldaña, a friend of Federico and member of the Granada town council elected in April 1936, was warned by a friend some time before Lorca fled from the Huerta de San Vicente that he should not go there, because the house was 'under observation'. Saldaña recalls hearing a persistent rumour that Lorca was suspected of being a 'Russian spy' and that he had a clandestine radio at the Huerta with which he was in contact with the Republicans.[10] Saldaña's evidence, along with what we know of subsequent visits to the Huerta by a group which ransacked the house in the search for incriminating documents, suggests that the persecution of the poet was now taking a semi-official turn.

Lorca decided that he would have to leave the Huerta before it was too late. But where could he go? Then he remembered his friend Luis Rosales who, like him, had returned to Granada shortly before the rising. He would be safe with the Rosales, all of whom were Falangists. Federico telephoned Luis immediately and soon afterwards the latter arrived at the Huerta by car.

Rosales is the only surviving participant of the tense discussion that now took place between him and the family (Federico, his sister Concha and their parents). His description of what was said has been repeated several times, usually inaccurately, in interviews given to Spanish and foreign journalists. The following account is taken from a tape-recorded interview that he gave me on 2 September 1966:

It must have been about 5 August when Federico telephoned me.[11] He told me that he was worried and asked me to go to his house, which I did. He explained to me that some individuals had been there twice during the day, mistreating him and going through his personal papers . . . In view of this I promised to help in any way they thought I could. I am the only surviving witness of the discussion—Federico's parents and sister Concha have all died. Well, Federico discussed the various possibilities open to him and I put myself at his disposal. The possibility of getting Federico into the Republican zone was discussed. I could have done this fairly easily and had already done it with other people—and brought people back from the Republican zone.[12] But

Federico refused. He was terrified by the thought of being all alone in a no-man's-land between the two zones. Nor would he consider going to seek refuge in Manuel de Falla's *carmen*. Federico had had a bit of a literary row with Falla about his *Ode to the Holy Sacrament*, which he had dedicated to him. It's a pretty unorthodox poem and Falla, who was very Catholic, didn't like it. Anyway Federico felt that to go there would be embarrassing and said that he would prefer to come to my house. And that's what we decided. He came that day[13] and was in my house for about eight days, until 15 August.[14]

While Angelina had no idea who Luis Rosales was she did recall that, before 'the gentleman' left the Huerta, he gave strict instructions to Concha that she was on no account to reveal the whereabouts of the poet after he was installed in Granada:

He told her that she was to say that Federico had fled across the *vega*, as everyone was doing in those days, and that, even if they said they'd kill her father or put them all in gaol, she wasn't to tell them where he'd gone.

Shortly after Federico arrived at the Rosales's house (on or about 9 August) another group of rebels went to the Huerta de San Vicente. This time they were looking for the poet and no one else. They returned soon afterwards. Both Couffon and Schonberg assume that Ramón Ruiz Alonso was the leader of this group. Couffon writes:

The first day he went to the Huerta to arrest his victim the latter had already flown. The house was too small, too simply constructed, for anyone to be able to hide there satisfactorily. Thus the poet was no longer at the Huerta. In spite of this he returned two or three times, ransacking the house and bullying García Rodríguez. On his last visit he was unable to resist the pleasure of threatening him:

'If you don't tell me where your son is hiding, I'll take *you* away instead'.

He struck the old man, who staggered under the blows. The poet's sister, in an attempt to discourage him, replied:

'But he's not in hiding. He's gone out, that's all. He's gone to read some poetry at a friend's house.'

Ruiz Alonso, pondering Conchita García Lorca's words, realised that the only poet in Granada with whom Federico could be hiding was Luis Rosales. He made enquiries, found that his hunch was correct and some time later arrived at 1 Angulo Street to arrest the poet.[15]

Schonberg, whose account is almost certainly based on Couffon, also takes it for granted that it was Ruiz Alonso who went to the Huerta[12], yet there are several difficulties about accepting such an assumption. In the first place, if Ruiz Alonso had really been looking for Federico, why would it have been necessary for him to return *two or three* times to the Huerta, when he could have bludgeoned the family into revealing the poet's whereabouts on his first visit? Secondly, and more importantly, no member of Lorca's family has ever been prepared to implicate Ruiz Alonso in what happened at the Huerta. Concha Montesinos, who was present when the house searches took place and who allegedly gave the CEDA ex-deputy the clue that led him to Angulo Street, never connected his name with these events.[17] Nor did Lorca's relatives in Granada when I questioned them about Ruiz Alonso.

On the other hand, there is no doubt that someone did go several times to the Huerta after Federico had left. Close relatives of the poet have described these visits to me. The house was turned upside down by a group of individuals who searched through the poet's papers, claiming that they were looking for letters from the Republican minister Fernando de los Ríos (whose friendship with the family was common knowledge), and even the grand piano was subjected to scrutiny in case it might conceal some secret cache of incriminating documents. These visits must have taken place between the date of Federico's removal to the Rosales's house (on or about 9 August) and 16 August, the date of his arrest, but we simply cannot be certain that Ruiz Alonso was involved in them.

In spite of this, Luis Rosales insisted during our conversation that the 'domesticated worker' did indeed go to the Huerta to detain the poet, whom he had placed under house arrest:

Ruiz Alonso went the last time, yes, that's certain, absolutely certain. The third time he went to arrest him at the Huerta. It had all been pre-arranged and, moreover, he said to the family: 'Didn't I tell him that he was under house arrest and that he wasn't to leave the Huerta?' Then he threatened them and Conchita said: 'Oh, all right. He's in his great friend Señor Rosales's house'. So it's certain that it was Ruiz Alonso who went the last time to the Huerta.

It should be borne in mind, however, that Luis Rosales did not yet know Ruiz Alonso and that he was not a witness to the latter's alleged visit or visits to the Huerta de San Vicente. We cannot, therefore, take his evidence on this point as being conclusive, however convenient it might be to do so.

The Rosales's spacious house in Angulo Street was situated only a few hundred yards away from the Civil Government where Commandant José Valdés Guzmán now held supreme power.

The house, which no longer belongs to the family, has been somewhat altered since 1936. The sitting-room where Federico used to read has been converted into a garage, a new flat has been built on what was previously a terrace on top of the house and many minor alterations have been effected. But the patio in the centre of the building remains unchanged, with its elegant columns and pots of flowers, and Gerardo Rosales, who showed me around, assured me that the general atmosphere of the place has changed little.

The Rosales's father, Miguel Rosales Vallecillos, had built up over the years a thriving haberdashery and hardware shop just off the animated Plaza de Bibarrambla, where jousts used to be held in Moorish times. He was one of the best-known merchants in the town and people respected him for his kindness and probity. He and Federico's father were on friendly terms and would often meet in the Casino with their other acquaintances to discuss the perennial topics of provincial life. They must have discussed, too, their respective children and their careers, and one can imagine the ironic humour with which Don Federico's friends would have regarded the progress of his elder son.

Don Miguel Rosales had produced a strangely assorted family. Luis, Federico's friend, was a talented poet and published his first book of verse, *Abril*, in 1935. Gerardo, the youngest son, also possessed considerable artistic ability and became an original painter and poet. José, Antonio and Miguel, on the other hand, were true Andalusian 'señoritos', much given to the pursuit of wine, women and song, and all passionately anti-Republican. José and Antonio, as we have seen, had joined the Falange at its inception. As a result they were often in trouble with the Republican authorities in Granada, José on one occasion incurring a brief spell of imprisonment for his political activities. Both José (widely known in Granada as 'Pepiniqui') and Antonio were office-holders in the Granada Falange and active plotters against the Republic. But Miguel had not belonged to the party before the Movement and only joined at the last moment. Despite this, he was one of the Falangists who took part in the events of 20 July, and still boasts of his bravery on that occasion. 'Many of the *camisas viejas* hadn't got the guts to go into the streets with the troops', he told me, 'but I did, even though I had only just joined up'. Antonio Rosales, an albino, died a few years ago (he is reputed to have been the most fanatical Falangist of all the brothers) but José and Miguel still live in Granada, where they are notorious for their noctambulous mode of life. Gerardo also lived in Granada until his death while Luis, resident in Madrid, was recently elected to the Spanish Royal Academy in recognition of his outstanding contribution to letters, both as poet and literary critic.

All the Rosales are highly unusual people: all have the same clear, blue eyes, the same superb command of language, the same impassioned energy, but they have exerted their abilities in different ways. Beyond doubt, they must have been a force to reckon with when the rising started in Granada.

When Federico arrived in Angulo Street he was haggard and frightened, but gradually he recovered some peace of mind and would spend hours entertaining the women of the house with stories about his experiences in New York, Buenos Aires and Cuba, or playing folk songs on the piano which they had installed specially in his room on the second floor, next to Aunt Luisa's. The women—Mrs Rosales, her daughter Esperanza and Aunt Luisa—adored Federico and did all they could to put him at his ease. Miguel Rosales recalls, not without scorn, that whenever a Republican aeroplane appeared over Granada Federico would hide under his bed in panic and could only be revived by several cups of linden tea prepared for him by the ladies.

The poet could not work under such conditions, although Couffon records that he touched up the manuscript of his play *The House of Bernarda Alba* and sketched out a plan for a collection of poems to be entitled *The Garden of Sonnets*. He did read, however, and made good use of the Rosales's well-stocked library of Spanish classics, rediscovering in particular the mediaeval monk-poet Gonzalo de Berceo, whose work he read enthusiastically to Gerardo Rosales. Aunt Luisa Camacho also recalled that Federico had recited parts of Berceo's *Miracles of Our Lady* to her.[18]

It has frequently been alleged by Nationalist propagandists that Luis and Federico collaborated at this time in the composition of a hymn in honour of the Falange fallen,[19] but Rosales categorically denied this during our conversation:

Federico wanted to collaborate with me in composing an elegy to *all* the dead of Spain, not just those of the Falange or of Granada. He at no time considered writing a 'Falangist' hymn. I myself have never, never said this. If they say that I did, either they have misunderstood me or have deliberately chosen to misrepresent my words.

How much can Federico have known about the Nationalist repression of Granada now being carried out with such ruthless efficiency? While he cannot yet have been aware of the full horror of what was happening, he must surely have sensed that there was death in the atmosphere and that the Rosales were hiding something. Lorca, whose work revolves around the themes of frustration and death! And after all, he knew that Manuel Montesinos, his brother-in-law, was in gaol, and must have been deeply concerned about him; perhaps he asked the Rosales to intercede on his behalf. Moreover he could observe the brothers' behaviour, their feverish comings and goings, their excitement, their gestures. Federico usually ate with the family and was so upset by the sight of the weapons that he begged his hosts to leave them outside the room. Frequently other prominent Falangists came to eat—Cecilio Cirre and José Díaz Plá, for example—and there was never any question of the Rosales hiding Lorca from the view of their colleagues. He was a guest in their house and as such seemed to be in complete safety.

But time was running out. Shortly before sunrise on 16 August, Manuel Fernández Montesinos was shot in the cemetery along with twenty-nine other prisoners.[20] On Montesinos's request the execution was witnessed by a priest of his acquaintance, and this man now had the unenviable task of informing Concha of her husband's death. Concha was in her flat in San Antón Street when she received the news, and Angelina remembered that she telephoned her parents at the Huerta de San Vicente to inform them of their loss. During the day the family joined her in the flat.

That same afternoon Federico was arrested at the Rosales's house and taken to the Civil Government.

It is at this point that the legend begins. A dozen or more scantily-documented and widely divergent accounts of Lorca's arrest and death have found their way into print, and a far greater number of vivid oral versions of what happened are available to the investigator in Granada.

All are agreed, however, on one basic fact: the man who went to Angulo Street and arrested the poet was Ramón Ruiz Alonso, the CEDA ex-deputy.

Ruiz Alonso is still alive, and in the spring of 1966 I had four long conversations with him in Madrid. He told me that I was only the second person in thirty years to ask him face to face for his own explanation of the part he played in the drama of Lorca's last hours, and expressed great pleasure that I had approached him so openly. He talked with a florid, emphatic facility and seemed perfectly at ease, as if he had rehearsed the scene a hundred times. I tape-recorded three of these conversations without Ruiz Alonso's knowledge, including the following essential declaration, which he made to me on the first afternoon we met:*

I am going to speak to you with utter sincerity, as if I were about to die. The moment will come, however, when I can add nothing further, not

---

* This was in my opinion the only scholarly procedure the circumstances permitted, however regrettable it might have seemed from other points of view.

because I want to hide something but because I honestly know no more.
I am going to speak to you with complete honesty, as if I were about
to die, as if I were before God. I am a Catholic, Apostolic and Roman
. . . and I'm going to speak to you as truthfully as if I were about to be
judged this very moment by Our Lord. What happened was as follows,
but don't ask me for exact dates or times of the day because I honestly
don't remember: the sixteenth, the seventeenth—I don't know exactly.
Well, one day . . . one of my assignments in Granada at the time was
with the Civil Government. I used to go there every day and they gave
me their orders. I had been an MP, and in the war I have my service
record, all perfectly in order, fighting under military command and
obeying orders. Well one day I went to the Civil Government and the
Civil Governor himself wasn't there. Actually he was visiting the
trenches on the Jaén front. When the Governor was absent his place
was taken by a Lieutenant-Colonel of the Civil Guard called Velasco.[21]
He said to me: 'We've got a tricky job for you, Ruiz Alonso. We've
discovered that García Lorca is hiding in such-and-such a street,
number so-and-so'.* I should explain to you that at that time in Granada,
in those circumstances, the poet—God rest him!—was, well, considerably disliked because, obviously, well, they used his plays, you know,
in the workers' club for [. . .]†. Then he said to me: 'Look, this
gentleman has got to come here to the Civil Government. The Governor
has told me that he wants him here by the time he gets back. But it's
terribly important to get him here without anyone laying hands on him
or interfering with him in any way, so the Governor has told me that
he is to be brought in by a person of standing. You're that person'.
Now obviously—and I don't want you to interpret this as pride on my
part; no, I'm a down-to-earth bloke myself and I believe in calling a

---

I have done my best to transcribe Ruiz Alonso's declaration with complete
accuracy, but the recording is slightly imperfect in places. Where it has proved
impossible to decipher a word or phrase satisfactorily, the omission is shown thus
[. . .]. In some cases I supply between brackets the general sense of what Ruiz
Alonso said, drawing on the detailed notes I made of our conversations before
transcribing the tapes.

* 'Resulta que en la calle tal número tal se encuentra el señor García Lorca'. Ruiz
Alonso did not seem to recall the name of the street where the Rosales lived, or
the number of the house.

† Ruiz Alonso told me at this point that in the Granada Workers' Club Lorca's
rural tragedy *Blood Wedding* (*Bodas de sangre*) was adapted for political purposes
and renamed *Dynamite Wedding* (*Bodas de dinamita*). Can there be any truth in this
extraordinary assertion?

spade a spade—yes, it's true, I *did* enjoy considerable prestige in Granada, for my integrity, for my work, for the work I had done throughout the province (I was an MP and a linotypist on the newspaper *Ideal*). Yes, it's true, I *did* enjoy considerable prestige. As I prepared to set off to the house belonging to . . .* Velasco [said to me]: 'You can take all the men you need as protection', [to which I replied] that my name was protection enough. As I went along Duquesa Street—the Civil Government wasn't then where it is now, it was in Duquesa Street—I had to pass in front of Police HQ. A policeman standing at an upstairs balcony saw me and asked: 'Where are you off to, Ramón?' 'To such-and-such a street, number so-and-so.' He replied: 'Ah, yes, to X's house.'

Now I was rather surprised at this since, well, X was none other than the *Provincial Chief of the Falange, Rosales, the Provincial Chief of the Falange*. I was surprised because I just couldn't believe that the Chief of the Falange was sheltering Lorca. I couldn't make head or tail of the thing [. . .] so I said to myself: 'I'm not going to *his* house [. . .]', and off I go instead to Falange HQ. 'Where is the Provincial Chief?' I demanded. I asked to see him and said to him: 'I've been given this assignment. They've told me that García Lorca is in your house. Tell me if he is or isn't. If you assure me that he's not, I'll go back and tell them: "It's turned out that the house you told me belongs to . . . I've spoken to him—a natural thing to do under the circumstances—and he's informed me that Señor García Lorca is not there. So you can take whatever steps are necessary."' Then he said to me: 'Look, Ramón, I'm not going to lie to you. Lorca *is* there. What will we do?' 'I don't know.' 'Do you think they'll harm him?' 'I don't think so.' 'Well, if they assure me that he's to be accompanied by an important person, well, then I see no objection.' 'At all events', I said to him, 'I have an idea. You go home and have a family meeting about it. Decide what you like. Meanwhile I'll wait here and then you can call me and tell me what you've agreed.' 'Fair enough.'

After quite a long time he came back. 'Well, Ramón,' he said, 'we've decided that perhaps it would be the best thing, you know [. . .]. But how did they find out that he was there?' 'I've no idea, none at all. Well, shall we go?'

When we arrived they were just finishing an afternoon cup of chocolate. I hadn't met Señor García Lorca before—God rest his soul! [I knew a little about his books but I'd never actually met him]. They

* Here Ruiz Alonso holds back Rosales's name in order to maintain suspense and give added effect to the final 'revelation'.

introduced us: 'How do you do? How are you?' 'Well, now', I said to him, 'how do you feel about all this?' 'The family think that the best thing is for me to go with you', he replied, '[but why do they want me?]'. 'I don't know. All I know is that they've told me that your safe arrival at the Civil Government is to be guaranteed . . . I have no other duty [. . .].' 'Well', he said, 'in that case let's go.'

We arrived at the Civil Government. Going up the stairs I couldn't prevent one of the men there, one of the men, from trying to give Señor García Lorca a blow with a rifle butt, but then I stepped between them. I tell you this to show you that I carried out my orders to the letter, carried them out honourably according to the dictates of my conscience, *my* conscience. I took him to a room there, accompanied by the Provincial Chief of the Falange, Señor Rosales—the three of us went together to the Civil Government. Once they were there I went to see the Governor, or rather Lieutenant-Colonel Velasco, who was acting Civil Governor. 'Lieutenant-Colonel Velasco', I said, 'the gentleman you entrusted to me and who I had to find is here with Señor Rosales, in whose house he was staying.' 'Yes, yes, I knew he was there', he replied. 'Do you need me further?' I asked. 'No', he answered, 'but I want to congratulate you on the way you have carried out your assignment.' 'Thank you very much, sir. Good day.'

Then I returned to the room where I had left the others. 'Well, what has the acting Governor told you?' they asked. 'That you have to wait here. Nothing can be done until the Civil Governor, Señor Valdés, gets back from the front. I've done all I have to do. Can I be of any further assistance to you?' Señor García Lorca offered me some cigarettes but I replied that I didn't smoke. I had a word with the orderly and told him that Señor García Lorca would like a plate of chicken broth. 'Anything else I can do for you?' I enquired. 'No, thank you', said Señor García Lorca. 'All I want is to thank you very much indeed and to be allowed to embrace you for having looked after me so well and brought me safely from the Rosales's house. I'll never be able to thank you sufficiently for your kindness.' 'Well, if I can do nothing more I'll be off', I said. Then I went back to Lieutenant-Colonel Velasco. 'I'm off now, sir', I said, 'are you sure that I can be of no further use?' 'Quite sure, thank you', he replied, 'see you tomorrow.' 'See you tomorrow.'

Next morning I returned to the Civil Government as I did every morning—it was one of my obligations—and they told me that Señor García Lorca was no longer there. *I swear to you before God that I know nothing more.* I have heard . . . they told me . . . I suspect that . . . it seems that . . .

I swear, with my hand on the Gospels, that I can tell you no more, because I know no more. I have told you *everything*. I swear to you now, as if I were swearing before a crucifix, that this is the whole truth. I swear this, as I said before, as if I were to appear this minute before God. I left him in the hands of the Provincial Chief of the Falange, Señor Rosales, in the room. This is the only part I played in the proceedings from beginning to end.

I have argued that we do not possess enough evidence to enable us to assert with confidence that Ruiz Alonso first went to detain Lorca at the Huerta de San Vicente before finally arriving at the Rosales's house in Angulo Street. In theory, therefore, when Ruiz Alonso insisted in another of our conversations that he knew nothing of this he may well have been telling the truth. But it is indisputable that his declaration, while it confirms his participation in Lorca's arrest, also contains more than one detail that casts doubt on its veracity.

The first inconsistency concerns the way in which the arrest was carried out. Ruiz Alonso claims that he set out alone on foot from the Civil Government and that he refused the armed support offered by Velasco ('my name is protection enough'). But there is conclusive evidence that Lorca's arrest was a large-scale operation.

Particularly corroborative is the testimony of a doctor well known in Granada, who was released from gaol on the afternoon of 16 August 1936. The doctor lived in Horno de Haza Street, off Duquesa Street, where the Civil Government was situated (see plan p. 87). As he entered Duquesa Street he found it thronged with militia and Assault Guards. Seeing a friend, José María Vialard Márquez, among the armed men, he asked what was happening. 'We're cordoning off Angulo Street', was the reply, 'García Lorca is in hiding there'.[22] The accuracy of the doctor's account has been confirmed to me many times in Granada by first-hand witnesses. Not only was the street surrounded but men were posted on the rooftops to prevent the poet's escape that way. It is clear that the Civil Government was determined that Lorca should not elude it, and equally so that Ruiz Alonso is not telling the truth about the arrest—unless, that is, his memory has failed him.

Ruiz Alonso asserts that, when he discovered to his surprise that Lorca was being protected by no less a family than the Rosales, he went immediately to Falange HQ and demanded to see the Provincial Chief, 'Señor Rosales'. But none of the Rosales was ever Provincial Chief of the Falange (that position was held at the time by Dr Antonio Robles Jiménez). It is true that José Rosales was one of Granada's three Falangist Sector Chiefs (*jefes de sector*) and that Antonio was the organisation's Provincial Treasurer, but these were positions of minor importance compared to that of Robles. And Miguel and Luis, as we have seen, only joined the Falange shortly before the rising began and never formed part of its hierarchy. At Falange HQ that afternoon of 16 August 1936, Ruiz Alonso spoke, not to the Provincial Chief of the party, but to the insignificant Miguel Rosales, whose account we must now consider.

It must have been about three o'clock when Miguel left home after lunch to walk back to Falange HQ, which was established in a building at the back of the monastery of San Jerónimo in Gran Capitán Street. Not long after his arrival there he received a frantic telephone call from his mother, who informed him that a group of individuals unknown to her had arrived at the house with a warrant for Federico's arrest. She had refused to discuss the matter since none of her sons was present, and she told Miguel that the men were now driving over to see him at Falange HQ.

A few minutes later Ruiz Alonso arrived and showed Miguel the warrant.[23] In the car with Ruiz Alonso were one of his Acción Popular colleagues, Juan Luis Trescastro, and two other men whose identities Miguel does not recall. The car, which belonged to Trescastro, was an Oakland, and had been requisitioned, like all the other private vehicles in Granada, by the Civil Government. In answer to Miguel's questions about the nature of the charges being preferred against the poet, Ruiz Alonso replied: 'He did more damage with his pen than others with their guns', and claimed that Federico was a 'Russian agent'.

When they arrived back in Angulo Street Miguel was amazed to find it alive with militia, and realised at once that resistance would be useless. He told me:

You can put this in your book. I hadn't got the guts to oppose them. With all those guns they might have killed the lot of us, including my parents and sister. I had no option but to hand Federico over, and anyway I reckoned that it could all be sorted out in the Civil Government. I never dreamt that they would kill him.

While Miguel helped Federico to get ready, Ruiz Alonso drank a coffee in the *patio*. Then the poet embraced the women of the house and quietly accompanied Miguel and Ruiz Alonso to the waiting car—quietly but, according to Miguel, trembling with fear. As they drove the short distance to the Civil Government— via Trinidad Street and Plaza de la Trinidad—Federico kept begging Miguel to intervene on his behalf with Valdés.

When they reached the Civil Government Valdés was not there, and it was Miguel's main interest to ensure that Federico did not fall into the hands of 'Italobalbo' who, as has been said earlier, was one of Valdés's most brutal accomplices, and renowned for the ferocity of his interrogations. After being searched by the guards on duty, Federico was taken to await the Civil Governor's return. Schonberg is incorrect in affirming that Miguel saw Valdés and received a promise from him that nothing would happen to Lorca.[24] Miguel also rejects many other details in Schonberg's narrative, particularly that Federico asked to see a priest or that he himself spent the whole night in the *vega* searching desperately for José.[25] In fact Miguel returned immediately to Falange HQ, from where he tried to telephone his brother, who was on a tour of inspection of Nationalist outposts. But he was unable to contact him and José did not return home until late that night. Nor did Miguel succeed in his efforts to contact Luis or Antonio.[26]

Now, have we any solid reasons for doubting the veracity of Miguel Rosales's account? Is it possible that the Rosales family has agreed to lie about certain aspects of what took place that afternoon?[27] To start with, let us remember that there is objective, disinterested evidence, from many sources, that Lorca's arrest was a large-scale operation mounted by the Civil Government. Whatever he may have said to the contrary thirty years after the event, Ruiz Alonso did have heavy armed support—plenty of it. Miguel

Rosales's lively description of the scene in the street merely confirms what many people in Granada, including the doctor already mentioned, have told me.

Then there is the car. Why should the Rosales invent an imaginary car if Ruiz Alonso and his associates had gone to their house on foot? Surely such a fiction would be unnecessary and unconvincing. But we are not dependent only on the Rosales for information about this aspect of the arrest. Juan Trescastro himself, before he died in 1947, never made any secret of the fact that he had participated in that afternoon's activities with Ruiz Alonso. He admitted openly that his Oakland had been used for taking Lorca to the Civil Government, and his chauffeur has confirmed that he was at the wheel of his employer's car on that occasion.[28]

Trescastro was a rich landowner, celebrated in Granada for his brawling and womanising, and is still remembered in the town for his excesses. A close friend of Ruiz Alonso (he was godfather to one of the latter's children), Trescastro joined Acción Popular shortly after the rising began.

Luis Rosales has always claimed that the other man with the 'domesticated worker' that afternoon was Luis García Alix, secretary of the local branch of Acción Popular and a close associate of Ruiz Alonso.[29] I have been unable to find conclusive proof of his participation in the poet's arrest (I was frustrated in my attempts to talk to García Alix in 1966, and he died in a car crash in 1971), although it is not unlikely that he was present. For the moment it is enough to accept that Ruiz Alonso's account of Lorca's arrest is most untrustworthy and that he was certainly accompanied by Juan Trescastro, in whose car the poet was taken to the Civil Government. All in all, it is Miguel Rosales's story of that afternoon's events in Angulo Street that seems to be the plausible one.

The news that Federico had been arrested and taken to the Civil Government spread quickly. While many of the town's inhabitants had doubtless never heard of the poet, there was certainly a substantial minority which was fully aware of his exceptional talents and fame. This minority included right-wing supporters who were now more or less engaged on the Nationalist side, decent folk who were in sympathy with the general aims of the

Movement without in any way condoning the violence that was hurrying away so many innocent *granadinos* to their deaths. It was upon these right-wing friends that Federico would have to depend for his salvation. And among these, very few indeed were in a position to help. Only the Rosales themselves, it seemed, could do anything to save the poet.

When Luis Rosales returned home that evening he was shocked to hear that Federico had been arrested and taken to the Civil Government. Luis immediately decided to confront Valdés, and set out for Duquesa Street later that night in the company of José and other Falangists, including Cecilio Cirre. They found that Valdés was not in the Civil Government:

There must have been a hundred people in the room. It was packed. Among them was Ramón Ruiz Alonso, whom I didn't yet know by sight. I knew no one there.[30] I said, with violent hatred: 'Who is this Ruiz Alonso who went to our house, a Falangist house, this afternoon, to remove without either a verbal or a written warrant someone staying under the roof of his superiors?'[31] I stressed the 'this Ruiz Alonso', and repeated my question a couple of times. Then—I was speaking with passion, with hatred in my voice—one of the individuals present stepped forward: 'I am *this* Ruiz Alonso', he declared. I demanded of him before the whole gathering (there were a hundred people there who could confirm the accuracy of this) how he had dared to go to my house without a warrant,[31] and to arrest my guest. He replied that he had acted on his own initiative. I said to him: 'You don't know what you're saying. Repeat it!' I was aware of the poignancy of the moment and wanted to be sure that both I and those present remembered the exact words spoken. So I repeated the question three times, and he replied each time: 'I acted on my own initiative.' Then I said to him: 'Salute and get out!' 'Who, *me*?' he replied. Cecilio Cirre was great, and got hold of Ruiz Alonso and shook him. To avoid more trouble Cirre said to him: 'You're speaking to a superior. Now salute and get out!' Finally Ruiz Alonso left.*

* Ruiz Alonso categorically denied that there was any such scene in the Civil Government that night. When I repeated Luis Rosales's account he burst out: 'It's all lies! All lies! I went home after leaving Lorca with Rosales and stayed there'. Cecilio Cirre, however, confirmed Rosales's narrative in a conversation I had with him in Granada in 1966.

Luis Rosales then made a statement before Lieutenant-Colonel Velasco, Valdés's second-in-command, in which he explained why he had taken Federico to his house:

In my statement I pointed out that Lorca had been threatened at his home on the outskirts of Granada, that he had sought my help, that he was politically innocuous and that, as a poet myself and as a man, I could not refuse my assistance to a friend who was being unjustifiably persecuted. I said that I would do the same thing again.

When the Rosales and their Falangist comrades left the Civil Government, José Díaz Plá, Local Chief of the Granada Falange and a lawyer by profession, helped Luis to draw up a careful declaration stating his reasons for protecting Lorca. Luis then sent a copy of this document to each of the following authorities in Granada: the Civil Governor (Valdés), the Military Commander (General González Espinosa), the Provincial Chief of the Falange (Dr Antonio Robles Jiménez), the Mayor of Granada (Lieutenant-Colonel Miguel del Campo) and Díaz Plá himself, the Local Chief of the Granada Falange. Rosales believes that a copy of this document may still exist in Granada, although the possibility is a slim one: much Civil War material was destroyed in order to avoid recriminations, and much more of it was just not preserved out of the chaos of those days.

Luis Rosales's attempts to vindicate himself in the eyes of his superiors were no more successful than his efforts to save the poet. He was expelled from the Falange by the Provincial Chief, Dr Antonio Robles, pending investigations into his conduct, and it even seems that his life may have been in danger.

They told me to stop wearing my Falangist shirt. For several days I was completely alone and the only person who stood by me was Díaz Plá. As a result of what had happened they imposed a huge fine on me—I don't remember how much, 50,000 or 75,000 pesetas—and eventually accepted me back into their ranks. They gave me the fine instead of killing me, or putting me in gaol, or what have you. It was my father, of course, who had to pay up.

At this time everyone in Granada was contributing money and valuables to the Nationalist cause, and the lists of subscribers appeared daily in *Ideal*. People were afraid of not being seen to contribute to the financing of the Movement*, and it is of interest that the name of the Rosales's father appears in *Ideal*'s lists on precisely 19 August 1936:

Don Miguel Rosales Vallecillos and his wife, a necklace and two brooches, three pairs of earrings, two lady's watches, a gentleman's watch and chain, three tiepins, a pair of spectacles, a crucifix, two bracelets, a signet ring, two rings and ten gold coins of various weights.[32]

Luis himself figures in the lists on 20 August: 'The Falangist Luis Rosales Camacho, a signet ring'[33], and these entries would seem to confirm partially what Esperanza Rosales, Luis's sister, has told me, namely that the fine imposed on the family was made to seem like a voluntary contribution to the war cause.

Luis Rosales was saved from further persecution by the intervention of a leading Falangist, Narciso Perales, to whom José Antonio Primo de Rivera had awarded the party's highest decoration, the *palma de plata*, for his part in events before the rising. To keep his son out of trouble Perales's father had sent him to Granada University, where he was studying when the Movement began. Few people in Granada were aware of his distinguished Falangist background, and when the rising broke out he did not push himself to the fore. He was, in fact, subordinate to Luis Rosales in the opening days of the insurrection and with him on 20 July when the Nationalists took Radio Granada. He was thus in a position to observe Rosales's conduct at first hand. Shortly before Federico's arrest, Perales went to visit the HQ of the Andalusian Falange in Seville, and when he returned to Granada it was with the authority

---

* They were also afraid of not being thought good Catholics. Soon after the beginning of the rising people began to sport Catholic badges on their lapels. These were known as *santos*, and on one occasion a member of the 'black squads' was heard to remark: 'What a lot of bloody Catholics we have around here. I know what I'd do to them!' (Conversation with Miguel Cerón, Granada, February 1966).

that corresponded to his rank. He found then that Lorca had already been killed, but was in time to intervene on Luis Rosales's behalf. Perales claims to have saved Luis's life by insisting that he was 'one of the few genuine Falangists whom he had seen in Granada', and believes that, if he had arrived back a few days earlier, he would have been able to save Lorca.[34]

None of the Rosales brothers saw Federico on the night of 16 August, or ever again.

Next morning, 17 August, José Rosales went once more to the Civil Government. This time he was able to confront Valdés, who had returned from his visit to the lines. Valdés told him that Lorca was no longer there and shouted: 'Now we'll have to see about your baby brother, won't we?'[35] He refused to discuss the matter further, merely repeating that the poet was no longer in the Civil Government. Rosales believed him and to this day refuses to accept that Federico spent more than one night there.[36]

But José had been misled by Valdés. The truth is that Lorca spent not only the nights of 16 and 17 August in the Civil Government, but almost certainly the first part of that of 18 August as well.

When Federico was taken away by Ruiz Alonso and his accomplices, Mrs Rosales informed his family immediately of the arrest. Next morning Lorca's mother sent Angelina, the Montesinos's nanny, to the Civil Government with food, tobacco and clean linen for the poet. My conversations with Angelina convinced me that Valdés lied to José Rosales on the morning of 17 August when he insisted that Lorca was no longer in the building. Here is what she and her daughter told me one afternoon in the summer of 1966:

Interviewer. So you went to the Civil Government with food for Federico?
Angelina. Yes, I saw him twice.
Interviewer. About what time in the day did you go?
Angelina. In the morning.
Interviewer. What did you take him?
Angelina. I took him a flask of hot coffee, a basket with food, tobacco.
Interviewer. With a name tag?
Angelina. No.

Daughter. No, not in the Civil Government, because there weren't any prisoners there. When my mother went to take food to Don Manuel in the gaol, she had to put a name tag on the basket.*

Interviewer. I see. So you took him a flask of coffee and a basket of food?

Angelina. That's right.

Interviewer. How many times a day did you go?

Angelina. Only once, in the morning.

Interviewer. You're absolutely sure?

Angelina. Of course. How could I forget? It nearly killed me. I was terrified. The first day I was sent I arrived trembling at the Civil Government. I asked the guards at the door: 'Is Señor García Lorca here?' 'Who are you looking for, what do you want?' they replied. 'I'm looking for Señor García Lorca.' 'And what do you want *him* for?' 'I've been sent with food.' 'I'm sorry, it's forbidden.' 'But why is it forbidden?' Then the other guard said: 'Oh, leave her alone, she's their servant. It's all right, you can go up.' I replied: 'But I can't go up by myself. Won't one of you go with me?' They took me upstairs to where Señor García Lorca was locked up. I was terrified!

Interviewer. I bet you were!

Daughter. They were terrible days.

Angelina. Even servants weren't safe. They'd shoot you for anything. Then one of the guards opened the omelette like this [*making the appropriate gesture*] to see if there was anything inside.† Señor Federico was locked in an upstairs room all by himself. There was no one else there, he was all alone. In the room there was a table, an inkwell, a pen and some writing paper—and a chair.

Interviewer. Was he writing, then?

Angelina. No, the things were just there. And a man at the door said: 'What a tragedy! What a tragedy for the son and for his father!' When I went in Federico said: 'Angelina! It's you!' and I said: 'You poor child!' 'Why have you come?' he asked, and I told him that his mother had sent me. While I was talking to him—you won't get me into trouble for saying this, will you? I'm terrified . . .

---

* Angelina took food to Manuel Fernández Montesinos in the provincial gaol every day until his execution on 16 August 1936. This explains her unshakeable confidence that Montesinos's death and Lorca's arrest took place on the same day. 'How could I ever forget it?', she said to me. 'Don Manuel in the morning and Señorito Federico that same afternoon'.

† In Spain omelettes are often eaten cold, placed between the halves of a loaf of bread.

Daughter. Everyone knows about it, Mamma. He knows more than you're going to tell him!

Angelina. Well, I was inside with Señor Federico and—they were at the door, pointing guns at us!

Interviewer. They had you covered?

Daughter. But that sort of thing is natural in wartime, Mamma!

Angelina. They wanted to see if I slipped him something.

Interviewer. How long did you stay?

Angelina. Only a few minutes. He didn't want to eat anything.

Interviewer. And you went there again the next day?

Angelina. Yes, and he hadn't eaten anything. Then, the third day, as I left the house in San Antón Street,* a man said to me: 'The person you're going to see in the Civil Government is no longer there.' But I knew nobody in Granada, I didn't know who he was, and I continued on my way. When I arrived at the Civil Government, they said to me: 'Senor García Lorca is no longer here.' 'Won't you tell me where he is?' I asked. 'We don't know.' 'Have they taken him to the prison?' 'We don't know.'

Daughter. A nice lot!

Angelina. I said: 'Can you tell me if he's left anything upstairs?' 'We don't know. Go up and see for yourself.' 'One of you'll have to go with me,' I replied. We went up to the room. It was empty. He'd only left the flask and a napkin.

Interviewer. Nothing else?

Angelina. Not a thing. Then I left the Civil Government and set out for the gaol, right across town.

Interviewer. Still carrying the basket and the things you collected in the Civil Government?

Angelina. Everything. I went to the gaol, and I asked them: 'Can you tell me if a gentleman called Señor García Lorca has been brought here from the Civil Government?' 'We don't know,' they replied, 'but come back later and we'll tell you—perhaps he's in one of the cells.' So I left the basket there and the tobacco. I returned the next day. Of course, he wasn't there. They'd already killed him . . . .[37]

During the two and a half days that Federico spent in the Civil Government, several people tried to intervene with Valdés on his behalf. One of these friends was Manuel de Falla. Falla, whom

---

* That is, the Montesinos's flat, in San Antón Street.

the Nationalists constantly urged to express his support for the Movement finally managed to leave Spain in 1939.[38] When he arrived in Buenos Aires he telephoned José Mora Guarnido, who had emigrated there several years previously, and asked him to come to his hotel. Mora was shocked to find that the composer, exhausted by the horror of the war and particularly by the repression of Granada, had aged beyond recognition.

Falla told him that, some months before the rising, he had been visited by a group of young Falangists who wanted him to compose a hymn for their organisation. He had refused as politely as possible, explaining that his Catholic conscience forbade him to compose music that might be used to inspire violence. But the young men had insisted, and eventually he agreed to instrumentalise a popular Spanish song to which they could put any words they chose.

When the rising started Don Manuel, terrified, shut himself up in his *carmen*. There he learned of the assassinations that were taking place in Granada, and indeed he can hardly have failed to hear the sinister firing from the cemetery every morning. Then one day they told him that Federico had been arrested. Falla, a gentle, timid man, knew that he must try to help his friend and accordingly set out for Falange HQ in search of the young men who had gone to see him about the hymn. Perhaps they could do something. When he found them he begged their assistance, and two of them accompanied him to the Civil Government. The building was packed with people and Falla sat on a bench while one of the Falangists went to make enquiries. When he returned his eyes were full of tears. It was too late, Lorca had been shot that morning.

The famous composer then went, broken-hearted, to the Lorcas' house, expecting that the family would already know the news. But he found that they were still hopeful that something could be done to save Federico's life.* Falla had not the courage to tell them the truth.[39]

---

* Marcelle Auclair, p. 396, states that Federico's father sought the advice of a lawyer, one Serrabona, believing in the possibility of obtaining a legal defence for his son. I have received confirmation of this, and it seems that Don Federico

We have established that Lorca spent the nights of 16 and 17 August in the Civil Government, that he was there on the morning of 18 August and that by the morning of 19 August he had been removed. Furthermore, we know from José Rosales's account that on the morning of 17 August Valdés was back at his desk in the Civil Government. Why did the Civil Governor lie to Rosales that morning, saying that Lorca was no longer there? The question is difficult to answer, but it seems that Valdés may have wanted time to think—without interruption from the Rosales. It would be a mistake to suppose that the Civil Governor was unaware of Lorca's importance or the damage that his death might do to the Nationalist cause at home and abroad, for he had been living in Granada since 1931 and knew perfectly well who Lorca was, who his friends were and what sentiments the poet had expressed in the Republican press.

By the time Federico arrived in the Civil Government Valdés had already given his assent to many executions. At least two hundred and thirty-six people had been shot in the cemetery by 16 August, and by all accounts Valdés had no qualms about signing death warrants. A Falangist priest in Granada said to me one day: 'Valdés would have killed Jesus and His Holy Mother if he'd got the chance'. The Civil Governor hardly slept during the first month of the Movement or even bothered to change his clothes. He was in a state of extreme nervous tension, and Miguel Rosales recalls that he incessantly drank cups of black coffee to stop himself falling asleep on his feet. Also, he was suffering from the internal complaint which eventually killed him. Valdés could not be expected to show mercy to anyone; only expediency might make him change his mind. Perhaps this is why he hesitated with Lorca, since it was most unusual for an 'undesirable' to be kept more than a few hours in the Civil Government before being taken out and shot or removed to the prison.

Valdés must have given the order for Lorca's execution at some point in time between the evening of 16 August and the early hours of the morning of 19 August.

---

gave 300,000 pesetas to the Nationalists on the advice of one of Valdés's accomplices who assured him that by doing so he would save the poet.

I believe that the fatal decision was taken after ten p.m. on 18 August, and with the official blessing of the supreme Nationalist authority in Andalusia. One of the members of the Civil Governor's clique was a man called Germán Fernández Ramos, who before the rising had played cards with Valdés in the Bar Jandilla and Café Royal. Fernández Ramos told a close friend how the order for Lorca's death was given. Valdés had a radio in the Civil Government which he used every night to contact his immediate superior, General Queipo de Llano, after the latter's customary harangue on Radio Seville. Valdés was worried about Lorca and one night—I believe that it must have been 19 August—he told Queipo that the poet had been arrested. 'What am I to do with him?', he asked, 'I've already had him here for two days'. Queipo's reply was immediate. 'Give him coffee', he rasped, 'plenty of coffee'. It was the savage General's favourite euphemism when ordering an execution. The Civil Governor did as he was told and next morning Lorca was dead.[40]

It seems that Queipo was indeed implicated in the poet's death. When Gerald Brenan was in Granada in 1949 people told him repeatedly that Lorca's death had been ordered in reprisal for the alleged assassination by the 'Reds' in Madrid of the Catholic playwright and Nobel Prize winner Jacinto Benavente.[41] But the story was yet another distortion of what actually happened, for Benavente's 'murder' was first reported on the night of 20 August, that is to say, *the day after Lorca was shot*. What is even more significant is that the lie was disseminated in Queipo de Llano's nightly broadcast from Seville, along with other false allegations of Red atrocities:

Amongst the delicacies which they [the Reds] have reserved for us figures that of having shot Benavente, the Quintero brothers, Muñoz Seca, Zuloaga and even poor Zamora. This is to say that these scum were determined not to leave anyone alive who excelled in anything. What must they be thinking in the civilised world of the men who have shot Benavente? When will the country recover from the loss of figures as outstanding as Benavente, the Quintero brothers and Zuloaga?[42]

But all the 'victims' of Marxist barbarity named by Queipo

were alive and well, and the allegations had no basis whatsoever in fact.[43] There is no reference to the alleged murders of Benavente, Muñoz Seca, the Quintero brothers or Zuloaga in any Nationalist newspaper before Queipo's broadcast of 20 August, and one must conclude that the fabrication was entirely a product of the General's twisted mind.[44]

Moreover the fact that four of the rumoured victims were, like Lorca, dramatists, is too close a coincidence not to have been intentional. It is clear that Queipo, aware that Lorca's execution had been a gross error, decided immediately to propagate allegations of 'commensurate' Republican atrocities in order to counteract the international outcry which he now realised must ensue.

Whatever the part played by Queipo in the decision to eliminate Lorca, Valdés must still be held most directly responsible for what happened, as indeed he must for the deaths of many hundreds of other innocent granadinos. This is not to suggest that it was Valdés who first decided to hound the poet (this question will be reviewed in Chapter Nine) but simply to affirm that, had he so desired, he could have prevented the crime from taking place.

In April 1937 Valdés was relieved of his post as Civil Governor by Franco, almost certainly on the instances of those Granada Nationalists who felt that too many people were being executed.[45] He died on 5 March 1939, before the end of the war, and never made any public statement about Lorca's death.[46]

Shortly after the event, however, he denied in private that he had any knowledge of the poet's execution. One evening towards the end of August 1936, Miguel Cerón, a conservative businessman who had been an intimate friend of Federico, was having a drink with some friends in the Café Royal. Sitting at another table was Valdés with a group of henchmen, including the Jiménez de Parga brothers. The Civil Governor greeted Cerón and his friends, who were discussing the Españoles Patriotas civilian militia of which Cerón had been made a Colonel, and asked for a contribution to a proposed blood bank. After a few moments of superficial conversation someone said, quite informally: 'You know, Valdés, that was a great mistake you made with Federico García

Lorca'. 'García Lorca?', the Civil Governor replied, 'we didn't kill García Lorca! He's just disappeared, that's all.'[47]

We will probably never know if there was a final confrontation between Valdés and Federico on 18 August 1936. Only one thing is certain: the poet was taken from the Civil Government and driven to the place of execution either late that night or in the early hours of 19 August.

17. *Above.* Víznar: the square, with the entrance to Archbishop Moscoso's palace on the right.

18. *Right.* The entrance to Archbishop Moscoso's palace district headquarters of the Falange in Víznar.

19. *La Colonia* where Lorca and other prisoners scheduled for execution were held. Ainadamar can be seen in the background.

Falange Española celebró ayer en Víznar una solemne misa de campaña

MUCHOS FALANGISTAS Y GRAN NUMERO DE FIELES RECIBIERON LA SAGRADA COMUNION

TERMINADA LA MISA FUE TREMOLADA LA BANDERA NACIONAL Y ANTE ELLA DESFILARON TODAS LAS FUERZAS

(De nuestro enviado especial)

En la plaza de Víznar, al pie de la sierra de la Alfaguara, para conmemorar la festividad de la Asunción de Nuestra Señora y el restablecimiento de la bandera roja y gualda, se celebró ayer una solemnísima Misa de campaña a la que asistieron mil quinientos falangistas armados de los pueblos de los alrededores, al mando del capitán Nestares. La inmensa mayoría de los asistentes recibieron la Sagrada Comunión y una banda de música interpretó escogidas composiciones y el himno de Falange en el momento de alzar.

Terminado el Santo Sacrificio de la Misa fué tremolada la bandera española desde un balcón de la plaza e inmediatamente desfilaron las fuerzas de Falange a los acordes de la banda.

El pueblo en masa asistió al brillante acto y aplaudió y vitoreó a las fuerzas defensoras del orden. El día de ayer fué de gran fiesta para Víznar.

* * *

A las tres de la madrugada se organizó una nutrida orquesta que recorrió las calles del pueblo para anunciar la inmediata salida del Rosario de la Aurora.

Este apareció en las puertas del templo al clarear el día, y con extraordinario acompañamiento de vecinos y falangistas recorrió las calles de Víznar en fantástica peregrinación piadosa.

Por las calles del recorrido los fieles entonaron las estrofas del Santo Rosario, acogidas con vítores y aplausos por la muchedumbre que presenciaba el cortejo.

LA MISA DE CAMPAÑA

Por la mañana la plaza principal del pueblo presentaba un aspecto admirable por los artísticos adornos de guirnaldas de papel de colores que se habían colocado, así como por la infinidad de flores situadas en distintos sitios.

Frente a la iglesia, en la acera de en frente de la plaza, se había levantado un artístico altar adornado bellamente con plantas y flores. Sobre él se elevaba un dosel rojo, en cuyo fondo se había puesto una M. inicial de María Inmaculada, formada con un lazo de los colores nacionales.

Delante del altar formaron las escuadras uniformadas de Falange Española de la capital que operan en la región de Víznar al mando del capitán Nestares.

A ambos lados de estas escuadras formaron en dos largas filas las escuadras de Falange de Alfacar, Nívar, Güevéjar y Cogollos Vega, juntamente con las de Víznar. En total las fuerzas de Falange que asistieron al Santo Sacrificio de la Misa se elevaban a mil quinientos hombres. Otros tantos, según nos informaron, completan el número de las fuerzas de aquella zona, pero no pudieron asistir estos últimos por estar prestando servicio.

Finalmente, en otro lugar de la plaza formaron los «santiaguillos» y en el lado del Evangelio se colocaron bancos para las señoras y señoritas, que en gran cantidad asistieron al acto. Al lado opuesto se situó la banda de música.

Junto al altar dieron guardia de honor cinco falangistas armados de fusil y el banderín de las fuerzas.

Da comienzo el Santo Sacrificio y en la multitud que llena la plaza se hace el silencio más profundo. Con extraordinario recogimiento, falangistas y público asisten a la Misa. Rostros curtidos por el sol y el viento radiantes de alegría y entusiasmo, pero recogidos por la solemnidad del espectáculo, cuerpos erguidos con el fusil al lado. Ambiente de profunda religiosidad. Este era el aspecto que presentaba ayer la plaza del pintoresco pueblo de Víznar.

Ambiente religioso y sublime, que se acentúa en el momento en que el sacerdote oficiante, después de convertir el pan y el vino en el Cuerpo y Sangre de Jesucristo, eleva a Dios y todas las fuerzas rinden sus armas, el pueblo se arrodilla y la orquesta interpreta el himno de Falange. Mientras tanto, el viento lejano nos trae el estampido del cañón, que con sus mortíferas balas destroza a los enemigos de la causa, hermanos de los allí reunidos, de cuyos labios se escapan en aquellos momentos ple-

20. *Ideal*, 16 August 1936: "Yesterday the Falange celebrated a solemn open-air mass in Víznar."

21. *Above*. Víznar: the *barranco*, showing the outline of one of the graves.

22. *Right*. The death certificate of Dióscoro Galindo González, who was buried in the same grave with Lorca.

Serie AB   N.º 169417

00379579

CERTIFICACION LITERAL DE INSCRIPCION DE DEFUNCION.— (1)

Sección 3ª.—
Tomo 15.—
Pág. 22 Vta.
Folio (2)

REGISTRO CIVIL DE PULIANAS.—
Provincia de GRANADA.—

El asiento al margen reseñado literalmente dice así: "En Pulianas a
seis de Septiembre de mil novecientos cuarenta
y uno, cumpliendo lo ordenado por la Superiori-
dad se procede a inscribir el siguiente Auto:—
Don Ramón Ruiz de Peralta y García licenciado en
derecho y Secretario del Juzgado de Primera Instancia número dos de esta Ciudad.— Doy fe. Que
en el expediente para inscribir la desaparición
de Don Dioscoro Galindo González conforme al Decreto de 8 de Noviembre de 1,936, se dictó auto
con fecha veintidos de Julio de mil novecientos
cuarenta teniendo por justificada dicha desaparición, y se mandó inscribir en el Registro Civil del Juzgado Municipal de Pulianas y la soli-
citante en el precedente escrito expone que el
fallecimiento de dicho señor lo podía probar con
los testigos Don Pedro Santos León y Don Gabriel
Reguera González y pedía que previos los trámites
legales se inscribiera la defunción de su esposo,
y acordado recibir declaración a dichos testigos,
han comparecido estos y manifestando que cono——
cían al señor Galindo González y día diez y ocho
de agosto de mil novecientos treinta y seis en —
la carretera de Viznar entre los términos de este pueblo y Pulianas vieron su cadáver, identifi
candolo por las circunstancias de ser cojo dicho
señor, pues le faltaba una pierna, habiendo dictaminado el ministerio fiscal que procede inscri
bir la defunción solicitada. Considerando: que
habiendo justificado la defunción de Don Diosco-

(Sello del Registro Civil)

ro Galindo González, procede sea inscrita.—Visto
el Decreto de 8 de Noviembre de 1,936 y disposi-
ciones posteriores = S.Sª. por ante mi el Secretario dijo: Se tiene por justificada la defunción
de Don Dioscoro Galindo González y en su virtud
inscríbase en el Registro Civil de Pulianas, al
Juez Municipal encargado del cual se libraré tes
timonio de este Auto con la oportuna orden.— Juz
gado de primera instancia número dos de Granada
a veinticinco de Agosto de mil novecientos cuaren
ta y uno.— Torcuato Casa=Ante mi Ramón Ruiz de —
Peralta y García.—El Auto inserto que ha quedado
firme por ministerio de la Ley, concuerda con su
original a que me remito, y para que conste en —
cumplimiento a lo mandado, pongo el presente que
firmo en Granada a primero de Septiembre de mil

CERTIFICA: Según consta de la página reseñada al margen, el Encargado

D. ....

.................................., a ...... de .... de 196...

(Firma del Secretario)   (Firma del Encargado)

de mil novecientos cuarenta y uno.— Ldo. Ramón
Ruiz de Peralta y García.—Rubricado.— Hay un se
llo en tinta que dice: Secretaría del Ldo. D. Ra
món Ruiz de Peralta y García.— Es copia literal
de su original a que me remito.— El Juez Munici
pal. F. Huete.— El Secretario. José Mª. Cuesta.
CERTIFICA: Según consta de la página reseñada
al margen, el Encargado D. Antonio Rodriguez Ma
rín.—
Pulianas a 27 de Marzo de 1,968.

Firma del Secretario.   Firma del Encargado.

Antonio Rodriguez

Importe de la certificación:
Tarifa tributaria, n.º 32 (er pólizas)   5,00 ptas.
Tasas (Decretos de 18-6-59, art. y ar-
ticulo 37, tarifa 1.ª)   32,00

C   Nº 290582   A

CERTIFICACION LITERAL DEL ACTA DE DEFUNCION

<table>
<tr><td>Libro 208.-</td></tr>
<tr><td>Folio 163.-</td></tr>
<tr><td>Núm. 542.-</td></tr>
<tr><td>Procedencia del documento en su caso: --</td></tr>
</table>

Don   Enrique Jimenez-Herrera Bejar.-
(Nombre y apellidos)

Juez Municipal   del numero uno de Granada.-

provincia de   idem.   , y Encargado de su Registro civil

CERTIFICO: *Que el acta al margen reseñada literalmente dice así:*

FEDERICO GARCIA LORCA.- Registro civil de Granada.- Juzgado municipal núm. 1.-
En la Ciudad de Granada a las doce y media del dia veinte y uno de Abril de
mil novecientos cuarenta, ante D. Enrique Jimenez-Herrera Bejar, juez municipal
y D. Nicolas Mª Lopez Diaz de la Guardia Secretario, se procede a inscribir la
defunción de D. Federico Garcia Lorca, hijo legitimo de D. Federico Garcia Rodriguez y de Dª Vicenta Lorca Romero, soltero, de 38 años de edad, natural de
Fuente Vaqueros y vecino de esta capital en callejones de Gracia, Huerta S.
Vicente el cual falleció en el mes de Agosto de 1936 a consecuencia de heridas
producidas por hecho de guerra, siendo encontrado su cadaver el dia veinte del
mismo mes en la carretera de Viznar a Alfacar.- Esta inscripción se practica
en virtud de auto dictado por el Sr. Juez de Instrucción de este Distrito en
armonia con lo dispuesto en el decreto de 8 de Noviembre de 1936 y orden de
19 del mismo mes y lo dictaminado por el Exmo. Sr. Fiscal de esta Audiencia;
habiendola presenciado como testigos D. Miguel Jimenez Bocanegra y D. Juan de
Dios Moya Villanova, de esta vecindad.- Leida esta acta se estampó el sello
del Juzgado y la firmarón el Sr. Juez y los testigos certifico.- Enrique J.
Herrera Bejar.- M. Gimenez.- Juan de D. Moya V.- Nicolas Mª Lopez.- Rubricados.
Hay un sello.-- -

23. *Left, top*. Ainadamar or Fuente Grande.

24. *Left, bottom*. Fuente Grande: the bungalows which now stand on the site of the ancient olive grove where Lorca was shot and buried.

25. *Above*. Federico García Lorca's death certificate.

26. A stamp bearing Lorca's portrait issued in the Republican Zone in 1938.

EIGHT

Death at Dawn: Fuente Grande

The Tower of the Vela commands a magnificent prospect of the *vega* of Granada and its circle of mountains and affords a fascinating view of the town itself. In his first book, *Impressions and Landscapes* (1918), the young Lorca evoked the colours, forms and sounds of a Granadine evening experienced from this vantage point:

The sun drops out of sight and from the Sierra innumerable cascades of musical colours come tumbling down onto the town and the hillside . . . and the musical colour fuses with the ripples of sound . . . Everything is resonant with melody, age-old sorrow, weeping. A terrible, irremediable sadness immerses the clustered houses of the Albaicín and the proud, reddish-green declivities of the Alhambra and Generalife . . . and the colour varies each minute and, with the colour, the sounds . . . There are pink sounds, red sounds, yellow sounds and sounds impossible to define in terms of sound or colour . . . then a great blue chord . . . and the nocturnal symphony of the bells strikes up.[1]

Beyond the Albaicín, the rounded, earthy hills move up once more from the edge of the *vega*, this time to end abruptly in the distance at the foot of a long, stark mountain which, seen from Granada, appears to be without growth of any sort. The sharp

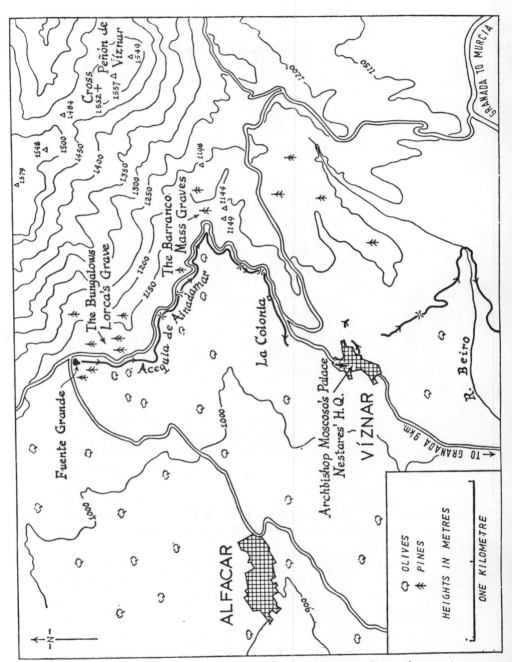

Map of Víznar showing the places mentioned in connection with Lorca's execution

dividing line between rock and vegetation is what most strikes the eye, and it produces an impression of cruel transition. This is the Sierra de Alfacar, the first in a line of parallel and increasingly lofty ranges which stretch north to Jaén, and whose highest peak, in the Sierra de Harana, rises to six thousand feet.

It was at the foot of this Sierra, at a point just on the line between rock and vegetation, that Federico García Lorca was shot.

Two villages, separated by little more than a mile as the crow flies, stand on the slopes below the mountain: Alfacar and Víznar. Alfacar (the name derives from the Arabic for 'potter') is situated several hundred feet lower than Víznar, from which it is separated by a sloping valley of olive groves. The village is famous in Granada for its excellent bread, but remarkable for little else. Víznar—here the word descends from the Arabic version of a still earlier place-name—is an attractive, steep-streeted little hamlet of dazzlingly white houses, against whose front walls strings of orange capsicums and pots of geraniums afford a brilliant contrast. While Granada swelters in the heat of summer, Víznar is fanned by cool breezes, and it was doubtless for this reason that the rich Archbishop Moscoso y Peralta built his palace here at the end of the 18th century when he returned from South America.

If the visitor plucks up enough courage to ask any of the older inhabitants of Víznar about what happened here during the Civil War, he will find them suddenly stiffen into an obstinate silence, for many have already come to their village asking such questions. Even if conversation on the topic is successfully initiated, the visitor will receive only evasive and misleading replies to his enquiries. The fact is that the people of Víznar, intimidated by the Civil Guard, are still too terrified to speak openly to a stranger about these matters.

At the outbreak of the war in July 1936, Víznar was rapidly converted into one of the Granada Nationalists' military outposts, because it was evident to the rebels that the village would become a position of considerable importance in the struggle to resist Republican incursions from the hilly country to the north-east of the capital. The area behind Alfacar and Víznar, indeed, remained more or less in Republican hands during the war, which explains why the Nationalists strove to make the foothill villages as impregnable as possible.

The commander of this military sector was the Falangist Captain José María Nestares, who has already been mentioned. Nestares established his HQ in Archbishop Moscoso's palace, and it was from here that he directed the military organisation of the area. Some years later a plaque was set up just inside the palace's front entrance to commemorate its role during the war:

The barracks of the First Granada Spanish Falange was established in this palace on 29 July 1936. Inside these walls it grew to become the First Bandera, then the First Tercio of the Traditionalist Spanish Falange of Granada, which in fierce combats maintained the security of our capital against the Marxist onslaught.

But Víznar was not only a military position. Had it been that alone its name would not be so notorious today. Víznar is remembered because it was above all a Nationalist execution place, a Calvary for many hundreds of men and women liquidated by the rebels. Nestares was in constant touch with Valdés in Granada (only five miles of bumpy, unsurfaced road link Víznar with the capital) and every night cars would arrive from the Civil Government and villages in the *vega* with batches of 'undesirables' to be shot at dawn. The cars from Granada had first to pass in front of Archbishop Moscoso's palace, and sometimes they would stop to exchange papers with the Falange HQ—then they set off up the hill.

Hugging the wall of the palace, a narrow street leads out of Víznar's little square, climbing steeply. On the right, the houses of the village. On the left, suddenly, the ground falls away past the palace walls down the hillside towards Alfacar. In the distance is the *vega*, with the Sierra de Elvira jutting out of it like an extinct volcano. Where the houses end, the street, now little more than a cart track, is joined above the village by the rough road that winds across the undulating countryside that lies between Víznar and the main road from Granada to Murcia.

The ground is new level. Directly ahead rises the Sierra de Alfacar; on its highest point stands a tall cross. And there is the abrupt transition from vegetation to rock which catches the attention from Granada, although it can now be seen that small clumps of pine and hardy plants manage to grow in the occasional loamy pockets between the boulders.

To the left, the vast sweep of the *vega*. Not a sound of human activity disturbs the silence, only the quiet gurgle from the *acequia* (watercourse) which runs just below the road.

The *acequia* now passes into an old, mill-like building half hidden among trees, and comes out on the other side. This building served as a summer residence for school-children before the rising and was known as *La Colonia* (The Colony) to local inhabitants. When the Falangists converted Víznar into a military position at the end of July 1936 the *Colonia* became a makeshift prison, and here the cars came each evening with groups of condemned men and women.[2]

A party of fourteen freemasons had been brought to the *Colonia* from Granada along with a few other 'criminals' (notably two professors from the University, Joaquín García Labella and Jesús Yoldi, and the town councillors Manuel Salinas and Francisco Rubio Callejón) and these men were forced to dig the victims' graves. Many of the grave-diggers were later executed themselves. I was fortunate to be introduced to two of the survivors, who provided me with a detailed account of how the *Colonia* functioned.

Although Captain Nestares was commander of the sector and, as such, deeply implicated in the Víznar killings, he was principally concerned with the area's military organisation and left the running of the *Colonia* largely to Valdés's men, many of whom belonged to the 'black squads', who, as described earlier, were men who enjoyed killing for killing's sake. Along with the 'black squad' volunteers were several Assault Guards forced by Nestares to take part in the executions as punishment for their lack of initial support for the Nationalist rising.[3]

The condemned men would usually arrive at one or two a.m., and were locked in a downstairs room until early morning. If they so desired the parish priest of Víznar would hear their last confession.[4] Upstairs were the quarters of the men who took part in the executions; soldiers were also billeted there. At least two women lived at the *Colonia*: María Luisa Alcalde González, an attractive and prominent left-winger from Granada whom Nestares was protecting and who cooked for the men, and an English girl, Frances Turner, who is said to have served as a nurse in Víznar. It has not been possible to trace either of these women.

At dawn the prisoners were taken out and shot (although killings often took place during the day and sometimes even at night), and then the grave diggers would arrive and bury them where they lay. Often the latter would find themselves staring at the corpse of a friend among the bodies awaiting burial.

Did Federico spend the last hours of his life in a cell at the *Colonia*? If he had arrived at the building before nightfall on 18 August, or if he were detained there for two days (as is frequently claimed in Granada), the grave-diggers, several of whom knew Lorca personally, would certainly have been aware of his presence among them. But both my contacts insist that Lorca cannot have spent more than a few hours, if that, at the *Colonia*, and are certain that he was not there when they went to bed that evening.

In Granada I heard many conflicting accounts of Lorca's last hours: there was no agreement about who drove him to Víznar, how or where he spent the night or whether he was tortured (several vivid narratives alleged that he had been brutally mistreated before being shot). I myself never met anyone who claimed to have been personally involved in the execution or to have seen Lorca immediately before his death. Published versions are understandably at variance. The Italian author Enzo Cobelli, for instance, spoke in Granada to a man called Luis García, a local landowner whose car had been requisitioned by the rebel authorities. García told Cobelli that the Civil Government had used him that night to drive Lorca to Víznar. Cobelli accepts García's story and is in no doubt that the poet was imprisoned for several hours at the *Colonia*.[5] Marcelle Auclair, on the other hand, heard that Lorca was driven to Víznar in a car belonging to a Granadine *señorito* called 'F. G. de la C.' [Fernando Gómez de la Cruz], who was himself at the wheel, having been ordered to present himself for duty that night in the Civil Government. According to this version Lorca was not taken to the *Colonia* at all, but was kept waiting till dawn in the little square of Víznar, seated in the requisitioned car between armed men; then he was driven directly to the place of execution.[6] The story sounds convincing enough, yet I have recently been informed on good authority from Granada that Gómez de la Cruz died before the Movement began.

Cobelli also spoke to a man who claimed to have stood guard outside the room where Federico and other condemned men were imprisoned. It was presumably from him that he obtained the following description:

Throughout the night of 19 August [sic], Federico García Lorca keeps up his cellmates' spirits. He talks and smokes despairingly (the poet always smoked a great deal—sweet tobacco which he had sent in huge quantities from abroad because he didn't like the Spanish 'black' brand). In the morning, when they came for him, he understood immediately that they were taking him on the 'paseo' (the walk of death). He asked at once for a priest, but unfortunately the parish priest of Víznar (when I saw him he was over eighty-five), who had been there all night, had left because they told him that there would not be any executions.[7]

One is hesitant to accept this account as adequate proof that Lorca was briefly imprisoned in the *Colonia*: so many seemingly convincing details supplied by ready talkers in Granada have later turned out to be inaccurate. The plain fact is that no one has yet come forward with conclusive, first-hand information about these last hours of the poet's life. Least of all Captain Nestares, who, more than anyone, is in a position to enlighten us.[8]

But whether Lorca spent some time at the *Colonia* or not (and I am inclined to believe that he did not), at least three other condemned men waited in Víznar that night for the dawn.

When I eventually located the grave-digger who buried Lorca, he told me that one of the other victims of that morning's executions, whose name he could not recall, was a one-legged school-master from the village of Cogollos Vega. Investigation quickly revealed, however, that the man in question was the school-master, not of Cogollos Vega but of another nearby village, Pulianas. His name was Dióscoro Galindo González. Like hundreds of other schoolteachers throughout Spain, Galindo, who was much loved by his pupils, died for his left-wing ideas. In Pulianas there was little difficulty in tracing his death certificate (see plate 22), where we read:

[. . .] these two witnesses have given evidence that they knew Señor Galindo González and that, on 18 August 1936, they saw his body on the road between Víznar and Pulianas, being able to identify it because the said gentleman was lame and had only one leg.

The discovery of this independent, documentary corroboration of the grave-digger's account convinced me that he was telling the truth when he insisted that he had buried Lorca and the school-master on the same morning, despite the slight differences in the dates: according to Galindo's death certificate he was killed on 18 August, whereas it is almost certain that Lorca was shot on 19 August. But the certificates were drawn up several years after the deaths and one cannot have automatic confidence in their accuracy. My faith in the grave-digger increased when later he courageously agreed to visit Víznar with me and point out the exact spot where the killings had taken place.[9]

The other men who knew they would die at dawn were Joaquín Arcollas Cabezas and Francisco Galadí Mergal, both small-time bullfighters (or, more correctly, *banderilleros*) from Granada. Galadí and Cabezas are named by the *Cruzada* as leaders of the column that was to have relieved Córdoba[10], and both men were known for the violence of their political activities. It has not been possible to locate their death certificates in Granada: perhaps no such documents exist in their case since their estates were too small to warrant their families' applying for a legal certificate attesting to their death.

If one now proceeds along the 'Archbishops's Road', as it is often called locally, leaving the *Colonia* behind and still accompanied by the *acequia* that winds on around the valley, crossed at intervals by little stone bridges, one arrives after a few minutes' walk at a sharp loop in the road where it passes over a small gorge. The *acequia* rushes across a narrow aqueduct below the road, and immediately beyond one observes a slope of bluish clay and pebbles, dotted with young pine trees, which stretches back up the hillside towards the first rocky outcrops of the Sierra de Alfacar.

This is the *barranco* of Víznar, somewhat melodramatically described by Couffon and Schonberg. Only a few dozen paces from the road, hundreds of bodies lie buried in the shale.

After passing through a clump of pines one comes out on to a flatter patch of grassy hillocks and dips, comprising an area of perhaps four thousand square yards. This is the unhallowed ground which covers the bodies of most of the victims despatched by the killers at the *Colonia*. Shallow graves were dug all over this slope, the bodies were tossed in and a thin covering of stones and soil was thrown over them. When Gerald Brenan visited the site in 1949 he found that 'the entire area was pitted with low hollows and mounds, at the head of each of which had been placed a small stone. I began to count them, but gave it up when I saw that the number ran into hundreds'.[11] By the early 1950s the evidence afforded by these headstones had been removed, though, for Schonberg comments that he saw not one during his visits to the place.[12]

No pine trees grew in the *barranco* in 1936. Those which are there now were planted by the Forestry Department after the war, and according to Couffon the whole area has been landscaped in order to mask the outlines of the graves.[13] But in many cases these were still clearly visible in 1967 (see plate 21).*

The largest pit in the *barranco*—it must hold at least a hundred bodies—was dug in what is in summer the dry, soft bed of a rush-edged dip, and in the rainy season becomes a pool full of toads.

* Six months after the publication, in June 1971, of the Spanish-language edition of this book, a friend wrote from Granada to say that the town council of Víznar has turned the *barranco* into a dumping-ground for the village's refuse, doubtless with the intention of hiding the graves.

Here it was easy for the grave-diggers to excavate a deep trench into which successive layers of corpses could be laid. The prisoners were brought to the pit tied together with rope or wire, and shot in the nape of the neck with pistols. They were then piled in heaps to await burial. There is no conclusive evidence that they were tortured before execution, or that they were ordered to run and then shot in the back (the infamous 'shot while trying to escape' procedure), although these charges are frequently made in Granada. Nor were the prisoners normally forced to dig their own graves.

In the early days of the Granada repression the men at the *Colonia* did not despatch their victims in the *barranco*, but in the olive groves that clothe the slopes of this wide valley. Federico was one of these early victims and, contrary to what has often been said, is not buried in the *pozos* (as the sinister pits in the *barranco* are known to local inhabitants).

The road now curves on around the valley, with the *acequia* still beside it, and in a moment one arrives at a group of modern bungalows standing on its right, an unexpected sight in this other-wise lonely spot. The bungalows are faced across the road by a copse of tall pines and just beyond these is the famous, horseshoe-shaped *Fuente Grande*.

The Fuente Grande has an intriguing history. The Arabs, not-ing the water-bubbles which rise continually from the depths of the spring, called it Ainadamar, 'The Fountain of Tears', a name by which the pool is still known. Ainadamar was apparently more vigorous in the past than it is now, for when Richard Ford visited it between 1831 and 1833 he found 'a vast spring of water which bubbles up in a column several feet high'.[14] The water is abundant and excellent to drink and the Arabs, always skilled in matters of irrigation, decided to construct a canal to carry it to Granada. The *acequia de Ainadamar* still flows around the valley to Víznar, drops down the slope to El Fargue and skirts the hills to the Albaicín, where until recently it supplied the whole quarter. But a new piped system was installed in Granada a few years ago, and the canal lost its former importance. Today it serves only to nourish the geraniums and jasmines of the Albaicín's gardens.

The Arabs admired the loveliness of the spring's surroundings, and a sizeable colony of summer residences soon appeared near the pool. No vestiges of the villas remain above ground, but several compositions by Arab poets in praise of Ainadamar's beauty have survived, most notably that by Abū 'l-Barakāt al-Balafīqī, who died in 1372 :*

Is it my separation from Ainadamar, stopping the pulsation of my blood, which has dried up the flow of tears from the well of my eyes?

Its water moans in sadness like the moaning of one who, enslaved by love, has lost his heart.

Beside it the birds sing melodies comparable to those of the Mausilī†, reminding me of the now distant past into which I entered in my youth; and the moons of that place‡, beautiful as Joseph, would make every Moslem abandon his faith for that of love.

It seems appropriate that the Fuente Grande, praised by the Islamic poets of Granada, should continue, six hundred years later, to bubble up its clear waters only a few hundred yards from the unacknowledged resting place of Granada's greatest poet. For it was to this spot that the killers drove Federico García Lorca and his three fellow prisoners in the dawn of 19 August 1936; here that they took the poet who had dared to say that the fall of Moorish Granada to Ferdinand and Isabella, the 'Catholic Monarchs', was a disaster.[15]

Where the bungalows now stand by the roadside there was, in 1936, a grove of ancient olive trees. Here Valdés's men led their victims. When the grave-digger arrived shortly afterwards he found the four bodies lying on the ground. He remembers particularly having noticed that the schoolteacher had only one

* Judge, historian and poet, born in Almería; one of the literary men who adorned the Granadine court at the zenith of its splendour in the 14th century. I am most grateful to my friend Dr James Dickie of Lancaster University for his researches concerning Ainadamar, undertaken on my behalf. He located this poem in al-Maqqarī, *Nafḥ al-Ṭīb* (Cairo, 1949), VII, p. 401. The translation is his, as are those of other Arabic descriptions of Ainadamar reproduced in Appendix E.

† A reference to Isḥāq al-Mausilī (that is, from Mosul), the most famous of all Arab musicians.

‡ In plain words, the local women.

leg and that Federico was wearing a loose tie—'you know, one of those artist's ties'.

He buried them in a narrow trench, one on top of the other, beside an olive tree.

Federico García Lorca's death certificate, drawn up in 1940 by the civil servants of the new regime, states:

[. . .] he died in the month of August, 1936, from war-wounds, his body having been found on the 20th day [sic] of the same month on the road from Víznar to Alfacar.*

* See plate 25. Lorca's death certificate is kept in the Audiencia of Granada, Juzgado no. 1. So many people have asked to see it that recently the Madrid authorities issued strict instructions that no further copies of it were to be provided. I am grateful to Dr Enzo Cobelli for kindly allowing me to publish a photograph of his copy.

NINE

The Motivation

In Chapters Seven and Eight it was my primary objective to establish the facts of the poet's arrest and death. We know with absolute certainty that Lorca spent two and a half days in the Civil Government before being shot officially on the orders of Valdés. This much is incontrovertible. It is also likely that General Queipo de Llano, the supreme Nationalist authority in Andalusia, gave his assent to the execution. Lorca, along with thousands of other victims, was eliminated by a system of terror set up for the express purpose of crushing all possible resistance by the Granadine populace to the Movement. His case was no more unusual than that of the dozens of other eminent men shot in Granada, including five harmless university professors. Yet someone must have initiated the proceedings that led to the poet's death, someone must first have decided that he should die. The question is: Who?

Almost all those who have described Lorca's last days name Ramón Ruiz Alonso not only as the man who arrested the poet but as the one responsible for his death, although widely different interpretations of the motivations behind his action are given.

Brenan and Couffon repeat the theory prevalent in Granada, according to which Ruiz Alonso exacted Lorca's death in reprisal for that of Jacinto Benavente. As we have seen, this theory is untenable.[1]

Schonberg believes that Ruiz Alonso was homosexual and jealous of the poet, and that this jealousy was exploited by another homosexual, the Granadine painter Gabriel Morcillo, who denounced the poet to the Nationalist authorities in order to save his own skin. This theory is rejected in Appendix D.

Enzo Cobelli affirms that Lorca was a pawn in a struggle for power being fought out between Valdés (Civil Governor), Nestares (the Army—Cobelli is unaware that Nestares, like Valdés, was an 'old shirt' Falangist as well as an army officer) and the Falange. Ruiz Alonso, a 'born informer', was persuaded by the Civil Governor to arrest Lorca and hand him over to Nestares for execution. Valdés hoped in this way to discredit the Army.[2] The theory is based on a serious misunderstanding of the situation in Granada at the time and can be dismissed.

By far the most convincing and well-documented explanation is that put forward by Marcelle Auclair. It is that Ruiz Alonso, on discovering that his political enemies the Falangist Rosales were protecting a 'Red', denounced them to Valdés, alleging that they were betraying the Movement. Valdés, whose sympathies lay more with the CEDA than with the Falange (one is hesitant to accept this), decided to make an example of the Rosales by having Ruiz Alonso arrest the poet. By this interpretation Ruiz Alonso's action was directed more against the Rosales than against Lorca.[3]

In our conversations Ruiz Alonso denied categorically that he had denounced the poet to Valdés, or had had any part in the persecution that led to his death; yet we have seen that there are many details in his account of the arrest that simply do not fit the facts, and which suggest that he has constructed an alternative version of what happened in Angulo Street on the afternoon of 16 August 1936.

In the early days of the rising, nobody could foresee clearly what course the war would take or what precise political system would emerge if the Nationalists succeeded in their bid for power, but it is evident from Ruiz Alonso's book on corporativism, published in 1937, what he, at least, envisaged. Evident, too, that he himself intended to play a significant role in the new state. Given the bitter antagonism between the CEDA and the Falange before the war, it is not unlikely that when the rising began in Granada Ruiz Alonso, who states in his book that he had been involved in the conspiracy against the Republic, was at pains to affirm his personality vis-à-vis the Falange, which had now achieved greatly increased status. And the only way to do this was to prove himself more 'Falangist' than the Falangists themselves and thereby to ingratiate himself with the all-powerful Valdés.[4]

It may well be, therefore, as Mme Auclair suggests, that Ruiz Alonso's motive in promoting Lorca's arrest was primarily to embarrass the Rosales brothers. But we must not forget that Lorca's harassment began *before he took refuge in Angulo Street.* If Ruiz Alonso himself did not go to the Huerta de San Vicente— and there is no conclusive evidence that he did—other individuals certainly ransacked the house several times before it became known that Lorca had gone to live with the Rosales. Since it is obvious that the poet's pursuers could not have anticipated his removal to Angulo Street, one may conclude that the subsequent embarrassment of the Rosales family was an unforeseen consequence of the determination of the poet's enemies to lay their hands on him whatever the obstacles.

It is the present writer's belief that the persecution which led to the poet's death was initiated, not by any one man but by a group of ultra-Catholic and like-minded members of Acción Popular, among whom Ramón Ruiz Alonso, as an ex-deputy of the CEDA, was the most influential.

It cannot be a coincidence that Juan Luis Trescastro, who accompanied Ruiz Alonso when Lorca was arrested, belonged to Acción Popular, nor that Luis García Alix, whom Luis Rosales insists was also in the car, was secretary of the party's local branch.

Of these three men only Ruiz Alonso is still alive: Trescastro died in 1947 and Luis García Alix, to whom I never succeeded in speaking, was killed in a car crash on 7 March 1971.[5]

Ramón Ruiz Alonso vehemently denied in our conversations that he denounced Lorca to Valdés, asserting that he merely carried out the order to 'accompany' the poet to the Civil Government.

Trescastro, however, talked freely about his participation in

Lorca's arrest and death, and I have spoken to several people who knew him personally. One of these, Miguel Cerón, told me that Trescastro died tormented by the memory of his activities during the Granada repression, and in particular his involvement in the Lorca affair. He admitted openly that he had been with Ruiz Alonso in Angulo Street, but insisted that it was Alonso and not he who had informed Valdés that Lorca was hiding in the Rosales's house.

Then there is the testimony of Trescastro's doctor, whom I met in Granada in 1971. He once brought up the subject of Lorca's death in the presence of Trescastro without knowing of the latter's involvement in it. Trescastro burst out:

I was one of the people who went to get Lorca in the Rosales's house. We were sick and tired of queers in Granada.[6]

Moreover, Trescastro boasted that he had actually participated in the killing of the poet in Víznar. One morning—probably that of 20 August 1936—Angel Saldaña, one of the few Granada town councillors to escape the Nationalist purge (see Appendix A), was sitting in the Bar Pasaje, familiarly known as 'La Pajarera', when Trescastro swaggered in and exlaimed for everyone to hear:

We've just killed Federico García Lorca. We left him in a ditch and I fired two bullets into his arse for being a queer.[7]

That same day the Granadine painter Gabriel Morcillo was having a drink in another café, the Royal, when Trescastro came up to him and announced:

Don Gabriel, we bumped off your friend the poet with the big fat head this morning.[8]

It seems that Juan Luis Trescastro's implication in Lorca's death is beyond doubt.

When I returned to Granada in 1971 I was also introduced to a

man who had been an Assault Guard before the war, a loyal
Republican who had had no option but to join the rebels. He told
me that he was on guard in Valdés's office one day when Lorca's
presence in the Rosales's house was denounced to the Civil
Governor by another member of Acción Popular, Jesús Casas
Fernández, a lawyer renowned in Granada for his fanatical
Catholicism. Casas Fernández lived in 4 Tablas Street, in a corner
house adjoining that of the Rosales, and had become aware that
Lorca was in hiding next door. Outraged that a Falangist family
should protect such a notorious Republican, Casas Fernández
went immediately to Valdés, who then consulted with his henchmen and decided to have the poet arrested. Casas Fernández died
some years ago, and I possess no further evidence to substantiate
this charge against him, but the Assault Guard's account is convincing (I have been able to verify that Casas Fernández did indeed
live next door to the Rosales), and adds further weight to the case
against Acción Popular.

Throughout our conversations Ramón Ruiz Alonso insisted on
his Catholic rectitude and the purity of his conscience before God.
One afternoon he said:

For me all men's lives are equally valuable, whatever the men's colour—
red, yellow, green or blue. We're all human beings made in the image
and likeness of God.

But on the night of 19 August 1936, not many hours after
Lorca was shot in Víznar, Ruiz Alonso expressed somewhat less
enlightened views on Radio Granada. In a harangue entitled
'Listen, Spanish proletariat' he said:

You who, ever since you were a child, have treasured an ideal in your
heart and are ready to die for it . . .
You who, hardened struggler, know full well the cruel bitterness of
life, and have passed the best days of your youth in deep sadness . . .
You who have always liked people to talk to you in tough, straightforward language . . .
You who have suffered hunger and persecution because you insisted on

following leaders who were rogues and traitors, men who always hide in the shadows, waiting for the best moment to assault banks and who then run away, leaving you abandoned, while the bullets tear through your flesh at the battlefronts . . .

Listen: the Marxist leaders, the scum, have engulfed you in tyranny and condemned you to slavery.

The men who call themselves your saviours are hypocrites and liars; they trample on your backs and live and prosper at the expense of your sweat and honest toil. At your expense, and wrapping themselves like cowards in the cloak of a prostituted companionship and brotherhood, they exacted from you in the Workers' Clubs contributions robbed from your salaries, and lived at their ease by exercising over you an abject, hateful and criminal despotism. Meanwhile your children were dying from hunger as a result of politically orientated and systematic strikes.

Sinister Red committees, made up of professional bullies and killers, forced you to join their union if you didn't want sorrow and poverty to invade your homes.

Spain is now standing squarely on her own feet to prevent the high prerogative of Human Liberty from being besmirched by the first scoundrel with a pistol to appear, or by a threat from the first street brawler to come along.

Indalecio Prieto, Largo Caballero, Fernando de los Ríos, Manuel Azaña, Casares Quiroga, Alejandro Otero . . . I accuse you before the whole world.*

More than this: before the generations which in the new Spain will build altars where Justice will be offered genuine homage.

Workers of Spain, my friends, brothers who listen to me—beyond the Alpujarras,† perhaps, or beyond the sturdy walls of the Alhambra, or perhaps even across the seas . . . shout with me now, shout until you are hoarse:

I accuse you.

* Republican politicians. Of Prieto and Caballero, Thomas writes that 'the antagonism between the two was almost the chief characteristic of the Spanish Socialist party' (p. 27). Casares Quiroga was Prime Minister when the rising began. Alejandro Otero, Professor of Gynaecology at Granada University, was the Socialist leader most hated by the Right there, with the possible exception of Fernando de los Ríos; both men were fortunate that the war did not find them in Granada.

† The Alpujarras, a high valley nestling among the southern slopes of the Sierra Nevada, lovingly described by Gerald Brenan in *South from Granada*.

I accuse you of having stained the glorious flag of the Spanish proletariat and—you vipers!—of having poisoned the souls of the workers.

I accuse you of having sullied the high ideals of redemption with the blood of our exploited companions, with the lives of our unyielding companions who retained in spite of everything their manly pride.

Rebellious proletariat:

Undefeated and undefeatable rebellion!

Rise up against them!

Your leaders . . . are hypocrites, because they deceived you.

Your leaders . . . are farcical, because it was nothing but a farce they enacted, while you, blinded, left bits of your life behind in the struggle for bread, bread which you won by the sweat of your brow and which they savoured with relish.

Your leaders . . . are criminals and bandits because they have bathed their hands in innocent blood and brought bereavement to an infinite number of humble, honest families.

Your leaders . . . are the aborted offspring of Humanity.

There is not and cannot be a Spanish mother capable of giving birth to these monsters who have made crime one of their principal weapons and assassination a way of life.

They always attack from behind!

The declaration of war was the result of an assassination from behind. A bullet in the neck of our glorious Calvo Sotelo.* They carry on the struggle with the same perfidious tactics: Dimas Madariaga falls, treacherously assassinated from behind.†

José Calvo Sotelo and Dimas Madariaga!

Your throne is on high above the stars.

Spanish proletariat: on your feet!

My incautious, idealistic fellow workers, who go on believing in an impossible utopia: you are still in time. But tomorrow may be too late.

Wake up and think over this:

The Fatherland which witnessed your birth . . .

Your holy mothers . . .

Your virtuous wives . . .

Your innocent, unsuspecting, virtuous children . . .

* This was untrue, since by the date of Calvo Sotelo's assassination (13 July 1936) the plans for the Nationalist rising were already well advanced.

† Dimas Madariaga, a founder member of Acción Popular and CEDA deputy to the Cortes for Toledo, was killed in the first month of the Civil War.

You who have always liked people to talk to you in tough, straight-
forward language, listen:
A sword's blade is strong and well-tempered.
The traitors' throats will be bathed in their own blood.
Make way for the new Spain![9]

The speech affords us a valuable insight into the workings of
Ruiz Alonso's—and by extension Acción Popular's—mind at the
time of Lorca's death, and shows clearly that impenitent Republican supporters could expect no mercy from *him*.

One of the Republicans most loathed by the Right in Granada
was the brilliant Socialist minister Fernando de los Ríos, who had
been Professor of Political Law at Granada University for many
years before moving to Madrid. In 1916 Don Fernando had listened
astonished as the young Lorca sat playing Beethoven on the piano
in the Arts Centre, and prophesied an outstanding future for him.
The professor had become a close friend of the family, and some
years later his daughter Laura married Francisco García Lorca,
Federico's younger brother. The friendship was well known in
Granada, and when the Huerta de San Vicente was ransacked after
Federico had fled to Angulo Street, the men claimed that they
were searching for letters from Don Fernando.

Ruiz Alonso hated de los Ríos, as can be seen from the reference
to him and other Republican leaders in the above broadcast. In his
book he writes:

I was a working man, a typographer, and a deputy to the Cortes for
Granada!
But:
Ramón Lamoneda was also a deputy to the Cortes for Granada, a work-
ing man and a typographer!
He was a Socialist: President of the National Federation of Graphic
Arts. His name figured on the list of candidates beside that of a Jew:
Fernando de los Ríos; he [Lamoneda] was the leader of the typo-
graphical workers of Spain. Mine figured in another list beside that of a
genius and a brave man: General Varela.[10]

In other words a Jew (or even, like Don Fernando, a non-Jew

with Jewish antecedents)—unlike a Spanish general—cannot be either a genius or a brave man. By such comments Ruiz Alonso reveals throughout his book an attitude of mind and a Catholicism radically different to the one which he claimed for himself in our conversations in 1967.

In Granada in August 1936 a person with Lorca's reputation and friends could not expect to escape death.

A man who had been a 'friend' of the poet before the Movement said to Miguel Cerón in 1936: 'If they've killed Federico they must have known what they were doing',[11] and a Granadine acquaintance of Mme Auclair told her recently that an individual there who now sings the poet's praises said to him a few years ago: 'If I had had a pistol and Federico were there in front of me, my hand wouldn't have trembled'.[12]

I have not the slightest doubt that Ruiz Alonso and his friends in Acción Popular detested Lorca and all he stood for, whatever they may say about him now, years later, when he is acclaimed as an outstanding poet and playwright, and I believe that enough evidence has been adduced in the course of this book to suggest strongly that the Granada branch of Acción Popular was responsible for the original denunciation that led to Lorca's arrest and death. The fact that Ruiz Alonso's name is not connected in Granada with arrests other than that of Lorca; that he was accompanied to Angulo Street by Juan Luis Trescastro and probably by Luis García Alix, both prominent members of Acción Popular; that Trescastro admitted to the part played by him in Lorca's arrest and actual death; that Ruiz Alonso's conversations with me in Madrid revealed many fundamental inconsistencies which could not be attributed merely to a fading memory; that Ruiz Alonso hated Fernando de los Ríos, with whose name that of Lorca was so closely connected; that he admits that Lorca was disliked in Granada on account of his contacts with the Left; that in all probability Jesús Casas Fernández, another member of Acción Popular, also denounced Lorca—all these and other details already discussed do not *prove* that Ruiz Alonso and Acción Popular were the first to decide that Lorca should die, but they certainly make it the most likely hypothesis.

That Lorca was disliked by traditionalist Spanish Catholics is beyond doubt. As an example of the feelings he aroused, the following quotation from an article published in London by the Marquis de Merry del Val in 1937 may be found appropriate. The Marquis is attacking a Statement issued in November 1936 by the Spanish Embassy, and his remarks demonstrate that he, at least, has no doubt that Lorca was a fervent, *political* adversary of Catholic Spain and that, as such, he deserved to die:

We encounter the same *suppressio veri* in the individual cases specified by the Statement. The 'Socialist' (read 'Communist') lawyers J. A. Manso, Rufilanchas, and Landovre, as also the poet García Lorca, whose literary merits were outshone by his political zeal, were all dangerous agitators who abused their talent and superior education to lead the ignorant masses astray for their own personal profit. In common with the other persons named, they were executed after a trial by court-martial.[13]

Lorca, whose liberal sympathies were well known and whose opinion of the reactionary middle class in Granada had been read there with anger when it appeared in the Madrid press just before the rising (see p. 43), could expect little mercy from the self-appointed guardians of the Faith who were now devoting themselves to ferreting out and destroying all those whom, with Merry del Val, they accused of being 'dangerous agitators'.

But this is not to say that Ramón Ruiz Alonso and his fellow members of Acción Popular were alone responsible for the death of the poet, as the Falange would have us believe. The fact that Lorca was taken to the Civil Government instead of being immediately shot in the street or by some roadside on the outskirts of the town—the usual fate of the victims of the 'black squads', for example—shows that in arresting him Ruiz Alonso was acting with the official blessing of no less an authority than the Falangist Civil Governor himself, and it is undeniable that responsibility for what was to happen to Lorca passed out of Ruiz Alonso's hands once he had left him in Duquesa Street. Henceforth Federico was at the mercy of Valdés. And Valdés—with the possible connivance of Queipo de Llano—chose to have him shot. Whoever first decided that Lorca should be arrested, and the evidence points to Ruiz Alonso and Acción Popular, the death itself was carried out officially, on the orders of Valdés.

Lorca spent two and a half days in the Civil Government, and it seems that no one in authority attempted to save him, despite the fact that his presence in Duquesa Street was well known and that the poet's father did everything in his power to obtain a reprieve. There was one man who could certainly have intervened: Monsignor Agustín Parrado y García, Cardinal Archbishop of Granada and one of the most influential prelates in Spain. But no help could be expected from a man who never once protested publicly about the mass killings that were taking place daily in the cemetery, and under whose direction the clergy in Granada had sided with the rebels from the start, identifying the Generals' insurrection with a Holy Crusade against the enemies of Christ and the 'true' Spain, the Spain of Ferdinand and Isabella, the Spain of sword and mitre.

In the last analysis, Federico, along with many of his friends and thousands of the humbler citizens of the Granada he loved so deeply, fell victim to the hatred of the Catholic Church and those whom he had termed 'the worst bourgeoisie in Spain'.[14]

Federico García Lorca was assassinated by an attitude of mind.*

* Ramón Ruiz Alonso left Granada shortly after the failure of the Pérez del Pulgar Batallion (see p. 70–1). According to a note published in *ABC*, Seville, on 2 April 1937, entitled 'Nationalist Propaganda at the Combat Fronts', Ruiz Alonso was by that time collaborating with Vicente Gay, head of Franco's propaganda department. Like Ruiz Alonso, Gay was a fanatical Catholic, anti-Semitic and an enemy of Fernando de los Ríos (see his book *Estampas rojas y caballeros blancos*, Burgos, 1937, *passim*).

TEN

Propaganda

Lorca's death was first announced in the Republican, not the Nationalist, press. The news took several days to reach Madrid, as was to be expected, for Granada was cut off from the Republican zone and rebel radio stations carefully avoided all immediate mention of the event.

On 1 September 1936 the following entry appeared in the Madrid newspaper *La Voz*:

An Incredible Piece of News
FEDERICO GARCÍA LORCA

The *Diario de Albacete* prints this item:

GUADIX. Rumours proceeding from the Córdoba front, which up to the present have not been proven false, reveal the possible shooting of the great poet Federico García Lorca, on the orders of Colonel Cascajo.*

La Voz was at first unwilling to believe this rumour, but on 8 September reproduced on its front page disturbing details of an interview given in Guadix to a correspondent of the Murcian newspaper *El Liberal* by a Republican who had escaped from Granada. This man was an intimate friend of Manuel Fernández

* Colonel Cascajo was commander of the Nationalist forces that took Córdoba.

Montesinos, and left the newspaper in no doubt that both Montesinos and his brother-in-law García Lorca had been shot. *La Voz*'s headline read THE EXECUTION OF THE GREAT POET GARCÍA LORCA HAS BEEN CONFIRMED.

But there was still general disbelief in Madrid that the poet could really have been assassinated. On 9 September 1936 *El Sol* wrote:

On the Alleged Assassination of García Lorca

Some colleagues in Madrid and the provinces give as proven the assassination of our glorious poet Federico García Lorca. Personally this paper has hesitated, and still hesitates, to accept this tragic confirmation because, although we may lack positively favourable news, it is nevertheless true to say that the evidence is not conclusive.

The information most likely to be accurate, proceeding from the Ministry of War and the Security Department, is not definitive, while on the other hand that which arrives from Andalusian sources is full of contradictions, it being variously affirmed that the assassination by the miserable insurgent forces took place in Córdoba, Guadix and Granada. A person just back from the siege of Córdoba tells us that the rumours circulating there located the assassination, without rhyme or reason, in Guadix. From there the event is transferred to Granada while, according to other sources, the great poet of the *Gypsy Ballads* was staying with his parents in their Huerta del Tamarit.*

It is quite likely that rumours about this foul deed, of which the traitors are perfectly capable, are based solely on the proven fact of the execution of Manuel Fernández Montesinos, Socialist mayor of Granada and husband of the poet's elder sister. Let us hope that we are not wrong, although we can expect anything from the vileness of soul characteristic of the accursed breed now bathing Andalusia and all Spain in blood!

The Nationalist press, aware that the fact of Lorca's death could no longer be concealed, embarked at this point on a deliberate policy of misrepresentation.[1]

On 10 September 1936 *La Provincia* of Huelva declared:

---

* The Huerta del Tamarit belonged to Federico's uncle, not his father. It is situated about half a mile away from the Huerta de San Vicente.

RADIO STATIONS CAPTURED BY THE REDS

Barcelona. Radio Unión and Radio Asociación are in the hands of the Central Committee of the Catalan Anti-Fascist militia.

The poet García Lorca was to have given a poetry reading last night over these stations but the reading failed to take place.

On the same day another Huelvan paper published a different account, making no bones about its dislike of Lorca:

THEY ARE KILLING EACH OTHER ALREADY! HAS FEDERICO GARCÍA LORCA BEEN ASSASSINATED?

Madrid, 9 September. It seems that the body of Federico García Lorca has been discovered among the numerous corpses that litter the streets of Madrid day in, day out.

Chaos amongst the Marxists has become so total that they no longer respect even each other.

Unable to escape from the Red fury, the author of *Gypsy Ballads* gained nothing from having been the 'correligionist' of Azaña in politics, in literature and in—how could one put it?—in doubtful sexuality.[2]

On 19 September 1936 the Nationalist press throughout Spain (with the notable exception of *ABC* in Seville) stated unequivocally that Lorca had been assassinated by the 'Reds' and stressed his connections with the Republic.

The *Diario de Huelva* announced:

THE POET FEDERICO GARCÍA LORCA SHOT IN BARCELONA

Barcelona. Today it has become known that the celebrated poet Federico García Lorca was assassinated by several extremists [i.e. 'Reds'] on 16 August. As the result of a denunciation he was discovered in the house of a businessman where he had been in hiding since the beginning of the revolution.

The same report figured in *La Provincia* of Huelva under the

headline FEDERICO GARCÍA LORCA SHOT IN
BARCELONA, while the *Diario de Burgos*, the most authorita-
tive rebel newspaper, affirmed that the poet had been killed in the
capital:

GARCÍA LORCA HAS BEEN SHOT

Paris. It is known that the poet García Lorca has been shot in Madrid by
Marxist elements.
In French literary circles the news has caused a shock since the poet's
left-wing ideas were well known.

Two days later, on 21 September, another Burgos daily, *El
Castellano*, announced:

THE POET GARCÍA LORCA SHOT WITH
THE WORKERS

Barcelona. A man from Barcelona who has succeeded in escaping from
Granada confirms that the poet García Lorca was shot on 16 August.
He was arrested in the house of a businessman called González.
200 workers were shot along with the poet.
García Lorca was spending the summer in his native village, Fuente
Vaqueros, and the rising caught him in Granada where he had gone to
take part in a music congress.

A strangely ambiguous report, this, which evidently emanated
from the same source as that published a few days earlier in the
Diario de Huelva but seemed also to suggest that the poet was
executed by the authorities in Granada.

ABC, the Sevillan daily, now controlled by Queipo de Llano,
avoided any direct reference to Lorca's death. The first, oblique
allusion to it appeared in a piece of double-think published on 27
September 1936:

The arrest of the Duke of Canalejas. Benavente. García Lorca
In a Red newspaper we read that the Duke of Canalejas has been arrested
on leaving an embassy where he was hiding. The papers also mention

the arrest of Fascist spies and name well-known people in that connection. And they insert an alleged letter from Don Jacinto Benavente,
whom they claim is in Valencia. A trick in connection with the death of
García Lorca—may he rest in peace.*

With regard to Benavente, we note an intention to mislead the public.
We hope that he is still alive. It would be ridiculous to start a quarrel
about it. Before long the truth will be established and confirmed. What
we *can* affirm is that the letter doesn't look at all like one by Don Jacinto.
Or else the illustrious author of *Holy Russia* is in a state of nerves—
Holy Russia, the only work by him that the newspapers remember
when, to create a fuss, they join the names of García Lorca—may his
soul rest in peace—and Benavente, to whom all honour if he's alive and
honour to his memory if he has succumbed.

M. SÁNCHEZ DEL ARCO

It can be seen from the above piece that the Nationalists now at
least conceded that Lorca had indeed been killed, while at the
same time deliberately avoiding all reference to the actual circumstances of his death. The journalist evidently assumes that his
readers are already acquainted with the fact of the death, and this
suggests that an official version of how it took place had been
broadcast over the Nationalist radio.†

By the beginning of October 1936 the Republican press was
reluctantly forced to conclude that the rumours about the assassination were based on fact. On October 2 *El Sol* published this
report:

MORE DETAILS ABOUT THE SHOOTING
OF GARCÍA LORCA

The president of the Granada FUE‡ has managed to escape from that
city to Murcia, where he has made new declarations that confirm the

---

* It will be recalled that the rumours about Benavente's death at the hands of the
'Reds' in Madrid sprang initially from Queipo de Llano's harangue on Radio
Seville on the night of 20 August 1936, and were put out to deflect public attention
from the death of García Lorca.

† Many people in Granada have told me independently that they heard the
Nationalist radio announce that Lorca had been killed accidentally by a stray
bullet or bomb.

‡ Federación Universitaria Española, the left-wing students' union.

outrages committed by the Fascists in the city by the Darro. The Granadine student has provided fresh information about the shooting of the great poet García Lorca. The author of *Yerma* was warned by various friends of the danger he was running on account of his connections with the Left, so he sought refuge in the house of another Granadine poet, Rosales, where he stayed until his presence there was denounced by a servant in league with the rebels. For having had García Lorca in his house, Rosales was on the point of being shot against the cemetery wall . . .

The European press was becoming increasingly interested in Lorca's death (in London *The Times* carried brief reports on 12, 14 and 23 September and 5 October), and it was at this point that H. G. Wells (a former guest of Lorca and his friends in Granada) sent his famous telegram to the military authorities of the town. On the front page of *El Sol*, 14 October 1936, we read:

A Plea from Wells

The rebel governor of Granada says that he does not know the whereabouts of García Lorca

London, 13. The writer H. G. Wells, president of the PEN Club in London, has sent the following message to the military authorities in Granada:

'H. G. Wells, president of the PEN Club of London, anxiously desires news of his distinguished colleague Federico García Lorca and will greatly appreciate courtesy of reply.'

The reply was as follows:

'Colonel Governor of Granada to H. G. Wells. I do not know whereabouts of Don Federico García Lorca.' Signed Colonel Espinosa.

El Sol followed the publication of the telegrams with a further article on 15 October in which it launched a vitriolic attack on Espinosa and went on to connect the name of Ramón Ruiz Alonso for the first time with the assassination, an interesting detail that shows how widely known the participation of the 'domesticated worker' in Lorca's arrest had already become:

Espinosa knows nothing about it. Or rather he chooses not to know anything about it, which unfortunately seems to confirm the treacherous death of the Spanish poet.
[. . .] Ex-Colonel Espinosa probably did not even know who García Lorca was. A reader in his moments of leisure of pseudo-pornographic novels and a devourer of all that foul, nauseous literature put out by our wretched right-wing scribblers, he never had either the opportunity or the desire to enter into communion with García Lorca's splendid work, pregnant with popular and poetic essences of a rare quality.
Ex-Colonel Espinosa will certainly have found out now, after receiving Wells's telegram, that there was once a poet called Federico García Lorca, and that he was murdered by the rabble led by Ruiz Alonso, the well-known paid assassin in the service of Gil Robles, for the simple fact of having put his distinguished pen at the service of the people. Faced with a *fait accompli*, ex-Colonel Espinosa decided that the most graceful attitude was to pretend that he knew nothing about it.

The death of the poet was becoming an increasing embarrass-ment to the Nationalists, and it was inevitable that they should now seek to exonerate themselves in the eyes of world opinion. To do this they would have to claim Lorca as 'one of their own' and either deny that they had taken any part in the killing or else ascribe it to the 'Reds'. Since it had become abundantly clear that Lorca could not have been shot by Republican extremists, Franco's propagandists decided to lay all the blame on unspecified assassins 'acting on their own initiative'. Only the Marquis de Merry del Val was unwise enough to state publicly that Lorca had been shot officially (see p. 134) and his mistake was never repeated.

The Falange quickly began to foster the legend that before his death Lorca was actively in sympathy with the aims of José Antonio Primo de Rivera (who had died some months after the poet, executed in Alicante by the Republicans).

On 11 March 1937 an article entitled 'They have killed Imperial Spain's greatest poet' appeared in the Falangist paper *Unidad* of San Sebastián. The author, Luis Hurtado, writes in the overblown style (quite untranslatable) of Spanish political rhetoric, and particularly the Falangist variety, and insists not only on the party's innocence in Lorca's death but that Lorca himself was virtually a Falangist:

I swear solemnly, by the friendship we once shared and by my blood shed in the noblest of tempests on the battlefield, that neither the Falange nor the Spanish Army had any part in your death. The Falange always forgives; and forgets. You would have been its greatest poet; for your sentiments were those of the Falange: you wanted Fatherland, Bread and Justice for all. Whoever dares to deny this is a liar, and his denial is the surest proof that he never wanted anything to do with you [. . .] The crime was in Granada, and there was no light to brighten the sky which you now possess. The hundred thousand violins of jealousy took away your life for ever [. . .] And yet I cannot resign myself to the belief that you are really dead; you cannot die. The Falange is waiting for you; its welcome is Biblical: Comrade, your faith has saved you. No one could have synthesised like you the religious and poetic doctrines of the Falange, glossing their clauses, their aspirations. They have killed Imperial Spain's greatest poet. The Spanish Falange, arms stretched in salute, pays homage to your memory.

Understandably, Hurtado's article infuriated Lorca's Republican friends, and shortly afterwards a riposte appeared in the Valencian journal *Hora de España*:

We would never have believed it possible that these despicable writers, Franco's vile 'singers of praise', could have gone so far, with their total lack of honesty, as to laud their victims when they think it is in their interests or those of their leaders to do so. The whole world has reacted with indignation to the cowardly assassination; they, for their part, have apparently received orders to confuse the issue as much as possible, burning incense before the memory of the dead poet and seeking, as far as possible, to blame the 'Reds' for the crime . . .[3]

Some months later another account of Lorca's death became available to those who were genuinely concerned to find out how the poet had died. On 15 September 1937 the Valencian paper *Adelante* published a sensational article entitled '*The crime was in Granada*': '*I witnessed the assassination of García Lorca . . .*' which claimed to be the report of an interview given to the journalist Vicente Vidal Corella by a Civil Guard forced to participate in Lorca's execution. The man had allegedly managed to escape to Valencia where he stated that the poet was executed by a group of Civil Guards near Padul, on the road from Granada to Motril. In December 1937 the essential part of this interview was reproduced by the Costa-Rican newspaper *Repertorio americano*, thereby spreading throughout South America the legend that Lorca had been shot by the Civil Guard.[4] Virtually the same account was published in Havana in 1939 and later in Brooklyn in 1940 by J. Rubia Barcia, who had also spoken to the escaped guard.[5] A small detail in Rubia Barcia's version reveals that the story about the Civil Guard's participation in Lorca's death was quite untrustworthy, but despite this it is still widely believed.*

Shortly before the contents of the *Adelante* article were disseminated in South America, the Nationalist authorities had decided that something should be done to counteract the wide, anti-Franco press coverage that was being given to the Lorca affair. Accordingly when the correspondent of the Mexican daily newspaper *La Prensa* guardedly asked General Franco in November 1937 for his views on the subject in the course of a long interview, the Caudillo had the text of his official reply ready. In answer to the question 'Have you [the Nationalists] shot any writers of world reputation?', he replied:

There has been a lot of talk outside Spain about a Granadine writer whose fame has spread far and wide, although I could not personally judge its dimensions; there has been a lot of talk about him because the Reds have used his name for propaganda purposes. The fact of the matter is that, in the early days of the revolution, this writer died in Granada mixed up with the rebels ['*mezclado con los revoltosos*']: one of the inevitable accidents of war. Granada was cut off for many days, and the idiocy of the Republican authorities who distributed arms to the

* For a discussion of this version of Lorca's death, see Appendix C.

people gave rise to the disturbances in one of which the Granadine poet lost his life.*

As a poet his death is most regrettable, and Red propaganda has made much capital out of the accident, exploiting the sensibility of the intellectual world; on the other hand these people never mention the following men who were assassinated in cold blood and with a brutality that would terrify even the most equanimous person: Don José Calvo Sotelo, Don Víctor Pradera, Don José Polo Benito, the Duke of Canalejas, Don Honorio Maura, Don Francisco Valdés, Don Rufino Blanco, Don Manuel Bueno, Don José María Albiñana, Don Ramiro de Maeztu, Don Pedro Muñoz Seca, Don Pedro Mourlane Michelena, Don Antonio Bermúdez Cañete, Don Rafael Salazar Alonso, Don Alfonso Rodríguez Santamaría (President of the Press Association), Don Melquiades Alvarez, Don Enrique Estévez Ortega, Don Federico Salmón, Father Zacarías G. Villadas, Don Fernando de la Quadra Salcedo, Don Gregorio de Balparda, and so many others, to list whom would make my reply interminable. I say it again: we have shot no poets.[6]†

Franco and his aides must have realised that his propagation of this version of Lorca's death had been an imprudence, and when the interview was reproduced in the official edition of Franco's collected declarations to the press the editors thought it politic to remove the Caudillo's last sentence.[7]

Shortly after Franco's *La prensa* interview his brother-in-law, Ramón Serrano Suñer, was appointed Minister of the Interior and Falange Propaganda Chief. Serrano had been head of the JAP (*Juventudes de Acción Popular*), the CEDA youth organisation, before the Nationalist rising and it was he who engineered its defection to the Falange in April 1936 after the CEDA's ineffectiveness had finally discouraged its younger members. When Serrano escaped from Madrid's Model Gaol in 1937 he made his way to Salamanca, where he quickly became one of Franco's closest accomplices. He was the principal architect of the famous

---

* Franco well knew that this was a lie. As we have seen, the Republican authorities in Granada did not distribute weapons to the workers.

† I have not personally investigated these cases, the enumeration of which does not absolve the Nationalists of the death of Lorca.

Decree of Unification promulgated on 19 April 1937, whereby all the parties of the Right were fused into one state organisation, the *Falange Española Tradicionalista de las JONS* which, to be sure, bore little resemblance to José Antonio Primo de Rivera's original movement. Franco, who had not been a Falangist before the rising, proclaimed himself National Chief of the new 'party' and put Serrano Suñer in charge of his propaganda machine. Serrano was thus in a position to control all news published in Nationalist Spain. He was also responsible for promoting abroad a climate of opinion favourable to Franco.

Ten years passed before Serrano Suñer himself made any public reference to Lorca's death. Perhaps he had learned a lesson from the Caudillo's mistake. During these years it was positively dangerous to talk openly about Lorca in Spain, and none of his books was tolerated, nor were his plays produced in Spanish theatres. But at last worldwide interest in the poet forced the regime to reconsider its position and in the early 1950s the thaw started.[8]

Since it was well known that Ramón Ruiz Alonso and other members of Acción Popular had participated in Lorca's arrest, and since, moreover, the CEDA no longer existed, the Franco authorities had little difficulty in deciding where to lay the blame for his death. Gerald Brenan takes up the story:

The first open blow in this controversy had already [by December 1948] been struck by the Falangist ex-minister, Serrano Suñer. In December 1947 he gave an interview to a Mexican journalist, Alfonso Junco, in which he asserted that the man who had given the order to kill Lorca was the Catholic Conservative deputy to the Cortes, Ramón Ruiz Alonso. Such an accusation could not of course be published in the Spanish press, but it conveyed accurately enough what the Falangists were saying. They were organising a whispering campaign to claim the poet for their friend and lay the blame for his death on the Clericals.[9]

Alfonso Junco has denied that his interview with Serrano Suñer was ever published[10], and it has become clear that the interview referred to by Brenan was given, not to Junco but to another

Mexican journalist, Armando Chávez Camacho, editor of *El Universal gráfico*. The interview appeared on 2 January 1948 and contained the following allusion to Lorca's death:

We knew a little about the death of García Lorca. Wanting to know more, we enquired. Serrano Suñer told us:
'I will complete your information. The leader of the group that took Lorca from his house and killed him was the right-wing deputy and ex-typographer Ramón Ruiz Alonso. He is still alive and kicking, and nobody molests him, in spite of the fact that the crime was stupid and unjust and that it did us great harm, for Lorca was an outstanding poet.'[11]

Serrano Suñer was far from happy that such a charge should be imputed to him in print, for he well knew that Lorca had been executed officially in Granada and that Ruiz Alonso, 'still alive and kicking' as he was, might be prepared to blurt the truth out publicly, were he to be openly blamed for Lorca's death. Serrano, therefore, wrote to Chávez Camacho to 'clarify' what he had said during their 'private' conversation. On 3 May 1948 Chávez published the most significant part of this letter in *El Universal gráfico*. It is a document of considerable interest, for while an interviewee can claim that his views have been misreported (as Serrano does), a letter affords no such loophole:

My dear friend,
[. . .] both of us lamented, in our private conversation, the tragic error committed by Nationalist Spain in the matter of the great Granadine poet's death. I argued that the crime had been deplored by many of us who were (and some who still are) leaders of the National Cause, which had itself no part in the crime, this being the work of a group of 'uncontrollables', the sort that take part, as a matter of course, in all upheavals. I was concerned to point out—and this without any equivocation—that not a single Falangist had participated in the crime.
And I'll go further now and add, if I didn't say it then, that it was precisely the few Falangists there were in Granada who acted as friends and protectors of the poet, whose adhesion to the Cause they envisaged. His death was brought about by those who least understood the generous,

Spanish ambition of the Movement, elements possessed of a provincial
and not easily definable rancour, and who were, needless to say, anti-
Falangist.

As proof of this I explained to you how public opinion had connected
with the perpetrators of the Granada crime the name of a CEDA
deputy who was naturally assumed to be in close touch with the militia
of Acción Popular who arrested García Lorca, although certainly without the intention of leading him to his tragic destiny. The arrest took
place in the house of the Falangist poet Rosales, who was protecting
him. As a result the story that the Acción Popular militia and the
deputy in question were responsible for the poet's death was no more
than a rumour that I adduced as proof of the anti-Falangist character
that public opinion gave to the crime from the first moment . . .

Serrano Suñer was careful to preclude all acrimony with Ruiz
Alonso himself, and the ex-deputy of the CEDA showed me a
letter from Serrano, dated March 1948, which contains more or
less the same sentiments as those expressed soon afterwards in his
letter to *El Universal gráfico*. Having denied that he ever accused
Ruiz Alonso of Lorca's death, Serrano goes on to tell him—Ruiz
Alonso!—that:

The death of Federico García Lorca was the work of a group of 'un-
controllables' during the confused situation of the first moments of the
Civil War but not, as has been said throughout the world, the work of
Falangist uncontrollables.

He adds:

Federico García Lorca was not in the enemy camp; in fact he was
coming over to us when stupidity and rancour went out to meet him on
the way.

It was not long before another prominent Nationalist apologist
referred, in equally imprecise and misleading terms, to the poet's
death. This time it was the turn of José María Pemán, a member

of the Spanish Academy, who exclaimed testily in an editorial in
ABC:

I do not think it will come as a surprise to anyone when I say that the
death of Federico García Lorca, the great Granadine poet, is still one of
the accusations most commonly levelled against Spain throughout the
whole of Spanish-speaking America. It is also clear that, in spite of the
continued bandying of this topic for polemical purposes, the simple
truth is making itself known, namely that the poet's death was a vile
and unfortunate episode, totally foreign to all official responsibility and
initiative ['un episodio vil y desgraciado, totalmente ajeno a toda
responsabilidad e iniciativa oficial'] . . .[12]

The ambiguity of this last sentence was doubtless intentional:
it could mean either that Lorca's death was not carried out by the
official authorities in Granada at the time or that those authorities
who carried it out acted in a totally irresponsible fashion. Such
casuistry has typified Nationalist writing on the subject.

Nowhere is this better shown than in *La estafeta literaria*, the
regime's 'official' literary review, which has occupied itself more
than once with the subject of Lorca's death.

The 1950s witnessed the appearance of three significant pieces
of research on the death, each involving personal investigations in
Granada, and each the work of a non-Spaniard. Gerald Brenan
was the first in the field with his chapter on Granada and Víznar
in *The Face of Spain*, and this account was reproduced shortly
afterwards in a French literary journal.[13] Meanwhile Claude
Couffon had been carrying out a more detailed piece of literary
detective work, and the resultant article was featured in *Le Figaro
Littéraire* on 18 August 1951.[14] Then, on 29 September 1956, the
same magazine printed Jean-Louis Schonberg's 'homosexual'
thesis under the following heading:

ENFIN, LA VÉRITÉ SUR LA MORT DE LORCA!
UN ASSASSINAT, CERTES, MAIS DONT LA
POLITIQUE N'A PAS ÉTÉ LE MOBILE.

At last the Nationalists had been presented with a convenient explanation of the poet's death, one all the more useful inasmuch as it was the product of a foreign pen. Brenan and Couffon had blown holes in the regime's previous propaganda, and their accounts were therefore totally unserviceable, but here was an article that lent support to the Nationalist argument that Lorca's death had been caused by individuals acting independently of official control. On 13 October 1956, a mere fortnight after the publication of Schonberg's article, *La estafeta literaria* carried the following banner headline on its front page:

THE FIGARO LITTÉRAIRE CONFESSES: AT LAST, THE TRUTH ABOUT GARCÍA LORCA'S DEATH! 'THE MOTIVATION HAD NOTHING TO DO WITH POLITICS'.

As the reader can see, the magazine is careful to omit from its headline version the phrase 'an assassination, certainly'. Its treatment of the substance of Schonberg's article is similarly devious, and reveals in every line a determination to distort the facts of Lorca's death. When one considers that Schonberg's article is itself most untrustworthy, the efforts of the propagandists seem even more clumsy:

At last, we for our part exclaim, the bluff has been called! Twenty years using García Lorca's death as a political instrument! Not that such a gambit is unique or original, of course: it can be seen on an international scale. But there we are, the death of the Granadine poet was available for exploitation without scruples or honesty, even if it meant committing a conscientious, vile and systematic swindle against people of good faith. Those public ceremonies, those solemn recitals of his work, that constant flaunting of his name as a victim, those crocodile tears—who could ever forget them?

Meanwhile in Spain, the true, honourable Spain, all the facts were there, waiting to tell the embarrassing truth which would show up the conspiracy for what it was. There is only one truth, and the person who has truth on his side is the best person to reveal and demonstrate it.

And here, in Spain, all the facts were there to reveal and demonstrate that truth. But, of course, nobody was interested in this outside Spain. How could the ripped garments be sewn up? Or the big political issues?

'DE POLITIQUE, PAS DE [sic] QUESTION'

Now, at last, a French writer, J. L. Schomberg [sic], author of the most complete and fully documented biography of the poet, has been in Spain several times between 1953 and 1956, has travelled all over Andalusia, visited villages adjacent to Granada and spoken to whomever he considered either useful or necessary. He has searched in archives and visited the relevant places. Finally, after all this, he has arrived at the following conclusion:

'De politique, pas question. La politique, c'était alors la purge qui vous évacuait sans préambule'. In other words, there was no question of a political motive. That is what this special correspondent writes in the third paragraph of the fifth column on page five of the *Figaro littéraire*, 29 September 1956.

Twenty years to admit the truth. Is truth so difficult to find? The point is, of course, that the problem or snag did not lie in finding the truth, but rather in allowing it to become known.

'L'AMOUR OSCUR* [sic], VOILÀ LE FOND DE L'AFFAIRE'

Bit by bit the writer and journalist tries to uncover the motives†. Blackmail? Revenge? Perhaps both, he replies openly and in print. But by whom? He also answers this:

'Reste alors la vengeance; la vengeance de l'amour oscur [sic].' Homosexual love's revenge, he writes in the first paragraph, column six of the fifth page.

From the time he wrote the *Ode to Walt Whitman* García Lorca knew perfectly well—continues the French writer and meticulous biographer —that he was the object of terrible hatreds. He was not unaware of the cesspool of humanity, full of pederasts, where they waited for him. 'Murderers of doves! No quarter! Death glints in your eyes. May the "pure", the "Classicals", shut the doors of the bacchanalia against you.'‡ And the journalist and biographer concludes: 'And here we have the crux of the matter'.

* That is, homosexual love.
† Here the *Estafeta* hurriedly passes over Schonberg's account of the Nationalist repression of Granada, which certainly could not have been reproduced in Spain.
‡ Disjointed quotations from Lorca's *Ode to Walt Whitman*.

HATRED IN EXCHANGE FOR SCORN

It is true that politically he had nothing to fear. True that he knew he had nothing to fear from the authorities. The authorities and the Falange were also his friends. He had taken refuge in the house belonging to the Rosales brothers. 'Ah, si Luis, l'ami qui adorait Lorca, avait été là.' And the Socialists and the Republicans. He was friendly with everyone. 'But it would be an error', he continues, 'to imagine that Federico, friendly with everyone, only attracted friendship in return. Beneath his affable manner he knew how to cultivate disdain. To this disdain the "impures" replied with hatred.'

'The accusation which led to the designation of Lorca's pursuer and executioner rested initially on nothing more than a personal vengeance which was completely independent of political, literary, religious or social considerations.'* 'This homosexual underworld, the bar in Elvira Street which gave him the key to two poems†, the gypsyism and the gypsy lads, all these lower levels of society that Lorca frequented as one of the confraternity, were treated by him with contempt, despite his personal nobility of character. It was precisely for this pride in his own superiority that they made him pay.'

It is to this conclusion that the writer and biographer J. L. Schomberg [sic] has come after a long and meticulous investigation into the places and people able to furnish him with the information he was seeking. At last the disreputable clique responsible for cooking up that deceitful tissue of lies has had its bluff—its political bluff—called.

At last, after twenty years! 'Voilà!'

This characteristic piece of Nationalist journalism was discussed widely in Spain and provoked the indignation of a leading ex-Falangist, the poet Dionisio Ridruejo. Ridruejo had been Director General of Propaganda (he was dismissed in May 1941) and was a close friend of Luis Rosales, from whom he had received a detailed account of Lorca's arrest. He now wrote an angry and courageous letter to the Minister of Information and Tourism, Gabriel Arias Salgado, which, according to Fernando Vázquez Ocaña, was 're-produced or discussed the world over'.[15]

* Schonberg had referred openly at this point to Ramón Ruiz Alonso.
† Here the anonymous *Estafeta* journalist reveals again his shaky knowledge of French. Schonberg had written: 'Cette pègre de l'amour obscur, ce bar de la rue d'Elvira *qui donne la clef de deux chansons* . . .' (my italics).

It was not, though, reproduced in Spain, and subsequent numbers of *La estafeta literaria* made no allusion whatsoever to the controversy. Nor indeed could they, for Ridruejo had placed the blame for the poet's death squarely on the shoulders of the rebel authorities in Granada:

Dear friend,

I cannot and will not allow to pass in silence and without protest the publication of an article that appeared recently in *La estafeta literaria* and in which, for despicable reasons, some paragraphs of the article on Federico García Lorca's death published by M. Schonberg in the *Figaro Littéraire* are reproduced and discussed. The *Estafeta* article is the kind that dishonours both its author, its publisher and those who read it without anger. I ask you to judge for yourself: the aim of the article is to wipe from the Nationalist Movement the stain cast on it by the poet's death; but the attempt fails and the author of the article, even were he an idiot, would have realised this. It is precisely what people have always said that remains true: that a system of political terrorism killed a man who, even from the most fanatical standpoint, ought to have been considered innocent. The article confirms his innocence, dissipates the possibility of a subjective justification based on a revolutionary necessity, while failing, at the same time, to disprove the fact that the poet died at the hands of the agents of the political repression of Granada, without anyone saying boo to them.

Why, then, this article? To my mind for only one reason: because the publication of Schonberg's paragraphs was a way of casting a shadow, a suggestion of moral degeneracy, on the memory of the victim. It was not so much a question of establishing that the reasons for his death, as hinted by the French writer, were not political as of proclaiming that they were 'homosexual'. Doubtless the editor of the *Estafeta*, Juan Aparicio, thought, with 'Christian' insight, that by diminishing the stature of the victim he would make the crime or the error more forgiveable.

It seems to me that this is going too far, that it is really a disgusting business and that all the laws of honour, pity and common decency have been trampled underfoot. I ask myself and you if the way Spaniards think is to be dictated by people capable of such foul behaviour. If this is to be so, we have sunk too low to command any respect at all . . .[16]

Unlike Ridruejo, the Falangist journalist Rafael García Serrano was happy to prolong the official campaign of misrepresentation.

In 1953 he had published a book which described the visit to South America of the Song and Dance Troupe of the Nationalist regime. In it García Serrano refers to Lorca's death (about which he was frequently quizzed by the poet's admirers) and, doubtless taking his cue from Serrano Suñer, ascribes total blame for the event to the CEDA and Ramón Ruiz Alonso, whom he is careful not to mention by name:

What is certain is that Lorca's death cannot be attributed to the Falange. He had taken refuge in a house belonging to two Falangists, in the hope of surviving those first confused moments which occur in all revolutions. The brother of the poet Luis Rosales was the provincial chief of the Granada Militia.* It was there that García Lorca found shelter. It has been asserted that he was composing an *Ode to the Falangist Dead*, and if this story has any basis in fact, it would be a good thing if Luis Rosales, who knows a great deal about the matter, were to say so. It was a group of right-wing militiamen, commanded by a certain CEDA deputy [. . .] who, taking advantage of the absence of the Chief of Militia and his brother, led García Lorca to face a Civil Guard firing squad, because the CEDA never had the guts to take firm decisions itself.[17]

The only original detail in García Serrano's tirade against the CEDA is his allegation that Lorca was shot by the Civil Guard. Such a charge had never before been made in a Nationalist publication and it must have considerably angered the force, no member of which had in fact intervened in the killing.

Twelve years later García Serrano returned, undeterred, to the subject of Lorca's death, publishing on 7 May 1965 a vicious leading article in *ABC* entitled 'A Note to Mme Auclair'. The French writer, who had been a close friend of the poet, was in Spain at the time, collecting material for a book on his life and work. Her opposition to the Franco regime was well known.

* This is inaccurate, as we have seen. José Rosales was never Provincial Chief of the Granada Falange Militia.

García Serrano begins pleasantly: Mme Auclair is interested in Lorca's travelling theatre, La Barraca, and he will give her the name and address of a friend who was a member of the company. But at the end of the article he reveals that his information will unfortunately be of little use to Mme Auclair because the friend in question was assassinated during the war—by the Reds. García Serrano repeats yet again the official story of Lorca's death and concludes:

That mistake for which we have all paid so dearly can be attributed only to the confused cruelty of a civil war that had just begun. The Rosales brothers and their comrades did all they could to obtain the reprieve that was so often impossible in the enemy zone, where no one complained . . .

In the course of his 'Note to Mme Auclair' the Falangist journalist refers to a recent article in *La estafeta literaria* which provided new details about Lorca's death. The item turns out to be a blatantly biased gloss on an account of Lorca's death by Saint-Paulien, which itself derives almost in its entirety from Jean-Louis Schonberg.[18] I reproduce some paragraphs from the article as a final example of this journal's lack of intellectual honesty (shown further by the fact that it does not even take the trouble to give the source of Saint-Paulien's and Werrie's pieces):[19]

Our excellent friend Federico García Lorca, the poet in New York who protests against the anglicisation of the Hispanic world [?]—a protest more important than the 'local colour' of his work which is so pleasing to those in search of 'typical Spanish' [sic]—was fortunate to live intensely, to know success in the fulness of youth and to find favour with the gods.
But he was unlucky in that dark passions cut down his life when his poet's heart was full of promise, of verses taking shape, verses which he was never able to utter. And after his treacherous death at the hands of the small men, his fame spread like a train of gunpowder across the hesitant and writhing continents of Europe and the Americas. Poor

Federico was converted overnight into an anti-Fascist hero, into the genius immolated by the Granada Fascists [. . .]

But there are also learned men determined to tell the historical truth. In France, as far as Lorca is concerned, this truth has been highlighted by many people. The most recent to do so are Paul Werrie and Saint-Paulien.

Saint-Paulien, a fine *lorquista*[20], accumulated a large amount of documentation in Spain, talking to people of all ideologies who knew Lorca or were his intimate friends. The legend of his death, he says, is a hoax as prodigious as that of *The Shoemaker's Wife**.

Lorca, writes Saint-Paulien, adducing numerous proofs, was politically innocuous, and never committed himself with regard to the Republic, despite the fact that it financed the *Barraca*; in his latter days he showed much interest in the Falange. José Antonio offered him an important post.† But Federico drew back and limited himself to cultivating the friendship of well-known Falangists such as Iturriaga and the Rosales brothers [. . .]

Saint-Paulien utilises the information collected by himself, quotes Federico's biographers González Caballero [sic] and J. L. Schonberg, and has recourse to Lorca's letters published in the *Revista de Indias* in Bogotá.

These well-known facts are analysed, given new life and described by Saint-Paulien in their full horror, the material and psychological horror of lives, deaths and crimes inspired by passion.

Let us have the decency not to mix or confound these things with a political crime that never existed.[21]

No more need be said to demonstrate the lack of seriousness shown by *La estafeta literaria* in its allusions to Lorca's death.

A year later, in the autumn of 1966, the Buenos Aires publishers Codex launched a weekly series of illustrated brochures on the Spanish Civil War. The series was distributed throughout the Spanish-speaking world and became immediately available to readers in Spain.

---

* A meaningless reference to Lorca's play *La zapatera prodigiosa*.

† Saint-Paulien states, p. 8, that there is in existence a correspondence between José Antonio Primo de Rivera and Lorca, and that one of the poet's letters to the Falange chief begins 'My dear friend'. I have found no evidence in support of this assertion, and it is hard to believe that, if the letters really existed, the Falange would have delayed their publication.

The tenth episode, *Andalusia: Confusion and Tragedy*, appeared on Spanish bookstands in November 1966. Largely dedicated to Queipo de Llano's putsch in Seville, the number also devoted considerable space to Lorca.[22] Most of the information on the poet's death was a rehash of Hugh Thomas's brief and rather inaccurate synthesis,[23] and as a result no mention was made of Lorca's detention in the Civil Government.

The explanation of Lorca's death ascribed to Ramón Pérez de Ayala, the Republic's ambassador in London, however, was startlingly new and provoked much comment. Although the editors claimed not to lend much credence to the account they nevertheless decided to publish it, ostensibly as one more example of the multiplicity of rumours surrounding the poet's death, but perhaps also to call in question the reputation of the Communist poet Rafael Alberti. Pérez de Ayala's version reads:

García Lorca, who, because of his connections with the Left, had gone, frightened, into hiding at the house of his great friend Luis Rosales, the Falangist poet, seldom sallied forth from his hiding place*. When he did so he was watched attentively by the excitable Nationalist militiamen, who regarded Federico with suspicion. It appears that on one of these occasions they questioned him and asked him where he was off to. Lorca replied that he was going to hand over some letters for friends and relatives in the Republican zone, which a well-known messenger had promised to deliver. The militiamen, probably Falangists, accepted his story with some scepticism. Some days later the voice of Rafael Alberti was heard over Madrid Radio referring to 'the great poet Federico García Lorca who was a prisoner of the insurgent traitors but who had not lost faith in the ultimate victory [of the Republic], and who for this reason had sent some lines of poetry to his friends in Madrid which he, Alberti, was now going to read there and then over the microphone'. Alberti proceeded to read some tremendous lines in which the rebel leaders were insulted in the most vile language; the poem could evidently not be imputed to Lorca, who was always correct and elegant in his expression. The lines bore the clear stamp of Alberti himself, who ended his broadcast by thanking Lorca for sending them and hoping for his speedy release.

* According to the Rosales, Federico never once left their house during his stay there: such an action would have been unthinkable in the circumstances.

It appears that the militiamen and Falangists who heard the broadcast
in the Granada zone were incensed with García Lorca, considering that
he had tricked them [. . .] This alleged act on the part of Lorca un-
leashed the fury of his fanatical accusers, who put him to death during
a confused spell of disorder and terror which has never been satisfactorily clarified . . .[24]

Alberti reacted quickly to this grotesque account and initiated
legal proceedings against Codex. He had in fact been in hiding in
Ibiza until 15 August 1936, when the island was liberated by the
Bayo Expedition, and could hardly have reached Madrid before
Lorca's death.

The Codex affair was widely covered in the Spanish press and,
while most journalists were sensible enough to dismiss the accusations against Alberti, the customary evasiveness about the poet's
death was again in evidence. We can be content with one example.
Jaime Capmany, writing in *Arriba*, concluded:

We must approach this version of the death of the great poet Federico
García Lorca with the same scepticism as the many and varied accounts
which up to now have circulated in books, periodicals and newspapers
both in Spain and abroad. The death of Federico García Lorca continues to be one of the enigmas of the first days of our war; a painful
enigma, the clarification of which can now only have an historical
meaning. These were days of general disorder and collective lunacy,
and if for many months everything was possible in one zone, it is not
surprising that for a few hours or a few days everything was possible in
Granada, including the death of García Lorca.[25]

Lorca's 'reinstatement' became virtually official on Sunday 6
November 1966, when *ABC*, the most widely read newspaper in
Spain, published a 'homage' to the poet on the occasion of the
thirtieth anniversary of his death.

The only reference in that issue to the death itself is to be found
in an article by Edgar Neville, 'The Works of Federico, the Nation's
Property'. The sentiments are predictable and require little comment:

Federico was killed by the disorder of the early moments, when evil men on both sides took advantage of the confusion to give free rein to their worst instincts and to revenge themselves on their enemies or on other people's success. It was a small-town crime, one might almost say a personal one, just like those that were committed on the other side against thousands of innocent creatures, some of them poets or authors, writers who had nothing to do with politics and who wanted nothing to do with them . . .

Referring to the 'evil men' responsible for Federico's death, Neville concludes:

It seems that some of those implicated have already died, but others are around still and wriggle out of their responsibility whenever anyone tries to shame them publicly.[26]

Which is, of course, an apt description of what the regime itself has been successfully doing for the last thirty years.

Six years passed before there was any further reference in the Spanish press to Lorca's death. Then, suddenly, a new controversy flared up. On 23 March 1972, a plaque commemorating the foundation of the Falange was fixed to the front of Madrid's Teatro de la Comedia, where the party was launched in 1933. The Nuria Espert production of Lorca's *Yerma* (which was received with acclaim in London some weeks later) was playing in the Comedia at the time, and the coincidence did not go unnoticed.

The day after the commemoration, the Catholic newspaper *Ya* published photographs of the ceremony which showed the plaque and the *Yerma* poster in close proximity, and Luis Apostúa commented in his daily column:

Other important political events yesterday were the reception of Archbishop Monsignor González as a Councillor of State and the uncovering of a plaque commemorating the foundation of the Falange on the front of the Teatro de la Comedia, where a drama by Federico García Lorca, who died in 1936, is currently playing. The Falange's return to an active role is evident ('*El retorno a la escena activa de Falange es bien visible*').[27]

The Falange had no doubt that the last sentence was double-edged, and that evening Antonio Gibello, editor of *El Alcázar*, took up the challenge on the party's behalf. He informed Apostúa that Lorca, hounded by militant Acción Popular youths, had taken refuge in a Falangist house, accused the CEDA of the poet's death and ended his article with a veiled allusion to Ramón Ruiz Alonso and the newspaper on which the latter worked in Granada, *Ideal* (which is owned by Editorial Católica, the Jesuit publishing company which also controls *Ya*).[28]

Next morning the Falangist daily, *Arriba*, added its voice of protest,[29] and Luis Apostúa proclaimed his innocence in *Ya*. How could the Falangists have read such a polemical intention into that innocuous sentence? Such an interpretation of what he had written was as absurd as it was gratuitous:

The return of the Falange to an active political role had already been noted with approval several times in *Ya*, because we believe that the future of Spain depends on the open functioning of authentic political groups.

Moreover, insisted Apostúa, he knew perfectly well that the Falange was not responsible for the poet's death. Indeed, he knew as well as anyone who *was* responsible.[30]

Next day an unsigned leading article in *Ya* reaffirmed the newspaper's absolute incomprehension of Gibello's charges.[31]

On 27 March Gibello fired his Parthian shot from the battlements of *El Alcázar*. He accepted Apostúa's clarifications but had one final query: if Apostúa really knew who killed García Lorca, would it not be a mark of courtesy to inform *Ya*'s readers, who must surely be *avid* for the facts?[32]

It was understandable that among all these innuendos and counter-accusations someone should have thought to ask Luis Rosales for his opinion. On 29 March *ABC* published the following letter:

To the editor of ABC

My dear friend,

Having been encouraged in an article by the well-known journalist Emilio Romero in your paper *Pueblo* to make a public statement concerning what I know about the death of Federico García Lorca[33], I wish now to say the following:

That painful event has exerted a decisive influence on my life and mode of being. To it I owe my deepest experience. As a result there is nothing I have desired more since 1936 than the opportunity to make a full and unconditional declaration in Spain about these matters. This I have already done more than once outside Spain.

Thanking you in advance for printing these lines.

Yours sincerely,

LUIS ROSALES

This letter highlighted the trivial nature of the controversy which was just then spluttering out in the Madrid press and proved that it was still impossible to write openly, 'unconditionally', about Lorca's death in Spain.

Or almost so, for a few weeks later a book appeared that contained the most daring account of it yet published in the country.[34] In his chapter 'Who killed García Lorca?', the author, José Luis Vila-San-Juan, had pieced the story together from Thomas, Brenan, Marcelle Auclair and myself, and was the first writer to state openly in Spain that the Nationalist repression of Granada had been 'very severe' and that Lorca was arrested on the orders of Valdés and imprisoned in the Civil Government before his execution. Blame had been laid publicly on the shoulders of the *authorities* in Granada for the first time, although Ramón Ruiz Alonso was still seen as the principal culprit.* Not only that: the author casually noted in passing that Valdés was an 'old guard' member of the Falange, which is precisely what the party has been trying to hide for thirty-seven years. Serrano Suñer's 1948 assurance that 'not a single Falangist participated in the crime' and the party's insistence

---

* Ruiz Alonso responded by initiating legal proceedings against Vila-San-Juan, without, so far as I know, any positive results to date. See *Sábado gráfico*, Madrid, 21 October 1972

on its spotless innocence in the Lorca affair could now be seen to be less than honest.

Vila-San-Juan had set the cat of intellectual honesty amongst the pigeons of deceit, and it is hard to believe that he had no official backing for his exposé, particularly in view of the fact that his chapter on Lorca was reproduced shortly afterwards in a glossy weekly.[35]

Moreover, some weeks later the Madrid magazine *Informaciones* gave Luis Rosales the opportunity he had been seeking. In an interview published on 17 August (the anniversary of Lorca's imprisonment), Rosales at last told his story, or part of it, in his own country and—most unexpectedly—quotations from the Spanish-language edition of the present book were reproduced, notably a passage indicating that Lorca was shot officially on the orders of Valdés.[36]

Clearly the authorities had decided on a change of approach, and this was confirmed a month later when, on 23 September 1972, José María Pemán of the Spanish Academy (whose contribution in 1948 to the Lorca debate has already been discussed) stated in *ABC* that, in his opinion, this book was written 'with intellectual integrity and without bias' and should therefore be made available in Spain.[37]

It seems that, finally, the regime has decided that so far as Lorca's death is concerned honesty, even if relative, is now the best policy.

ELEVEN

Conclusion

More than thirty years have now passed since the Spanish Civil War ended, yet the country is still in the grip of a political system which denies basic human freedoms. There is rigid censorship (particularly of books on the war), a police with wide powers to interfere in the lives of ordinary people, active suppression of free speech and no right to strike or elect parliamentary representatives. Despite the 'economic miracle' achieved by industrialisation, booming tourism and foreign investment, Franco's regime, in the words of one modern historian, 'retains to this day its original character as a reactionary military dictatorship'.[1]

The damage done to the psychological health of Spain during these years is incalculable. Carrying out research on the Granada repression has made one aware of a collective evasiveness and unease which, on the intellectual level, produces extraordinary hypocrisy and dishonesty. In this book it has been part of my purpose to demonstrate the deviousness with which the Nationalists have sought to exonerate the Movement for Lorca's death, and I believe that my analysis of what has been published on the subject indicates an almost pathological inability to face up to the guilt of the immediate past. The same process has been studied on a far greater scale by Herbert Southworth, whose meticulous examination of what Nationalist historians have written about the war

reveals their carelessness and lack of integrity.[2] When one considers
the brilliance and promise of Lorca's generation, it is painful to
contemplate the state of Spain today, where assassins can hold
public office, thinkers and artists are persecuted and a Picasso exhibition can be wrecked by fanatics in the name of Jesus Christ.

It is Lorca's poetic achievement, not his death, that remains and
will always remain an enigma.

Even if the regime were to put at our disposal tomorrow the
documents relating to the poet's death which must exist in official
archives, even if Ramón Ruiz Alonso, Nestares, the Rosales family
and those other people who possess first-hand information about
the repression were to tell us all they know, the mystery of Lorca
the poet and the man would continue to challenge us. Perhaps it
was inevitable, in some way we cannot understand, that Lorca,
whose entire work is concerned with the search for love and fulfil-
ment, should have been murdered in the Granada which had not
only formed him but given him a feeling of solidarity with all
those who are prevented by a cruel society from realising their
true potential.

Had Federico not died that morning in Víznar, the thousands of
other innocent, but less well known, *granadinos* liquidated by the
rebels might have been forgotten. As it is they will be remembered
long after those responsible for the repression have passed into
oblivion.*

* In Section 2 of the Bibliography I make a few suggestions which may assist the
English-speaking reader new to Lorca to establish some personal contact with the
poet's work.

APPENDIX A

A complete list of town councillors holding office in Granada between February and July 1936

This list was published by *Ideal* on 10 July 1936. By that date only the first twenty-four councillors on the list still held office. All those marked with an asterisk were executed. Alejandro Otero, who was particularly loathed by the Nationalists, was lucky to be out of Granada when the rising began.

*Manuel Fernández Montesinos (Socialist)
 Francisco Gómez Román (Independent)
*Rafael Gómez Juárez (Socialist)
*Juan Fernández Rosillo (Socialist)
*Constantino Ruiz Carnero (Left Republican)
*Rafael Baquero Sanmartín (Left Republican)
*Antonio Dalmases Miquel (Socialist)
*Francisco Ramírez Caballero (Socialist)
*José Valenzuela Marín (Socialist)
 Miguel Lozano Gómez (Left Republican)
*Enrique Marín Forero (Left Republican)
 Antonio Ortega Molina (Independent)
*Jesús Yoldi Bereau (Left Republican)
 Alejandro Otero (Left Republican)
*Maximiliano Hernández (Socialist)
*Francisco Rubio Callejón (Left Republican)
*Virgilio Castilla (Socialist)
*Juan Comino (Socialist)

*José Megías Manzano (Socialist)
  Cristóbal López Mezquita (Independent)
*Manuel Salinas (Left Republican)
*Wenceslao Guerrero (Socialist)
  Rafael Jiménez Romero (Independent)
*Luis Fajardo (Left Republican)
*Rafael García Duarte (Socialist)
  Antonio Alvarez Cienfuegos (CEDA)
  Federico García Ponce (Socialist)
  José Martín Barrales (Left Republican)
  José Pareja Yévenes (Left Republican)
  Eduardo Moreno Velasco (CEDA)
  Claudio Hernández López (Left Republican)
  Juan Félix Sanz Blanco (CEDA)
  Angel Saldaña (Independent)
  Carlos Morenilla (CEDA)
  José Antonio Tello Ruiz (CEDA)
  Indalecio Romero de la Cruz (CEDA)
*Ricardo Corro Moncho (Left Republican)
*José Palanco Romero (Left Republican)
*Francisco Menoyo Baños (Socialist)
*Pablo Cortés Fauré (Socialist)
  Eduardo Molina Díaz (CEDA)
  Germán García Gil de Gibaja (CEDA)
  Fermín Garrido Quintana (CEDA)

APPENDIX B

Deaths Attributable to the Nationalist Repression of Granada (Capital and Province)

The total number of deaths caused by the Spanish Civil War has generally been calculated in that country at one million. While it is not yet possible to arrive at a really accurate figure it nevertheless now seems that the total of about 600,000 estimated by both Thomas[1] and Jackson[2] is nearer the mark.

These two historians differ noticeably in their breakdown of this estimate, however, and Thomas attributes far less deaths than Jackson to Nationalist *paseos* and executions (which he believes are unlikely to have totalled more than 50,000).[3] Jackson is of the opinion that 200,000 people were executed by the Nationalists *during* the war and that, from 1939 to 1943 a further 200,000 prisoners were either executed or died from disease and malnutrition. Until carefully documented studies of the repression in each Spanish province have been carried out there can be no certainty on the matter, although it is fair to say that Thomas's figure of 50,000 for the whole country must be too low.

In 1940 Granada (the capital) had, in round figures, 155,000 inhabitants,[4] and we have seen that, at a very minimum, 4000 people were killed by the rebels in the town and its immediate surroundings (particularly Víznar). The real total was unquestionably higher, and if one includes the many outlying villages of the *vega* which were gradually occupied by the Nationalists, it seems that an aggregate of 4500 victims for the area must be an absolute minimum.

In the capital, as we have seen, very little resistance was offered to the Nationalists, so that executions there could not properly be termed reprisals. This was not so of other towns throughout the province, some of which did not fall into rebel hands until the end of the war. They paid dearly for their obstinacy.

Guadix (pop. 26,000) and Baza (pop. 20,800), for example, remained behind the Republican lines until March 1939. No figures are available for the executions that took place there, but on the basis of procedure elsewhere these are likely to have totalled at least 500 for each town. Motril (pop. 20,500) on the Granada coast was taken by the Nationalists in January 1937, six months after the Movement began. Gollonet and Morales list the names of approximately seventy right-wing supporters killed there by the 'Reds' before the town fell (pp. 240–61); if this figure is accurate, and if the ensuing reprisals followed the ratio of ten to one reported in many Andalusian and Castilian villages,[5] then we might expect a figure of, say, 700 executions for Motril. Certainly 500 would be a safe estimate. Another large town that suffered a brutal repression was Loja, on the road from Granada to Málaga. Loja (pop. 24,000) has always been a key position in the wars of this area, and its capture on 18 August 1936 by General Varela signified an important advance for the Nationalists. Again there must have been many hundreds of executions.

All these towns have a sizeable population and the slaughter there was consequently on a greater scale than in the many villages and smaller towns scattered throughout the province. Yet the killings in these were numerous and totalled together would add several thousand victims to the list. In Lanjarón, for example, about 480 people were shot.[6] Alhama de Granada (pop. 9,900) was taken by troops from Granada on 22 January 1937, and many executions followed in reprisal for the strong resistance offered by the inhabitants. The same procedure was repeated in almost every town and village of the province, especially in the coastal ones that lay in the path of the Nationalist advance on Málaga; of these Salobreña and Almuñécar suffered particularly.*

We arrive, then, at the following estimate:

Granada and immediate surroundings	4500
Guadix, Loja, Baza	1500
Coastal towns (Motril, Salobreña, etc.)	1000
Other towns and villages in the province	2000
	9000

* A brief comparison with Málaga may be found helpful here. Málaga (pop. 138,000) fell to the rebels in February 1937 and executions took place on a massive scale, Italian firing squads assisting the Nationalists. If 4000 people were shot in Granada, we can be sure that the total was much higher in Málaga, where resistance to Franco had been fierce and numerous right-wing supporters were killed.[7]

It must be stressed that this is a conservative estimate. An acquaintance of mine who has had access in an official capacity to documents kept in the Granada *Audiencia* (Municipal Courthouse and legal archives) insists that a total of 25,000 victims would be nearer the truth. Moreover his figure coincides almost exactly with the estimate arrived at by one of Professor Jackson's contacts, a notary who had lived all his life in Córdoba and been a member of the CEDA. In 1946 this man decided to determine as accurately as possible the number of Nationalist executions in Andalusia. After careful research (which has of course never been published) he estimated 26,000 executions for the province of Granada, 32,000 for Córdoba and 47,000 for Seville.[8]

Even if we accept a figure of approximately 10,000 victims for Granada, this is already a fifth of Thomas's total for the entire country. Yet in Madrid, Burgos and Barcelona alone, in each of which cities executions continued unchecked right up to 1943, the number of victims was probably ten times as high as in Granada.[9]

Perhaps some day historians will be able to document these sordid events and arrive at accurate figures for the executions. At the moment such research is obviously out of the question.

APPENDIX C

The Origins of a Rumour: Federico García Lorca and the Spanish Civil Guard

It was probably inevitable that Lorca's death should have been attributed to the Civil Guard.

His *Ballad of the Spanish Civil Guard* had become one of the most famous poems in the language and lines from it were on everybody's tongue:

> The horses are black.
> The horseshoes are black.
> On their capes shine
> Stains of ink and wax.
> Their skulls are made of lead,
> that is why they cannot weep.
> Up the road they come
> with their souls of patent leather . . .

The poem evokes the traditional struggle between the Civil Guard (founded in 1844 to suppress banditry) and the gypsies, whose lawlessness and refusal to be assimilated into Spanish society have always made them particularly odious to the authorities. In the ballad a band of forty *civiles* attacks an unsuspecting gypsy village busily celebrating Christmas Eve. But Lorca's poem is far more than a mere concession to Andalusian local colour: for him the gypsy symbolises the deepest elements in the human personality, the ultimate source of laughter and tears, while the brutal Civil Guard embodies the oppressive forces of 'civilisation' which seek to stamp out vitality and spontaneity. The poem has, therefore, a relevance far beyond the confines of Southern Spain.

The Civil Guard was offended by it. In 1936 (eight years after the appearance of the *Gypsy Ballads*) a case was brought against Lorca by a man from Tarragona who claimed that the poet had grossly insulted the force. 'He would be satisfied with little less than my head', laughed Federico afterwards. The poet had no difficulty in persuading the judge of his 'innocence', but the incident revealed the extent to which his work was capable of irritating the Spanish reactionary mentality.[1]

When Federico's death began to be known in Spain it was natural to assume that the Civil Guard had been implicated.

What started out as an assumption soon attained the status of accepted fact. On 15 September 1937 the Valencian socialist daily *Adelante* carried a sensational article on its front page which was to have immediate repercussions throughout the Spanish-speaking world:

THE CRIME WAS IN GRANADA, HIS GRANADA.
'I SAW GARCÍA LORCA BEING ASSASSINATED' . . .

'Federico was chased by a hail of bullets from the Civil Guard as he upheld, before dying, the justness of our struggle', relates a witness to that crime.

He did not want to tell me his name because he has five brothers and a mother in the other Spain. The black Spain. The Spain of crimes and treachery. And crime and treachery would visit the five boys and the poor old woman who have remained behind, thinking about the other son, absent from their side. But even though we may not know his name it's all the same. What matters is to hear the true, spine-chilling account of that terrible crime: the assassination of our poet Federico García Lorca.

The man is from Granada. Along with him are several others who have escaped from the enemy zone and now live in this happy, welcoming Valencian barracks where the atmosphere of hatred that permeated those where the treacherous plot against the Spanish people was hatched is entirely lacking.

Numerous soldiers throng the spacious courtyard: the men who escaped, almost a thousand of them, from the battlefronts of Aragon.

At my side a young lad notices my curiosity and draws my attention to the strange uniforms of the soldiers, some of whom are mere boys, almost children.

'Did you escape too?'

'Yes, but not just now. Those chaps are from the Aragonese fronts. I got here from Granada'.

'García Lorca's Granada . . .'

'Yes.'

The lad suddenly looks upset, stops talking and lowers his head.

'Did you know García Lorca, then?'

'No, but I've read a lot of his books. I knew his work and quite a lot about his life . . . The awful thing is that I also know how he died.'

'Did you see him in front of the firing-squad?'

'Federico García Lorca didn't die that way. His death was something I'll never forget, something so monstrous, so criminal, that I'll always remember it. Even when I close my eyes I can still see it. Federico was mown down as he ran by the Civil Guard's bullets.'

That terrible room in the Civil Guard barracks

'I was a member of the Civil Guard in Granada. Although I was totally un-interested in politics I sympathised with the Cause of the ordinary people be-cause I'm an ordinary chap myself. And even if I hadn't sympathised with the Cause, I would have been forced to do so by the terrible succession of crimes and assassinations committed in the early days of the rebellion. Crimes carried out with sadistic refinement, with ghastly cruelty, all over the place and at all hours of the day. So much so that all the things I could tell you about the people assassinated and the form the assassinations took, would be only a pale imitation of the truth . . . That awful room in the barracks, full of inquisitorial instru-ments of torture! It was ghastly. I could never have believed that the human spirit could sink so low—and with such a refinement of cruelty. There were truncheons, iron clubs, knives, tongs . . . Someone had even devised a club bristling with razor-sharp blades with which he used to beat his victims to make them divulge where the workers were hiding—the workers were terrified by the crimes committed against so many of their comrades and had hidden wherever they could in an effort to escape from the worst sort of death.

Luckily I managed to pretend that I was unwell, and so avoided having to live through all that horror or to take part in crimes.

> '*Their skulls are made of lead,*
> *that is why they cannot weep*'.

That day I was on guard duty. I saw this young man entering the barracks. He was pale, but walked with serenity. It was Federico García Lorca. When I saw him I understood at once that a tremendous tragedy was about to occur. García Lorca signed his death warrant the day he put his name to the famous ballad about the Civil Guard . . .

They told me they had found him in the French Legation. They tricked him into leaving the building and then arrested him. He got no more of a trial than any of the other victims before him, naturally, and that same night he left the barracks escorted by a picket of Civil Guards. It's terrible to have to admit it, but I was one of them. The cars pulled off along the road to Padul. The sinister convoy stopped about ten miles from Granada. It was eight o'clock. The head-lamps lit up the man walking to his death. His silhouette stood out against the depths of the night. The picket formed up behind the lamps, where the victim couldn't see it.

García Lorca walked steadily, with magnificent serenity. Suddenly he stopped, and turned to face us, as if wanting to speak. This caused a great sur-prise, especially to Lieutenant Medina, who was in command of the picket.

And he spoke. García Lorca spoke with firmness and a steady voice. His words betrayed no weakness and he begged no forgiveness. They were manly words in defence of what he had always loved: liberty. And he praised the people's Cause, which was his, and the good work they were doing in the face of such barbarity and crime.

Those words spoken with the fire of passion made a tremendous impression on the men with the guns. For me it was like a penetrating light that burned into my brain. The poet continued speaking . . .

But he never finished. Something terrible, something monstrous and criminal happened: Lieutenant Medina, shouting dreadful curses, fired his pistol and urged his Civil Guards on against the poet.

The spectacle was appalling. Clubbing him with rifle-butts, firing at him (some of us stood petrified with terror at the sight), they hurled themselves on García Lorca, who ran followed by a tremendous hail of bullets. He fell about a hundred yards away and they went after him to finish him off. But Federico stood up again, pouring blood, and with terrible eyes stared at the men, who drew back in horror. All the Civil Guards got back into their cars and only the Lieutenant remained with him, pistol in hand. García Lorca closed his eyes for the last time and slumped to the ground that was already saturated with his blood.

Medina stepped rapidly forward and emptied three rounds of bullets into poor Federico's body.

There they left the poet, unburied, outside Granada, *his* Granada . . .

VICENTE VIDAL CORELLA[2]

On 10 December 1937 the substance of this article was reproduced in the course of a speech delivered before the Democratic Anti-Fascist League of Costa Rica by Vicente Saenz. The speech was published a few days later in the influen-tial Costa-Rican weekly, *Repertorio americano*, and was widely read and dis-cussed in Central and South America.[3]

But there was more to come, for Vidal Corella was not the only journalist who had talked to the Civil Guard from Granada. So too had J. Rubia Barcia, a teacher from Granada who had known Lorca. Rubia Barcia delayed two years before publishing his version of the Civil Guard's declaration, which first appeared, in Havana, in 1939. Adopting the 'omniscient narrator' technique, he describes Lorca's arrival at the Civil Guard barracks:

Sergeant Remacho, head of the local Civil Guard 'black squad', was waiting for him. Young, tall and corpulent, he affords a striking contrast to the physical weakness of the author of *Gypsy Ballads*.* In this room there are pizzles, pincers and clubs which have been used on other occasions to force useless declarations out of condemned men. Until eight that night they remain together.

Meanwhile groups of Civil Guards chat in the courtyard. Some, a small minority, leave, unable to bear the screams of the victims under torture. Others, among whom Francisco Ubiña Jiménez, an ex-schoolteacher, stands out, make witty comments each time a scream of pain is heard. The scene is interrupted by the arrival of Staff-Sergeant Tomás Olmo. It is time for the list [of those to be shot]. The Civil Guards are already drawn up and the trucks await their load of men to be killed that night. Federico García Lorca will doubtless be among them. But the plans are changed. Better for him to go alone, by himself, with five *civiles* under the command of Lieutenant Medina. These will be the men entrusted with the execution.

Everything is ready. The only person missing is the prisoner himself, who now appears escorted by two Civil Guards who hold his arms. Blood is flowing from his face and hands. Nevertheless he maintains his dignity. He is shoved and jostled into the truck, which moves off. In it are the Civil Guards Francisco Ubiña Jiménez, the bloodthirsty ex-schoolteacher; Burgos, who used to be a clerk in the Military Commandery; Carrión, no less celebrated than the first man for his ferocity; and finally the new recruits, Corpas Jiménez and José Vázquez Plaza, who are unable to conceal their terror as newcomers to the assassination business. Sitting with them is the sadistic Lieutenant Medina, the father of three priests.†

They stop about half a mile from Padul, on the road from Granada. The

---

* Properly, Romacho. Romacho was also a Falangist, and is listed by Gollonet and Morales with Valdés's early accomplices (see Chapter Five, n. 17, above). In Granada one hears frequently of his brutality during the repression. It appears that he is still alive.

† I have not investigated these allegations. Ubiña and Burgos, I gather, still live in Granada. It can be deduced that either Corpas Jiménez or Vázquez Plaza is the escaped Civil Guard.

moment has arrived. Night has already fallen and the headlamps are on. The prisoner is ordered to walk six yards away from the truck . . .

The description of the shooting that follows corresponds almost exactly to that given by Vidal Corella and indeed a comparison of the two writers' versions reveals quite clearly that they spoke to the same man. Rubia Barcia's article was reproduced a year later in New York[4] and shortly afterwards John A. Crow referred closely in another article on the poet's death to Vidal Corella's original *Adelante* account as quoted by Vicente Saenz in *Repertorio americano*.[5]

But there was a snag that those who repeated the story about the Civil Guard's complicity in the poet's execution had failed to notice. The 1940 publication of Rubia Barcia's article was introduced by the following explanation:

One day during the wartime summer of 1937 the author of this article, a friend of Federico García Lorca, was summoned to the Almirante Barracks in Valencia, which at that time had been converted into a provisional gaol for prisoners and escapees from the Nationalist zone, to hear the unsolicited confession of a Civil Guard who had been a member of the picket that shot the great Granadine poet. Seemingly a simple, straightforward country type, he had passed over to the loyal troops after being forced to commit this and other crimes that were repugnant to his conscience. *He did not know the first thing about the poet, but one afternoon, in the 'Cultural Corner' of the barracks ['Rincón de Cultura'], he saw a picture of him which he recognised; unable to conceal his emotion, he exclaimed: 'We killed that man as well'*. And then, with a moving simplicity, he began to speak . . . [my italics]

Thus it is evident that, on 19 August 1936, the date of Lorca's death, the Civil Guard in question did not know the poet by sight or even, apparently, by reputation. In 1937 he had seen a photograph in Valencia of a man who resembled a prisoner whose execution he witnessed *a year earlier*, been told that it was of the famous poet Federico García Lorca, and gone on to conclude that he had been present at the execution. The legend of the Civil Guard's participation in Lorca's death was the result, first, of a faulty piece of identification made one year after the event and, second, of an over-readiness on the part of two journalists to give credence to an unsubstantiated declaration.

One question remains unanswered: who was the *real* victim of that night's brutal killing by the Civil Guard? We will probably never know.

APPENDIX D

Jean-Louis Schonberg and his 'Homosexual Jealousy' Thesis Concerning Lorca's Death*

In his book *Federico García Lorca. L'homme—L'oeuvre* (Paris, Plon, 1956), Jean-Louis Schonberg offered the first coherent explanation of why the poet was killed. His chapter on the death appeared separately in *Le Figaro Littéraire* a few weeks before the book's publication and produced widespread interest in France and Spain (see pp. 149-53).[1]

Having denied, on the flimsiest of evidence, that the death had a political motive, Schonberg concludes: 'Reste alors la vengeance; la vengeance de l'amour obscur' (p. 106). The *non sequitur* is obvious and the second inference strikes one as particularly unjustified, for even if Lorca had been killed in revenge that revenge need not necessarily have had a homosexual basis. It might, for example, have been motivated by jealousy—jealousy of the poet's talents, his fame, etc.

Determined to prove that the assassination was the outcome of a homosexual rivalry, Schonberg proceeds to build up the details of his case.

The first question he must answer is: who was Lorca's homosexual rival? He tackles the matter obliquely. To start with we are told that the murder squads were recruited from the low world of 'communistes retournés et de pédérastes' (p. 107). It is difficult to see what evil qualities Communists and pederasts share

* I have recently been given reason to believe that this is a pseudonym. In 1955 Albert Camus, then at Gallimard, received a letter from a certain Baron L. Stinglhamber offering the manuscript of his book *García Lorca. L'homme et l'oeuvre* for publication. Camus rejected it. It seems that 'Schonberg' is Baron Stinglhamber, although I have not followed up this clue myself. All quotations from the French-language editions of Schonberg's book are given in the original French in order to avoid distortion.

as a matter of course, and in fact there is simply no evidence that the Granada killers, whatever their individual political histories, were noted for their pederastic inclinations. Schonberg insinuates that these men entertained a violent, homosexual hatred of Lorca which was then exploited by someone who was determined that he should die. He reminds us that in his *Ode to Walt Whitman* the poet had established a distinction between 'pure' and 'impure' homosexuals, accusing the latter of being 'assassins of doves', and goes on to affirm that it was precisely because Lorca had spurned the 'impure' members of the homosexual confraternity in Granada that they decided to kill him, just as they did with another 'pure' homosexual, Constantino Ruiz Carnero.[2]

Now, whose was the sinister mind behind all this? Schonberg begins by insinuating that the culprit was Ramón Ruiz Alonso, and it follows that he must make Ruiz Alonso not only a homosexual but an 'impure' one at that:

Parmi ces loups, doit-on compter le chef lui-même des bandes noires, Ramón Ruiz Alonso, sur qui deux témoignages laissent peser le soupçon d'inversion sexuelle? (p. 107)

I have already insisted that Ramón Ruiz Alonso was not a member of these squads, let alone the 'chef lui-même'. As regards the man's alleged homosexuality there can be little doubt either. In Granada, a town well known for its active disapproval of those who cannot or will not conform to the demands of conventional sexuality, I never once heard such a charge. On the contrary, Ruiz Alonso is remembered as a lady's man. When I informed him that doubts had been cast on his virility, he burst out:

I can assure you that I am and always have been very virile, very virile. So he thinks I'm a queer! If M. Schonberg wants proof of my interest in women let's see him send me his wife and daughters for a fortnight. They could take him back some accurate documentation on my sexual preferences!

This crude sally, typical of the man, would of course be inadequate proof in itself (many a Spanish *macho* with hidden insecurities must have made similar claims) but the fact remains that if Ruiz Alonso has homosexual tendencies he has also been capable of fathering two famous daughters, the film actresses

Emma Penella and Elisa Montes. The 'suspicions' of Schonberg's 'two witnesses' are in my opinion without foundation and, if Ruiz Alonso was jealous of Lorca at all, it is likely to have been for other reasons.

Schonberg proceeds to describe how this homosexual Ruiz Alonso, discovering that Lorca was hiding in the Rosales's house, had his 'black squad' cordon off the street. I have shown that Lorca's arrest was not effected by the murder squads, however, but by a formidable array of soldiers and police acting on instructions from the Civil Government. Once again Schonberg is either misinformed or else imposing his assumptions on what really happened: since the members of the squads were all perverts it *must* have been they who arrested the poet.

According to Schonberg this group of homosexuals, turncoat Communists and pederasts frequented a bar in Elvira Street. Federico was a member of the confraternity, but because he was 'noble' and 'pure' he scorned the others and so they decided to kill him:

C'est justement cette morgue supérieure qu'on lui a fait payer. Le meurtre de Lorca, couvert par la politique, absous par la complicité du clergé de Grenade, qui ne risqua ni une intervention ni une protestation contre l'odieux massacre des innocents, sort d'une guerre de hannetons. C'est un règlement de comptes entre invertis. (p. 113)

A settling of accounts between homosexual rivals. But who was Lorca's enemy? At the end of his tortuous exposition Schonberg finally gets to the point and makes a totally unexpected and unsubstantiated accusation:

Un règlement où la jalousie, la perversité de don Gabriel Morcillo, peintre d'éphèbes, ne restèrent pas plus étrangères qu'au crime du bar de la rue Elvira commis par un de ses élèves. Entre Lorca et Morcillo s'était creusé une cassure empoisonnée, traîtresse . . . Mais devenu personnage officiel et peintre du Régime, pour avoir su à temps retourner sa veste, Morcillo est tabou. D'autres que lui se sauvèrent, au même prix, le prix d'une délation. (pp. 113–4)

Schonberg made it quite clear in his reply to a letter by Claude Couffon criticising his article (both letters were published by Le Figaro Littéraire on 13 October 1956), moreover, that he stood by his accusation:

Quant au dénonciateur, nommé en toutes lettres, le lecteur saura bien le trouver.[3]

So the well-known Granadine painter Gabriel Morcillo was responsible for Lorca's death. Ramón Ruiz Alonso was involved in the arrest and entertained a homosexual jealousy towards the poet, but Morcillo was the original *informer*, the homosexual rival who was determined to 'settle accounts'.

The charge is a serious one, all the more so since Schonberg produces not a shred of evidence to support his allegations. Federico, in fact, had never been a close friend of Morcillo, as Schonberg implies when he talks of the poisoned rift that opened between them, although it is true that the painter does have the reputation in Granada of being a homosexual (despite which he is married with a family). I met no one in the town who ever suggested that Morcillo was in any way involved in the poet's death. Indeed several friends of both Morcillo and Lorca, especially Miguel Cerón, rejected Schonberg's accusation as monstrous. Some months after the publication of the Spanish-language edition of this book an acquaintance wrote from Granada:

Gabriel Morcillo heard the news of Lorca's death in the Café Royal. He himself told me about it. He was drinking a beer when Trescastro himself came up to him on purpose and said: 'Don Gabriel, we bumped off your friend the poet with the big fat head this morning'. Morcillo says that his hand trembled and that he got back to his *carmen* as quickly as possible and hid in his garden for two months. I know him well. Schonberg's disgusting accusation is nonsense. Like all the other artists and intellectuals in Granada, Morcillo was terrified.

Who was the source of Schonberg's information about Morcillo? Why does he not provide us with the evidence on which his accusation rests? Moreover the other murder referred to by Schonberg, the one committed in the infamous bar in Elvira Street (which I have been unable to identify), had nothing to do with Morcillo either. The student in question, who apparently murdered an old homosexual, was the protégé, not of Morcillo, but of a South American painter who was living in Granada at the time (some ten years or so ago). Schonberg has accused Morcillo of Lorca's death without producing any evidence. Such a procedure is intolerable.

In a footnote appended to the above exposition, Schonberg tells us that:

Le dossier de Lorca aux archives du ministère de l'Intérieur confirme le nôtre. Un récent article de la *Tribune de Genève* à propos de la représentation de *Yerma*, s'exprime dans le même sens. (p. 114)

The first sentence of this footnote would lead the unsuspecting reader to the conclusion that Schonberg had himself seen the dossier to which he so confidently refers. Yet in the later Swiss edition of his book, *A la recherche de Lorca* (Neu-châtel, A la Baconnière, 1966), we learn that this is not so. In this book, which is little more than a reworking of the original French edition, Schonberg appends two new paragraphs to his homosexual 'settling of accounts' explanation of the poet's death.

In the first of these he refers again to the file on Lorca kept in the Ministry of the Interior in Madrid, and informs the reader that, although he himself has not seen the dossier, the information he possesses about it proceeds from a com-pletely trustworthy source (p. 120).

The second sentence of the footnote refers to an article that appeared in the *Tribune de Genève* 'à propos de la représentation de *Yerma*' shortly before the publication of the French edition of Schonberg's book, in October 1956. The author does not refer the reader to the exact article in question, and a search through the paper's files is therefore necessary if one wants to judge for oneself to what extent it 'confirms' his thesis. Two brief articles on Lorca appeared at about that time in the *Tribune*, but only one of them referred to the current production of *Yerma* in Geneva. This was published on 8 December 1955, under the title '*Yerma* à la Comédie', and made no allusion whatsoever to Lorca's death. It seems, therefore, that Schonberg's reference must be to the second article. Entitled 'Une fleur de sel et d'intelligence' à la bouche/ Il y a vingt ans/ FEDERICO GARCÍA LORCA', it appeared on 31 May 1956, signed by Jacques Givet. But this short article, which contains an obtuse and skimpy com-mentary on the poet's last days, is based neither on personal research nor on an adequate knowledge of Lorca's work. Givet seems to be quite unaware of the investigations of Brenan, Couffon and Schonberg himself, and claims that little is known about the circumstances of the poet's death except that he was executed without a trial. He does assert, however—and this is probably what drew Schonberg's attention—that:

Il serait hasardeux d'affirmer, comme on s'est risqué à le faire, qu'on a voulu tuer en lui le poète de la révolution espagnole, puisqu'il n'était pas, politique-ment parlant, engagé dans la bataille.

Is Schonberg referring to Givet's article, which in no sense 'confirms' his own theories? Or to another item, published about the same time but which has escaped one's notice despite a careful search? It would be helpful if Schonberg could indicate exactly which article in the *Tribune de Genève* 's'exprime dans le même sens' as the Ministry of the Interior dossier which he himself has not seen.

Having investigated these pieces of so-called confirmation which Schonberg adduces in support of his 'homosexual' thesis we can now proceed to consider his further clarifications.

In the Second Preface to the Mexican edition of his book, *Federico García Lorca. El hombre—La obra* (Mexico, Compañía General de Ediciones, S.A., 1959), Schonberg seeks to defend himself against those critics who have shown their dissatisfaction with certain aspects of the French 1956 edition, and produces three new pieces of 'corroboration' with which to confound them.

First, he announces that he has received a 'signed' letter from a man who knew Lorca, Luis Rosales and other members of that group, and who confirms that the account he has read in Schonberg's book is accurate. The author then goes on to reveal that the source of his correspondent's information about Lorca's arrest and death is—Luis Rosales! This would lead us to expect that Rosales's version and that of Schonberg coincide, but nothing could be further from the truth. Rosales has told me that he completely rejects Schonberg's thesis, along with numerous other details of his account. Rosales can hardly have told Schonberg's anonymous correspondent that Lorca was killed for homosexual motives, therefore, since he has never held this opinion, and he certainly has never imputed the responsibility for Lorca's death to the painter Gabriel Morcillo, as Schonberg does. Thus the letter is worthless as confirmation of the latter's thesis.

Schonberg's next reference is to a note published in the Jesuit literary journal *Brotéria. Revista contemporânea* (Lisbon, no. 5 (1956), pp. 480 –1). The author of this snippet, which is entitled 'A morte de García Lorca', is a certain 'M.A.' who claims to have himself investigated Lorca's death in Granada. He has come to the same conclusion as Schonberg, he informs us, and proceeds disdainfully to dismiss Couffon's *Figaro* article as a 'novel'. M.A. brings no new information whatsoever to bear on the subject of Lorca's death, in spite of his alleged personal researches, and his 36-line note cannot therefore be taken as a worthwhile 'confirmation' of Schonberg's thesis.

The final piece of new 'evidence' with which Schonberg seeks to combat the opinions of his critics is, without a doubt, the most flimsy:

To these true testimonies which confirm our own, should we add the confession of a famous singer, an old friend of Lorca's, whose confidences pertaining to the poet's death were well-known in Parisian literary circles? (p. 18)

The reader can decide for himself what might be a fitting reply to that question.

This leaves the additional material contained in the Swiss edition of Schonberg's book, which has already been briefly mentioned in passing. Here Gabriel

Morcillo is no longer named in full as the man responsible for the poet's death: he is now designated 'Don G.M.' (p. 119). And Schonberg has discovered what the Ministry of the Interior's file on Lorca, which he himself has not seen, says about the reasons for his death:

Au dire de qui l'a su, et qui l'atteste sous la garantie d'une voix tout-à-fait autorisée et peu suspecte, outre le coup dans le dos de M., un autre bras, celui du Commandeur [Valdés?], s'est exercé par l'entremise de Ruiz Alonso. Moins odieuse que la première, pour autant qu'une vengeance puisse trouver son excuse, c'était la vindicte du père outragé d'un triste adolescent entraîné dans le vice par Lorca; pour joindre sur sa tête, au drame de la trahison, celui de l'assouvissement d'une justice immanente. De Thesée cette fois, l'ombre irritée, sur le coupable s'abattait. (p. 120)

It seems certain that there is indeed an official dossier on Lorca in the Ministry of the Interior, and it may even contain these accusations. But it would be ludicrous to imagine that such a file, compiled by the very people who for more than thirty years have been seeking to exculpate the Movement for the poet's death, could possibly be trustworthy. By repeating these charges without producing any supporting evidence, Schonberg has further weakened his case. In fact he has totally failed to substantiate his a priori theories concerning the alleged homosexual motives for the poet's death. His arguments cannot withstand close scrutiny, his research is careless and it can be seen that he seeks to shift the ultimate responsibility for Lorca's death from the leaders of the rising in Granada onto the shoulders of private individuals acting more or less on their own initiative. It was for this reason that his 'revelations' were received with such delight in Spain and, as we have seen (in Chapter Ten), Franco's propagandists lost no time in appropriating for their own purposes the essential details of his account. Thanks to Schonberg, Lorca's death could, from 1956 onwards, be explained away as a sordid 'affaire de moeurs' (p. 113) and the Nationalist authorities in Granada be freed of responsibility for the crime.

APPENDIX E

Further References by Arab Authors to Ainadamar*

1. *Ibn al-Khaṭīb* (1313–74). The greatest of Granada's Arab historians, vizier to Mohammed V and teacher of the poet Ibn Zamrak, whose odes cover the walls of the Alhambra, Ibn al-Khatib himself possessed a palace in Ainadamar. First, his prose description of the spot:

Concerning the Fountain of Tears, it is inclined towards the South Spring†
and located on the skirts of Mount Alfacar. It overflows with water which is
channelled along the road, and enjoys a marvellous situation, blessed with
pleasant orchards and incomparable gardens, a temperate climate and the sweet-
ness of its water, in addition to the several prospects it commands. There are to
be found well-guarded palaces and well-attended places of worship, lofty residences and fortified buildings amidst a landscape verdant with myrtle. The idle
rich have foregathered there to the cost of the learned and the wise who
formerly dwelt there, and have drawn on their resources to expend them therein.
State employees have vied one with another enviously in the purchase of property until, in the course of time, it has become the talk of the world, beauty
finding in it its own reflection such that mention of it is frequent in poetry and
on the tongues of the eloquent amongst those who abide there and those who
go to visit it.[1]

* I am indebted to my friend Dr James Dickie of Lancaster University for the
information and translations contained in this appendix, and remember with
pleasure our many visits together to Ainadamar.
† Perhaps this was what is today called the *Fuente Chica* ('Small Pool') in Alfacar.

After this enthusiastic description, Ibn al-Khaṭib cites verses from two of his own poems, the second of which he had inscribed inside a dome of his palace near the pool:

Oh Ainadamar, how many years like pearls shed in the course of our acquaintance could you perhaps restore! When your soft breezes blow cold and damp during the night, an ardent passion for you agitates me.

If Ainadamar were a real eye(*), then . . .(†).

Neither has it ever ceased to be a race-course for the horses of orgy and amusement, nor its soft accommodation to form an abundant pasture.

[So brilliant is it that] the Pleiades themselves want to be its residence; the Dog-star wants to praise it [for its abundance even in the canicular heat] and al-Mu"‡ to watch over it.

2. *The alfaquí Abū 'l-Qāsim ibn Qūṭīya.* Lines from three poems quoted by Ibn al-Khaṭib:

I spent the night in Ainadamar, feasting in its pastures, and in its dwelling places I had my fill of love.

Whenever the East Wind blows it carries me its scent and evokes the spectre of the lost loved one.

It was a night of amorous union in Ainadamar when its stars amongst all others presaged good fortune,

in which one could behold beauty unrolling its mystery and the shadow of hopes long on the hills.

We spent the night, and there were flowers in the garden of the cheeks and cheeks amongst the roses in the garden,

and red were our apples and full and swollen our pomegranates in the centre of the breasts;

and a violent passion and a beautiful woman learned from our livers§ the limits and extent of love.

---

* *'Ain* means both eye and spring in Arabic (Translator's note).
† Scribal errors render the Arabic text unintelligible at this point (Translator's note).
‡ Al-Mu" is a star or constellation, and to identify it with certainty one would have to consult astronomical treatises. It does not figure in the dictionaries (Translator's note).
§ To the Arabs the liver is the seat of love (Translator's note).

Of a certainty, Ainadamar enchains the beholder's eyes, so free your eye in contemplation of its . . .*,

and pause at that spot, if you are inclined to love, for on its hills wild cows pasture;

and shake therein the hand of the narcissus in greeting, kissing the cheeks of companionship amidst the flowers;

and take them freely in the valleys and on the mounds where they shall assuage the thirst of your thoughts.

Such a spring is a wine matured by Time itself, so fear not, in drinking of it, that there befall you the vicissitudes of the times.

It could speak to you of Chosroes and of Sāsān before him, and could inform you about a mortal vine become immortal.†

O tempora, o mores! Not a vestige of Ainadamar's palaces remain above ground today. The spring's resources have been exploited by modern entrepreneurs, however, and a swimming pool was built a few years ago near the Fuente Grande. There is now a hotel, and bungalows are in demand in the vicinity. Ainadamar has been rediscovered by a new generation of *granadinos*, most of whom must be unaware of its Arab or more sinister, recent associations, and at weekends the place is alive with picnickers from the capital.

* See note (†) on p. 184.
† Sāsān gave his name to the Sassanian Dynasty of the neo-Persian empire, founded by Ardashir I in AD 226, and of which Chosroes I (531–597) was the most powerful ruler. The Sassanian empire was conquered by the Arabs in 637, less than a century before they invaded the Iberian Peninsula.

APPENDIX F

An Anonymous Ballad on the Death of
Garcia Lorca

One afternoon in the summer of 1966, Dr Sanford Shepard, Professor of Spanish at Oberlin College, USA, and his wife Helen were walking in the garden of their delightful *carmen* in Granada. Among the flowers Mrs Shepard noticed a soiled piece of paper with writing on it. Picking it up, she was surprised to find herself reading a poem on Lorca's death, scribbled in longhand on a sheet of notepaper bearing the heading 'The National Institute of Social Security Employees' Confraternity of Our Lady of Perpetual Succour' ('Hermandad de Nra. Sra. del Perpetuo Socorro de Funcionarios del Instituto Nacional de Previsión').

The poem narrates the burial of the poet by grief–stricken gypsies on the slopes of the Cerro del Aceituno (The Hill of the Olive Tree), which rises behind the Albaicín and is crowned by the Church of Saint Michael. Lorca, in his *Ballad of Saint Michael*, had evoked the pilgrimage which winds up through the Albaicín every 29 September to reach the church and pay homage to the dazzling image of the Archangel by Bernardo Mora, and somehow it seems appropriate that the anonymous ballad should locate the poet's burial place there. The elegy has little artistic merit, but is touching in its simplicity and genuine emotion:

> Calle Real de Cartuja
> y la Cuesta de Alhacaba,
> Plaza Larga y Albaicín,
> a hombros de seis gitanas.

Por siete cuestas arriba
al filo de la mañana,
va Federico García
a hombros de seis gitanas.

Al Cerro del Aceituno
se lo llevan a enterrar
solo gitanos delante
solo gitanos detrás,
y solo suena en el aire
un cante, la soleá.

Soleá con la soleá
(escarcha) en aquella aurora
(moja) tus huesos llorando
Soleá, Soleá Montoya.

Up Real de Cartuja Street and Alhacaba Hill, through Larga Square and the Albaicín, on the shoulders of six gypsy women.

Up the seven hills goes Federico García, just as dawn is breaking, on the shoulders of six gypsy women.

To the Cerro del Aceituno they take him to be buried, with only gypsies in front and only gypsies behind and only one strain sounding in the air, the soleá.

The soleá, oh the soleá, (frost) in the dawn (wets) your bones with its weeping, Soleá, Soleá Montoya.*

* The *soleá* (the Andalusian pronunciation of the word *soledad*, solitude) is a flamenco song that expresses grief and suffering. Soledad Montoya, an embodiment of the soleá, appears in Lorca's ballad *Romance de la pena negra*.

NOTES

Throughout the notes, Federico García Lorca, *Obras completas* (Madrid, Aguilar, 5th edition, 1963) is referred to as 'Aguilar' and *El Defensor de Granada* is referred to as *El Defensor*.

CHAPTER ONE

1. Richard Ford, *A Handbook for Travellers in Spain* (London, John Murray, 1845), p. 367.
2. To be more precise, Lorca's mother was born on 25 July 1870 at 10 p.m., in 1 Solarillo Street, Granada. Her parents were Vicente Lorca, a native of Granada, and Concepción Romero, from Atarfe in the *vega*. Details from the Register of Births for Granada, 1870, no. 126, kept in the Town Hall.
3. Aguilar, pp. 1754–5.
4. *Id.*, pp. 1770–1.
5. *Id.*, p. 298.
6. Karl Baedeker, *Spain and Portugal. Handbook for Travellers* (Leipzig, 2nd edition, 1901), pp. 379–80.
7. Victor Hugo, *Grenade*, in *Les Orientales* (1829).
8. See note 1 above.
9. Aguilar, p. 43.
10. Ford, p. 363.
11. Aguilar, pp. 7–8.
12. José Mora Guarnido, *Federico García Lorca. Testimonio para una biografía* (Buenos Aires, Losada, 1958).
13. J. B. Trend, 'A Poet of Arabia', in *Alfonso the Sage and Other Spanish Essays* (London, Constable, 1926), pp. 155–61.

14. Conversation with Miguel Cerón, Granada, July 1971.
15. Aguilar, p. 1700.
16. *Id.*, p. 129.
17. *Id.*, p. 124.

CHAPTER TWO

1. The *Nuevo Ripalda enriquecido con varios apéndices* (14th edition, 1927), quoted by J. B. Trend, *The Origins of Modern Spain* (Cambridge, 1934), p. 63.
2. Gerald Brenan, *The Spanish Labyrinth* (Cambridge, 1960), p. 53.
3. *Id.*, p. 236: 'A bare two weeks after the proclamation of the Republic, the Cardinal Primate of Spain, Mgr Segura, had issued a violently militant pastoral against the Government'.
4. All details from José Venegas, *Las elecciones del Frente Popular* (Buenos Aires, Patronato Hispano-Argentino de Cultura, 1942).
5. The Electoral Law of 1932 had given the vote to Spanish women for the first time, and it has sometimes been suggested that the Left's defeat at the polls in 1933 was partly due to the fact that the Catholic women of Spain voted against the government that had enfranchised them. One of the Socialist candidates for Granada in 1933, for example, has described how even the nuns in that constituency were given a special dispensation by the ecclesiastical authorities to issue forth from the perpetual seclusion of their convents and vote against the Republic (María Martínez Sierra, *Una mujer por caminos de España*, Buenos Aires, Losada, 1952, p. 87). The author almost seems to imply that the good sisters' votes were decisive. The truth is probably that the female vote made little difference, if any, to the outcome of the election. In the vast majority of cases the women would have voted with their menfolk, the only result of their participation in the election being to increase the number of votes cast for all the parties. See Venegas, p. 19.
6. Brenan, p. 265.
7. *Id.*, p. 267.
8. *Id.*
9. *Id.*, p. 269.
10. *Id.*, pp. 286-9.
11. *El Defensor*, 21 November 1933.
12. *Id.*, 15 December 1934.
13. Marcelle Auclair, *Enfances et mort de Garcia Lorca* (Paris, Seuil, 1968), pp. 330-2.

CHAPTER THREE

1. *El Defensor*, 17 February 1936, p. 4.
2. *Id.*, 19 February 1936, p. 4.
3. *Id.*, 17, 18, 19 February 1936, *passim*.
4. Brenan, p. 298.
5. *Id.*, pp. 298–9.
6. *El Defensor*, 9 March 1936.
7. *Id.*, 22 February 1936.
8. *Id.*, 21 February 1936.
9. *Id.*, 10 March 1936.
10. A. Gollonet Megías and J. Morales López, *Rojo y azul en Granada* (Granada, 1937), p. 37.
11. *El Defensor*, 12 March 1936.
12. *Historia de la Cruzada Española*, the official Nationalist history of the war. Details in the Bibliography, section 5. All references are to Vol. III, book xi. Henceforth, *Cruzada*. This ref., p. 276.
13. *Cruzada*, p. 280.
14. *Ideal*, 25 August 1936. *Ideal* does not mention that the train was carrying a consignment of dynamite. This detail was given to me by Miguel Rosales, who commanded the expedition.
15. Gollonet and Morales, pp. 41–7.
16. *Id.*, p. 47: 'The [new] Civil Governor is a faithful servant of the high officials of the Masonic Order and of Judaism'.
17. *Id.*, pp. 41–2; *El Defensor, passim; Cruzada*, p. 276.
18. José María Gil Robles, *No fue posible la paz* (Barcelona, Ariel, 1968), p. 558.
19. *El Defensor*, 4 May 1936.
20. Brenan, p. 302.
21. Stanley Payne, *Falange. A History of Spanish Fascism* (Stanford University Press and Oxford, 1962), p. 95.
22. *Cruzada*, p. 275.
23. Details from a potted biography of Valdés published in *Ideal*, 25 July 1936.
24. Conversation with José Rosales, Granada, April 1966.
25. Claude Couffon, 'Le crime a eu lieu à Grenade . . .', in *A Grenade, sur les pas de García Lorca* (Paris, Seghers, 1962), pp. 59–115. These refs., pp. 70 and 98. This is the definitive text of Couffon's article, 'Ce que fut la mort de Federico García Lorca', in *Le Figaro Littéraire*, Paris, no. 278, 18 August 1951.
Jean-Louis Schonberg, 'Enfin la vérité sur la mort de Lorca! Un assassinat, certes, mais dont la politique n'a pas été le mobile', in *Le Figaro Littéraire*, no. 545, 29 September 1956. The article was reproduced in Schonberg's book

Federico García Lorca (Paris, Plon, 1956), pp. 101–18, from which all references are taken.

26. *Cruzada*, p. 276.

27. Gollonet and Morales, p. 53 *et seq.; Cruzada*, p. 276.

CHAPTER FOUR

1. José Luis Cano, *García Lorca. Biografía ilustrada* (Barcelona, Ariel, 1962), p. 119.

2. *Id.*, p. 119.

3. *Id.*, pp. 119–20.

4. *Id.*, p. 120.

5. *¡Ayuda!*, Madrid, no. 7, 1 May 1936. A copy of the text was given by María Teresa León, wife of Rafael Alberti, to Robert Marrast, who published it in French translation in his article 'La dernière interview de García Lorca', *Les Lettres Françaises*, 14–20 November 1963.

6. Marie Laffranque, 'Pour l'étude de Federico García Lorca. Bases chronologiques', in *Bulletin Hispanique*, Bordeaux, 1963, pp. 333–77. This reference, p. 375.

7. Cano, p. 122; *El Sol*, Madrid, 23 May 1936.

8. Dámaso Alonso, *Poetas españoles contemporáneos* (Madrid, Gredos, 1958), p. 173.

9. Aguilar, p. 1812.

10. Gabriel Celaya, 'Un recuerdo de Federico García Lorca', in *Realidad. Revista de cultura y política*, Rome, no. 9, April 1966.

11. Aguilar, p. 1814.

12. *Id.*, pp. 1816–7.

13. *Id.*, p. 1813.

14. The interview was given to Antonio Otero and appeared in the Madrid review *Mundo gráfico* on 24 February 1937. Robert Marrast published a French translation of it in 1963 (see note 5 above) and Otero reprinted it in the original Spanish in *La Torre*, Puerto Rico, no. 48, October–December 1964.

15. Extracts from the memoirs of Antonio Rodríguez Espinosa, Lorca's first schoolteacher, translated by Marie Laffranque and published in her *Federico García Lorca* (Paris, Seghers, Collection 'Théâtre de tous les temps', 1966), pp. 107–10.

16. Hugh Thomas, *The Spanish Civil War* (London, Eyre and Spottiswoode, 1961), pp. 120–7. This quotation, p. 125.

17. Rafael Martínez Nadal, 'El último día de Federico García Lorca en Madrid',

in *Residencia. Revista de la Residencia de Estudiantes*, commemorative issue published in Mexico, December 1963, The article is reprinted in Martínez Nadal's '*El público*': *Amor, teatro y caballos en la obra de Federico García Lorca* (Oxford, The Dolphin Book Co. Ltd, 1970), pp. 9–15.

18. Marcelle Auclair, p. 369.
19. See note 15 above.
20. Couffon, p. 70.
21. See note 15 above.
22. Dámaso Alonso, p. 173.
23. Among Lorca's personal papers contained in the packet was the manuscript of a surrealist play, *El público*, which is still in the possession of Martínez Nadal. Nadal has recently published a detailed study of the play (see note 17 above).
24. Ramón Ruiz Alonso, *Corporativismo* (Salamanca, 1937), p. 15.
25. Conversation with Ruiz Alonso, Madrid, 1966.
26. Ruiz Alonso, pp. 249–50.

CHAPTER FIVE

1. Thomas, pp. 131–4.
2. *Id.*, p. 134.
3. *Id.*, p. 135.
4. *Id.*, pp. 136–8; *Cruzada*, pp. 169–85.
5. *Ideal*, 19 July 1936, p. 2.
6. *Cruzada*, p. 183.
7. *Thomas*, p. 138.
8. Gollonet and Morales, pp. 64–5.
9. *Ideal*, 19 July, p. 3.
10. Gollonet and Morales, pp. 65, 69, 82.
11. In Granada I spoke to a man who knew Torres well and who was with him in gaol. It seems that the Civil Governor was completely unaware of the plot against the Republic until it was too late.
12. *Cruzada*, p. 278.
13. *Ideal*, 19 July, p. 2.
14. *Cruzada*, pp. 278–9.
15. *Id.*, pp. 279–81.
16. *Id.*, pp. 281–2.
17. *Id.*, p. 284. According to Gollonet and Morales, the Falangists accompanying Valdés were: Enrique Iturriaga, José Rosales, Cecilio Cirre, José Gámiz González, Aureliano Castilla, José Nestares, Alberto Sánchez, José Díaz Plá,

José Rubí Fernández, Fernando Estévez, José Molina Plata, Peregrín Rodríguez Muñoz, Vicente Alonso, Manuel Garrido Márquez, Pablo Sierra,
Manuel Romacho, José Alvarez, Santiago Cardel, Antonio Rosales, Commandant Tapia, Ramón López Cuervo, Gonzalo Martínez Gandía and
Santiago de la Torre.

18. *Ideal*, 21 July, p. 1.
19. *Cruzada*, p. 284.
20. *Ideal*, 21 July, p. 3.
21. *Id.*
22. *Cruzada*, p. 288.
23. Published in *Ideal*, July 21, p. 1.
24. *Cruzada*, p. 286.
25. *Ideal*, 21 July, p. 1.
26. *Id.*, p. 4.
27. *Cruzada*, p. 288.
28. *Ideal*, 22 July, p. 4.
29. *Id.*, p. 1.
30. *Id.*, 23 July, p. 4.
31. *Id.*, p. 3. According to the *Cruzada*, p. 297, these aeroplanes had been sent
    from Madrid to protect Republican bombers attacking Seville. Their pilots,
    unaware that Armilla was in rebel hands, were arrested on landing.
32. *Ideal*, 23 July, p. 3.
33. *Id.*
34. *Id.*, 24 July, p. 3.
35. *Cruzada*, p. 289.

CHAPTER SIX

1. *Ideal*, 26 July 1936, p. 3; *Cruzada*, p. 289.
2. *Cruzada*, pp. 287–8.
3. *Ideal*, 22 July, p. 5.
4. *Cruzada*, p. 289; Gollonet and Morales, p. 165.
5. *Id.*, p. 289.
6. *Id.*; *Ideal*, 4 August 1936, pp. 1, 3–4.
7. *Ideal*, 31 August 1936, 3 September, p. 5.
8. Personal communication from Ramón Ruiz Alonso, 1966.
9. *Ideal*, 6 September 1936, p. 5.
10. Couffon, p. 89.
11. Personal communication from one of the members of the Españoles Pat-
    riotas who was forced to take part in the executions in the cemetery.

12. Helen Nicholson (Baroness de Zglinitzki), *Death in the Morning* (London, Lovat Dickson, 1937), p. 33.

13. *Id.*, p. 82.

14. Brenan, *The Face of Spain* (London, Turnstile Press, 1950), p. 130.

15. I have myself seen the cemetery records, from which these details proceed.

16. Brenan, *op. cit.* p. 135.

17. *Id.*, p. 132.

18. This information proceeds from Don José García Carrillo, a close friend of Ruiz Carnero who was with him in prison. García Carrillo (who died recently) miraculously escaped execution. It was he who kindly allowed me to reproduce the moving photograph of Ruiz Carnero and García Lorca in his possession (see plate 1).

19. Cf. Nicholson, p. 34: 'Asta went on: "He [Santa Cruz] was planning to blow up the town, and had already mined the river-bed beneath the Reyes Católicos"—the principal street of the town. "They found papers on him that proved everything. He had powerful friends, and he must have been guilty beyond all doubt, since they couldn't save him. But it's a dreadful shock to all of us who knew him!"' Miss Nicholson's political naïvety was equalled, it would seem, only by that of her daughter.

CHAPTER SEVEN

1. Aguilar, p. 1603.

2. Conversation with Miguel Cerón, Granada, 1966.

3. Claude Couffon, 'Ce que fut la mort de García Lorca', in *Le Figaro Littéraire*, no. 278, 18 August 1951.

4. Claude Couffon, 'Le crime a eu lieu à Grenade', in *A Grenade, sur les pas de García Lorca* (Paris, Seghers, 1962), pp. 59–115. All future references are to this edition.

5. *Id.*, p. 92.

6. Conversation with Manuel Montesinos, Granada, 1967.

7. *Ideal*, 10 August 1936, p. 4.

8. Schonberg, p. 106.

9. Cf. Marcelle Auclair, p. 381, note: 'There has been talk of anonymous letters which added blackmail to threats of death. According to Luis Rosales, neither Federico nor his family ever mentioned these during his conversations with them when all the disturbing circumstances [concerning the visits to the Huerta] were discussed'.

10. Conversation with Angel Saldaña, Madrid, 27 May 1966. Cf. Nicholson, p. 72: 'They [the Reds] were well served by their spies within the town.

When our troops went out to fight the Red columns our aeroplanes usually went along to protect them, and inside a quarter of an hour of their leaving the Red planes would be bombing Granada. It was obvious that a secret wireless apparatus was being used to communicate the movements of our troops to the enemy'.

11. Luis Rosales's estimate was accurate enough. As has been shown, the exact date was probably 9 August.

12. According to Marcelle Auclair, p. 382, Luis Rosales had been made head of the Motril sector. The town, on the coast of Granada, remained in Republican hands until January 1937.

13. Recently Luis Rosales has informed me (London, 7 December 1972) that he and his brother Gerardo drove with Lorca that evening to Angulo Street. It appears that Luis telephoned Gerardo from the Huerta, asking him to come with a taxi.

14. Luis Rosales agreed in our conversation that Lorca may have been arrested on 16 August, as I believe. For further evidence that Lorca was arrested on 16 August see p. 98 and footnote p. 106.

15. Couffon, pp. 102–3.

16. Schonberg, p. 110.

17. See Franco Pierini, 'Incontro a Spoleto con la sorella di Federico. Quella notte a Granada . . .', in *L'Europeo*, 17 July 1960. In the interview Concha Montesinos talks about her brother's arrest without mentioning Ruiz Alonso.

18. Couffon, p. 99.

19. What seems to have been the first reference to the alleged hymn appeared in an article by Guillermo Camacho Montoya, 'Por qué y cómo murió García Lorca', in *El Siglo*, Bogotá, 15 November 1947.

20. I have myself seen this entry in the cemetery records. See also the photograph of Montesinos's tomb, plate 11.

21. Ruiz Alonso was undoubtedly telling the truth about Valdés's temporary absence. On 18 August 1936 General Varela, who for several weeks had been advancing on the town from Cadiz, finally took Loja, thereby breaking the 'siege' of Granada. The Granada garrison took part in the operation, which was described at length in *Ideal*, 19 August 1936. *Ideal* did not appear on 17 August (it being the traditional practice in Spain that daily newspapers are not published on Mondays), so that we are deprived of information concerning Valdés's movements on Sunday 16 August, the date of Lorca's arrest. From references in *Ideal* on 18 August it is evident that Valdés was personally involved in preparations for the assault on Loja, and we may not unreasonably assume that on 16 August he was visiting Nationalist outposts. The province of Jaén borders on Granada to the north and north-west and,

since Jaén was in Republican hands, the line between the two territories was known as the 'Jaén front'.

There are frequent references in *Ideal* to Velasco's deputisation for Valdés. On 18 August 1936, p. 3, for example, we read: 'Lieutenant-Colonel Velasco received the representatives of the press on behalf of the Civil Governor, who was absent from his desk owing to the unavoidable pressures of his position'.

22. The doctor has recently informed me that Vialard Márquez died soon after the end of the war.

23. Luis Rosales does not accept that there was a written warrant for Lorca's arrest, and believes that Miguel is imagining this detail. I am inclined to believe myself that there was a warrant.

24. Schonberg, p. 111.

25. *Id.*

26. Details given to me in the course of numerous conversations with Miguel Rosales in Granada, 1966 and 1967.

7. Couffon, pp. 103–4, states that Ruiz Alonso captured Lorca on the terrace on top of the Rosales's house as he was trying to escape across the roofs. All the members of the Rosales family with whom I spoke (Luis, José, Miguel and Esperanza) categorically denied this, yet it seems that Couffon heard this version from Aunt Luisa.

28. This man was still living in Granada in 1967. I have promised not to give his name here.

29. Luis García Alix's name appears frequently in *Ideal* at this time.

30. According to Marcelle Auclair, p. 382, Luis Rosales returned to Granada on 13 July, just a few days before Lorca. He had been in Madrid for several years, and as a result was not in touch with the political life of his home town.

31. See note 23 above.

32. *Ideal*, 19 August 1936, p. 6.

33. *Id.*, 20 August, p. 4.

34. All details from Auclair, pp. 442–3.

35. Valdés was referring to Luis Rosales, whom he disliked because of an altercation that took place between them just before the Movement began. See Auclair, pp. 441–2.

36. Conversations with José Rosales, Granada 1966.

37. In Granada I spoke to two men who were in gaol at the time and saw Lorca's basket being passed around. 'I didn't know that Federico was here!', someone exclaimed.

38. See, for example, *ABC*, Seville, 7 October 1937 where, under a photograph of Falla and José María Pemán, a fanatical supporter of the Nationalists, we read: '*Granada. The Poet and Musician of the Crusade*. Here, in a tranquil

corner of his Moorish *carmen* "La Antequeruela", we see the glorious composer Manuel de Falla with the great poet José María Pemán, collaborators in the splendid patriotic poem *The Poem of the War*, of which both are the authors'.

39. José Mora Guarnido, pp. 199–201.

40. Personal communication from Antonio Pérez Funes, 1967. Pérez Funes, who died in 1971, knew Fernández Ramos well and believed that the latter's account was accurate.

41. Brenan, *The Face of Spain*, pp. 137–8.

42. *Ideal*, 21 August 1936, p. 2.

43. Jacinto Benavente, dramatist, 1866–1954; Joaquín Alvarez Quintero, dramatist, 1873–1944; Serafín Alvarez Quintero, dramatist, 1871–1938; Pedro Muñoz Seca, another dramatist, was assassinated in Madrid on 28 November 1936, three months after Lorca's death; Ricardo Zamora, a famous footballer, was still alive in 1966. Who was 'Zuloaga'? According to *Ideal*, 23 August 1936 (see plate 12), this was a certain José Zuloaga, 'a potter with a wide reputation'. But no such person existed, and it seems that 'José' Zuloaga was an amalgam, intentional or otherwise, of the painter Ignacio Zuloaga, who died in 1945, and Juan Zuloaga, the latter's cousin (son of the famous potter Daniel Zuloaga), who died recently.

44. On 18 August 1936 *Ideal* made a passing reference to the death of Zamora in Madrid. On 22 August the newspaper published photographs of him and Benavente on its front page (see plate 13) and of the Quintero brothers on p. 8; on August 23 *Ideal*'s front page carried photographs of 'José' Zuloaga and Pedro Muñoz Seca, the latter being designated in the caption as 'our most popular and productive national dramatist' (see plate 12).

45. I was repeatedly told on good authority in Granada that a deputation headed by Lieutenant Mariano Pelayo of the Civil Guard travelled to Burgos to complain to Franco about the continuing brutality of the repression being imposed by Valdés. On 22 April 1937 *Ideal* announced that the Civil Governor had resigned, and published a farewell message from him in which he apologised to the people of Granada for the severity he was forced to demonstrate during his occupancy of the Governorship but asserted that his conscience was clear before God (see plate 14).

46. On 14 June 1937 *Ideal* reported that Valdés was to be sent to Tetuán to take command of a unit of the Regulares (African Army). It is possible that he was later wounded in action, for it is stated on his tomb in Granada (see plate 15) that he died 'for God and Country'. The main cause of his death, however, is almost certain to have been tuberculosis or cancer.

47. Conversation with Miguel Cerón, Granada, December 1965.

CHAPTER EIGHT

1. Aguilar, p. 1573.

2. Brenan, *The Face of Spain*, p. 144, writes: 'It was known, our guide told us, as La Colonia. Before the military rising it had been a sort of Brown House for the Falangists of Granada, where they had met and received training. They had also brought their girls here and danced'. I have found no evidence in Víznar or Granada to support these statements.

3. I was able to draw up a list of details about fourteen of the *Colonia* killers, but see little point in giving their names here: most of these men have since died.

4. The parish priest of Víznar in August 1936 was José Crovetto Bustamente, whose name appears frequently in the pages of *Ideal* during these months. Schonberg, who visited Víznar three times between 1953 and 1956, spoke to the old parish priest, presumably the same man, but found him uncommunicative about his spiritual ministrations to the condemned men (p. 115).

5. Enzo Cobelli, *García Lorca* (Mantua, Editrice La Gonzaghiana, 2nd edition, May 1959), p. 77.

6. Auclair, pp. 407–8.

7. Cobelli, p. 78.

8. In the summer of 1966 I gave English lessons to Nestares's daughter at their Granada home, in the hope of eventually being able to discuss Lorca's death with him. Nestares's visiting card reads 'Infantry Colonel (Retired)': that he never received further promotion was probably due to his serious mishandling of the famous Peñón de la Mata operation against a Republican position, in which hundreds of Nationalists lost their lives. The lessons were conducted in Nestares's study, which contains, among other mementoes of the war, a framed diploma from Hitler's chancellery which reads: 'Im Namen des deutschen Reiches/Verleihe ich/dem Oberst-Leutnant/José María Nestares/das Verdienstkreuz/des Ordens vom deutschen/Adler/erster Stufe/ mit Schwertern/Berlin den 5 Juni/Der deutsche Reichskanzler'. Nestares's daughter repeated to me her father's version of Lorca's death: he was a friend of the poet, and when he heard about the arrest he rushed to Granada from Víznar to intervene on his behalf. But it was too late, and Lorca had already been killed 'by a certain individual acting on his own initiative'. When I plucked up the courage to approach the subject with Nestares, he shied away from the question like a frightened stallion. 'It was all a mistake', he said. 'The sort of mistake that occurs in all civil wars, when innocent people die because they just happen to be there when the trouble starts . . . he was a friend of mine . . . he had left-wing acquaintances. . . it was all a mistake'. No more information was forthcoming and in the interests of

safety I pursued the matter no further: the rest of the discussion was devoted to less dangerous topics, such as furniture and Irish stamps (on which Nestares is an expert). Nestares is an influential man in Granada—and a rich one. He possesses a splendid house, half a dozen estates and a large block of apartments, 'El Ancla', in the summer resort of Almuñécar on the Granada coast. He is reputed in Granada to have become wealthy as a result of the appropriation of property belonging to the victims of the repression. If there is one person who knows the exact details surrounding Lorca's execution it is Nestares, who doubtless will take his secrets to the grave.

9. I cannot for the moment risk giving the grave-digger's name. In 1967 he was still living in Granada.

10. *Cruzada*, p. 280.

11. Brenan, *The Face of Spain*, p. 145.

12. Schonberg, p. 117.

13. Couffon, p. 114.

14. Richard Ford, *A Handbook for Travellers in Spain* (London, John Murray, 4th edition, 1869), p. 372.

15. Aguilar, pp. 1816–7.

CHAPTER NINE

1. Brenan, *The Face of Spain*, pp. 137–8; Couffon, p. 102.

2. Cobelli, pp. 65–76.

3. Auclair, pp. 390–3.

4. It seems that Ruiz Alonso joined the Falange in the early days of the rising. According to Miguel Rosales, José Díaz Plá, Local Chief of the Granada Falange, sent for Ruiz Alonso a few days after Lorca's arrest and ripped the Falangist emblem from his shirt with the words: 'You filthy bastard, we're not having *you* in the party' (Conversation with Miguel Rosales, Granada, 16 August 1966). I have not been able to confirm these details.

5. Friends in Granada who knew García Alix told me that he always refused to discuss the subject of Lorca's arrest, which perhaps suggests that he was involved in it. He is buried in Granada cemetery, Patio 2, Section 8, Bóveda 5.

6. Personal communication from the doctor, whom I cannot yet name, Granada, July 1971.

7. Conversation with Angel Saldaña, Madrid, 27 May 1966.

8. Personal communication from a writer well known in Granada, July 1972.

9. *Ideal*, 20 August 1936, p. 8.

10. Ramón Ruiz Alonso, *Corporativismo*, p. 134. Varela was one of the National Front candidates in the reconvened Granada election of May 1936.

11. Conversation with Miguel Cerón, Granada, 1966.

12. Letter from Marcelle Auclair, 2 May 1968.

13. The Marquis de Merry del Val, 'Spain: Six of One and Half a Dozen of the Other', in *The Nineteenth Century*, London, March 1937, p. 368.

14. See p. 43.

14. See p. 43.

CHAPTER TEN

1. Angel del Río, *Federico García Lorca* (Hispanic Institute in the United States, 1941), p. 24, wrote that, shortly after the news of Lorca's death reached Madrid, the following United Press despatch appeared in the newspapers: 'A report from Murcia states that a copy of the Granadine daily, *Ideal*, dated 20 August, which arrived in that city, includes the name of the poet Federico García Lorca in the list [of executed prisoners] for 19 August'. Many later writers have accepted the accuracy of this report, yet *Ideal* made no such reference to the poet's death on 20 August 1936. Lists of executed prisoners rarely appeared in *Ideal*'s columns and allusions were never made to the victims of the 'Black Squads'. Many years were to pass before *Ideal* printed Lorca's name.

2. This reference, quoted in French translation by Marcelle Auclair, p. 417, is probably from *El Diario de Huelva*. The snide allusion to Lorca's homosexuality is typical of the traditionalist, Catholic mentality of the Spanish Right which was responsible for his death. Cipriano Rivas Cherif—well-known theatre director, nephew of Manuel Azaña and close friend of Lorca—has written: 'From Geneva I was unable to pick up the war-time ravings of the Falangist Radio Nacional, but someone with the precise job of listening to the enemy broadcasts heard, more than once, the voice of José María Pemán (not yet the voice of Pemán the Academician) labelling Federico, Margarita Xirgu [the Catalan actress who played many of Lorca's protagonists] and me as sexual inverts' ('Poesía y drama del gran Federico. La muerte y la pasión de García Lorca', in *Excelsior*, Mexico, 13 January 1957).

3. S.B., 'La muerte de García Lorca comentada por sus asesinos', in *Hora de España*, Valencia, no. 5, May 1937, pp. 71-2.

4. Vicente Saenz, 'Consideraciones sobre civilización occidental a propósito de Federico García Lorca', in *Repertorio americano*, San José de Costa Rica, 18 December 1937.

5. J. Rubia Barcia, 'Cómo murió García Lorca', in *Nuestra España*, Havana, no. 2, 1939, pp. 67-72, and *España Libre*, Brooklyn, 1 March 1940.

6. Ricardo Saenz Hayes, 'Para *La Prensa* hizo el general Franco importantes declaraciones', in *La Prensa*, Mexico, 26 November 1937.

7. Francisco Franco, *Palabras del Caudillo. 19 Abril, 1937–7 Diciembre, 1942* (Madrid, Editora Nacional, 1943), pp. 439–51.

8. The first edition of the Aguilar *Obras completas* of García Lorca appeared in 1954. The bibliography had been carefully vetted, and titles referring too obviously to the poet's death had been mutilated or omitted altogether. In the *Chronology* the final entry, for 1936, reads: 'August 19. Dies (*Muere*)'.

9. Brenan, *The Face of Spain*, p. 137.

10. In a conversation with the British Embassy in Mexico in July 1966 (letter to me from the Embassy, 22 July 1966).

11. Chávez Camacho reproduced the original article and Serrano Suñer's letter in his book *Misión de prensa en España* (Mexico, Editorial Jus, 1948), pp. 372–4.

12. José María Pemán, 'García Lorca', in *ABC*, 5 December 1948.

13. Gerald Brenan, 'La vérité sur la mort de Lorca', in *Les Nouvelles Littéraires*, 31 May 1951.

14. Couffon, see note 3, Chapter Seven.

15. Fernando Vázquez Ocaña, *García Lorca. Vida, cántico y muerte* (Mexico, Grijalbo, 1957; 2nd edition, 1962), p. 381.

16. The text of Ridruejo's letter is reproduced by Vázquez Ocaña (see note 15 above), pp. 381–2, and was probably taken from the Mexican newspaper *Excelsior*.

17. Rafael García Serrano, *Bailando hacia la Cruz del Sur* (Madrid, Gráficas Cies, 1953), pp. 330–1.

18. Saint-Paulien, 'Sur la vie et la mort de Federico García Lorca', in *Cahiers des Amis de Robert Brasillach*, Lausanne, no. 10, Noël 1964, pp. 7–10.

19. Paul Werrie has kindly supplied me with a copy of his article: 'Lettre d'Espagne: García Lorca a reparu sur scène à Madrid', in *Ecrits de Paris*, February 1961, pp. 91–5. It contains no allusion to Lorca's death.

20. I am not aware that Saint-Paulien has written anything else on Lorca.

21. *La estafeta literaria*, no. 314, 27 March 1965, p. 36.

22. *Crónica de la guerra española. No apta para irreconciliables* (Buenos Aires, Editorial Codex, 1966), no. 10, October 1966, pp. 224–5, 227, 237–8.

23. Thomas, pp. 169–70.

24. As for note 22 above, p. 227.

25. Jaime Capmany, 'Lorca y Alberti'. Unfortunately the cutting of this article, sent to me by a Madrid friend, is undated. It appeared in *Arriba* during the spring of 1966.

26. Edgar Neville, 'La obra de Federico, bien nacional', in *ABC*, Madrid, 6 November 1966, p. 2.

27. Luis Apostúa, 'Jornada española', in *Ya*, Madrid, 24 March 1972, p. 5.

28. Antonio Gibello, 'García Lorca y Luis Apostúa', in *El Alcázar*, Madrid, 24 March 1972, p. 2.
29. — '¿Qué pretenden?', in *Arriba*, Madrid, 25 March 1972, p. 3.
30. Luis Apostúa, 'Jornada española', in *Ya*, 25 March 1972, p. 5.
31. — 'Esto pretendemos', in *Ya*, 26 March 1972.
32. Antonio Gibello, 'La verdad ocultada', in *El Alcázar*, 27 March 1972, p. 3.
33. Emilio Romero, 'La Guinda', in *Pueblo*, Madrid, 27 March 1972.
34. José Luis Vila-San-Juan, '¿Quién mató a Federico García Lorca?', Chapter Six of *¿Asi fue? Enigmas de la guerra civil española* (Barcelona, Nauta, 1971, appeared April 1972), pp. 104–18.
35. *Sábado gráfico*, Madrid, no. 790, 22 July 1972, pp. 67–71.
36. Luis Rosales, interview with Manolo Alcalá entitled 'Luis Rosales recuerda los últimos días de Federico García Lorca', in *Informaciones*, Madrid, 17 August 1972, pp. 12–13.
37. José María Pemán, 'Las razones de la sinrazón', in *ABC*, Madrid, 23 September 1972.

CONCLUSION

1. Gabriel Jackson, *The Spanish Republic and the Civil War. 1931–1939* (Princeton, 1965), p. 497.
2. Herbert R. Southworth, *Le mythe de la Croisade de Franco* (Paris, Ruedo ibérico, 1964).

APPENDIX B

1. Thomas, Appendix II, 'The Casualties of the War', pp. 631–3.
2. Jackson, Appendix D, 'Deaths Attributable to the Civil War', pp. 526–40.
3. Thomas, Penguin (1965) edition, p. 789.
4. All the population figures quoted for the province of Granada refer to the 1940 census, and are taken from Gonzalo Gallas Encinas, *Granada. España en paz* (Madrid, Publicaciones españolas, 1964), pp. 30–1.
5. Jackson, p. 534.
6. Personal communication from Don Antonio Pérez Funes, 1967.
7. For information on the Málaga repression see: Arthur Koestler, *Spanish Testament* (London, Gollancz, 1937), pp. 209–54, and Antonio Bahamonde y Sánchez de Castro, *Un año con Queipo. Memorias de un nacionalista* (Barcelona, 1938), pp. 127–36.
8. Jackson, p. 535. See also Queipo de Llano's broadcast, reported on 26 July 1936 in *Ideal*, p. 2, and elsewhere in the Nationalist press, during which he said: "For each person killed by them [the 'Reds'] I will kill ten, inexorably; in several places this has already been more than done."

9. Jackson, *Id.*; Herbert R. Southworth, 'Their Man in Madrid' (an adverse review of Crozier's and Hills's books on Franco), in the *New Statesman*, London, 29 December 1967, writes: 'More than 35,000 were executed in Barcelona alone from 1939 to 1941'. In a letter published in the same journal on 19 January 1968, Southworth added that this figure proceeds from a book 'published in Spain in 1942 by Father Martín Torrent, Chaplain of the Prisión Celular of Barcelona'.

APPENDIX C

1. Interview given to Antonio Otero in 1936. For details, see Chapter Four, n. 14, above.
2. Vicente Vidal Corella, 'El crimen fue en Granada. "Yo he visto asesinar a García Lorca . . ." "Federico fue cazado a tiros por la Guardia Civil cuando defendía, antes de morir, la verdad de nuestra lucha", relata un testigo de aquel crimen', in *Adelante*, Valencia, 15 September 1937, p. 1.
3. For details see Chapter Ten, note 4, above.
4. J. Rubia Barcia, 'Cómo murió García Lorca', in *Nuestra España*, Havana, no. 2, 1939 and *España libre*, Brooklyn, 1 March 1940.
5. John A. Crow, 'The Death of García Lorca', in *Modern Language Forum*, Los Angeles, XXV (1940), pp. 177–87.

APPENDIX D

1. For details, see Chapter Three, note 22, above.
2. Constantino Ruiz Carnero was shot officially (see p. 78), not for any 'sexual' reason.
3. 'Enfin la vérité sur la mort de Lorca: une lettre de M. Claude Couffon et la réponse de M. J.-L. Schonberg', in *Le Figaro Littéraire*, 13 October 1956.

APPENDIX E

1. All quotations, verse and prose, are from Ibn al-Khaṭīb's history of Granada, *al-Iḥāta fī akhbār Gharnāta*, ed. by 'Abd Allāh 'Inān (Cairo, 1955), I, pp. 127–8.

SELECTED BIBLIOGRAPHY

This bibliography lists only those sources which I have consulted myself: it makes no claims to be exhaustive. Sources referred to in the text, appendices and notes are indicated by an asterisk.

1. *The principal Spanish-language editions of Lorca's work*
GARCÍA LORCA, FEDERICO, *Obras completas*. Introduced and selected by Guillermo de Torre (Buenos Aires, Losada, 1938–1942, 7 vols. Several later editions).
*GARCÍA LORCA, FEDERICO, *Obras completas*, ed. by Arturo del Hoyo (Madrid, Aguilar, 1954, and successive editions). In this book all references are to the 5th edition, 1963.

2. *English-language editions of Lorca's work*
There is no complete English-language translation of Lorca, and those which exist of separate works are unsatisfactory. Perhaps the best and most readily available texts for the English-speaking reader new to Lorca are the bilingual anthology of his poetry by J. G. Gili, with a sensible introduction (Penguin Books), and that edited by Donald M. Allen (New Directions), and for the plays *Three Tragedies* (*Blood Wedding, Yerma, The House of Bernarda Alba*), translated by James Graham-Luján and Richard L. O'Connell and introduced by Francisco García Lorca (published by New Directions in the U.S.A. and Penguin Books in Britain). The best critical book on Lorca in English is still Edwin Honig *García Lorca*, published by New Directions in the U.S.A. and Jonathan Cape in Britain.

3. *Bibliographies consulted for initial information on Lorca's death and the subsequent polemic*
ROSENBAUM, SIDONIA, bibliography included in RÍO, ANGEL

DEL, *Vida y obra de Federico García Lorca* (New York, Hispanic Institute in the United States, 1941), pp. 75–99.

HOYO, ARTURO DEL, bibliography included in the Aguilar edition of the *Obras completas* of García Lorca (see above).

4. *Principal sources consulted for general information on Granada*

*BAEDEKER, KARL, *Spain and Portugal. Handbook for Travellers* (Leipzig, 2nd edition, 1901).

*BRENAN, GERALD, *South from Granada* (London, Hamish Hamilton, 1957).

*FORD, RICHARD, *A Handbook for Travellers in Spain* (London, John Murray, 1845, 2 vols; Carbondale, Southern Illinois University Press, 1966.)

*GALLAS ENCINAS, GONZALO, *Granada. España en paz* (Madrid, Publicaciones Españolas, 1964).

GARCÍA GÓMEZ, EMILIO, *Silla del moro y nuevas escenas andaluzas* (Madrid, Revista de Occidente, 1948; Buenos Aires, Espasa-Calpe, 1954).

GALLEGO Y BURÍN, ANTONIO, *Guía de Granada* (Granada, 1946).

GÁMIR SANDOVAL, ALFONSO, *Los viajeros ingleses y norteamericanos en la Granada del siglo XIX* (Universidad de Granada, 1954).

MOLINA FAJARDO, EDUARDO, *Manuel de Falla y el 'cante jondo'* (Universidad de Granada, 1962).

*MORA GUARNIDO, JOSÉ, *Federico García Lorca y su mundo. Testimonio para una biografía* (Buenos Aires, Losada, 1958).

RUIZ CARNERO, CONSTANTINO, *Siluetas de 'Constancio'* (Granada, 1931).

SECO DE LUCENA, LUIS, *Anuario de Granada* (Granada, 1917).

SECO DE LUCENA, LUIS, *Granada. Guía breve* (Granada, 2nd edition, 1919).

SECO DE LUCENA, LUIS, *Mis memorias de Granada* (Granada, 1941).

*TREND, J. B., 'A Poet of Arabia', in *Alfonso the Sage and Other Spanish Essays* (London, Constable, 1926).

5. *Sources consulted in connection with the history of the Spanish Republic and the Civil War*

ARRARÁS, JOAQUÍN, *Historia de la Segunda República Española* (Madrid, Editora Nacional, 1957; 3rd edition, 1964).

*BAHAMONDE Y SÁNCHEZ DE CASTRO, *Un año con Queipo. Memorias de un nacionalista* (Barcelona, 1938).

*BRENAN, GERALD, *The Spanish Labyrinth* (Cambridge, 1943; in my book I refer throughout to the 1960 paperback edition).

CARR, RAYMOND, *Spain, 1808–1939* (Oxford, 1966).

CROZIER, BRIAN, *Franco. A Biographical History* (London, Eyre and Spottiswoode, 1967; Boston, Little, Brown, 1968).

Cruzada Española, Historia de la. Literary editor, Joaquín Arrarás; artistic editor, Carlos Saenz de Tejada. (Madrid, 1939–1943, 35 vols.). Vol. III, book xi, contains the official Nationalist version of the rising in Granada.

Defensor de Granada, El. Left-wing newspaper founded in 1879.

GARCÍA VENERO, MAXIMIANO, *Falange en la guerra de España; la Unificación y Hedilla* (Paris, Ruedo ibérico, 1967).

*GIL ROBLES, JOSÉ MARÍA, *No fue posible la paz* (Barcelona, Ariel, 1968).

*GOLLONET Y MEGÍAS, ANGEL, and MORALES LÓPEZ, JOSÉ, *Rojo y azul en Granada* (Granada, Prieto, 1937).

G. ORTIZ DE VILLAJOS, CÁNDIDO, *Crónica de Granada en 1937, II año triunfal* (Granada, 1938).

HILLS, GEORGE, *Franco. The Man and his Nation* (London, Robert Hale, 1967; New York, Macmillan, 1968).

Ideal. Granadine Catholic newspaper founded by Acción Popular in 1931. Still published.

*JACKSON, GABRIEL, *The Spanish Republic and the Civil War* (Princeton, 1965).

*KOESTLER, ARTHUR, *Spanish Testament* (London, Gollancz, 1937).

*MARTÍNEZ SIERRA, MARÍA, *Una mujer por caminos de España. Recuerdos de propagandista* (Buenos Aires, Losada, 1952).

*NICHOLSON, HELEN (Baroness de Zglinitzki), *Death in the Morning* (London, Lovat Dickson, 1937).

*PAYNE, STANLEY, *Falange. A History of Spanish Fascism* (Stanford University Press and Oxford, 1962).

PAYNE, STANLEY, *Politics and the Military in Modern Spain* (Stanford University Press and Oxford, 1967).

PEERS, E. ALLISON, *The Spanish Tragedy, 1930–1936* (London, Methuen, 1936).

RIESENFELD, JANET, *Dancer in Madrid* (London, Harrap, 1938).

*RUIZ ALONSO, RAMÓN, *Corporativismo* (Salamanca, 1937).

SOUTHWORTH, HERBERT R., *Le mythe de la Croisade de Franco* (Paris, Ruedo ibérico, 1964).

SOUTHWORTH, HERBERT R., *Antifalange. Estudio crítico de 'Falange en la guerra de España' de M. García Venero* (Paris, Ruedo ibérico, 1967).

*THOMAS, HUGH, *The Spanish Civil War* (London, Eyre and Spottiswoode, 1961; Penguin Books, 1965; New York, Harper and Row, 1961).

*TREND, J. B., *The Origins of Modern Spain* (Cambridge, 1934; New York, Russell & Russell, 1965).

TUÑÓN DE LARA, MANUEL, *La España del siglo XX* (Paris, Librería Española, 1966).

*VENEGAS, JOSÉ, *Las elecciones del Frente Popular* (Buenos Aires, Patronato Hispano-Argentino de Cultura, 1942).

6. *Sources consulted in connection with the death of García Lorca and the subsequent polemic. Arranged in chronological order. Sources based on original research or first-hand information are indicated by a dagger.*

*— 'Una noticia increíble. Federico García Lorca', in *La Voz*, Madrid, 1 September 1936, p. 2.

*— 'Se ha confirmado la ejecución del gran poeta García Lorca', in *La Voz*, 9 September 1936, p. 1.

*— 'Sobre el supuesto asesinato de Federico García Lorca', in *El Sol*, Madrid, 9 September 1936, p. 1.

*— 'Emisoras intervenidas por los rojos', in *La Provincia*, Huelva, 10 September 1936, p. 2.

*— '¡Ya se matan entre sí! ¿Ha sido asesinado Federico García Lorca?', in *El Diario de Huelva*(?), 10 September 1936.

*— *The Times*, London, 12 September 1936, p. 11, also 14 September p. 12, 23 September, p. 12, and 5 October, p. 11.

*— 'En Barcelona ha sido fusilado el poeta Federico García Lorca', in *El Diario de Huelva*, 19 September 1936.

*— 'García Lorca ha sido fusilado', in *Diario de Burgos*, 19 September 1936.

*— 'En Barcelona. Federico García Lorca, fusilado. Otros fusilamientos', in *La Provincia*, Huelva, 19 September 1936, p. 2.

*— 'El poeta García Lorca fue fusilado con los obreros', in *El Castellano*, Burgos, 21 September 1936.

*SÁNCHEZ DEL ARCO, M., 'Detención del duque de Canalejas. Benavente. García Lorca', in *ABC* Seville, 27 September 1936.

*— 'Nuevos detalles del fusilamiento de García Lorca en Granada', in *El Sol*, Madrid, 2 October 1936, p. 3.

*— 'Una gestión de Wells. El gobernador faccioso de Granada dice que ignora el paradero de García Lorca', in *El Sol*, Madrid, 14 October 1936.

— 'Ante el asesinato del gran poeta español Federico García Lorca', in *El Sol*, Madrid, 15 October 1936, p. 4.

MACHADO, ANTONIO, 'El crimen fue en Granada: a Federico García Lorca', in *Ayuda*, Madrid, 17 October 1936. The famous elegy was reproduced the world over.

TORRES RIOSECO, A., 'El asesinato de García Lorca', in *Repertorio americano*, San José de Costa Rica, 7 November 1936.

*HURTADO ÁLVAREZ, LUIS, 'A la España imperial le han asesinado su mejor poeta', in *Unidad*, San Sebastián, 11 March 1937, p. 1.

MACHADO, ANTONIO, 'Carta a David Vigodsky', in *Hora de España*, Valencia, no. 4, April 1937.

*S. B. [SÁNCHEZ BARBUDO?], 'La muerte de García Lorca comentada por sus asesinos', in *Hora de España*, no. 5, May 1937.

†*VIDAL CORELLA, VICENTE, 'El crimen fue en Granada. 'Yo he visto asesinar a García Lorca . . .' 'Federico fue cazado a tiros por la Guardia Civil cuando defendía, antes de morir, la verdad de nuestra lucha', relata un testigo de aquel crimen', in *Adelante*, Valencia, 15 September 1937, p. 1.

*SAENZ HAYES, RICHARD, 'Para *La Prensa* hizo el General Franco importantes declaraciones', in *La Prensa*, Buenos Aires, 26 November 1937.

*SAENZ, VICENTE, 'Consideraciones sobre civilización occidental a propósito de Federico García Lorca', in *Repertorio americano*, San José de Costa Rica, 18 December 1937.

GONZÁLEZ CARBALHO, JOSÉ, *Vida, obra y muerte de Federico García Lorca* (Santiago de Chile, Ercilla, 2nd edition, 1941).

CAMPBELL, ROY, 'Flowering Rifle. A Poem from the Battlefield of Spain' (London, Longmans, Green and Co., 1939); included in *The Collected Poems of Roy Campbell* (London, The Bodley Head, 1957).

MARTÍNEZ NADAL, RAFAEL, introduction to F. García Lorca, *Poems* (London, Dolphin, 1939, 1942).

†*RUBIA BARCIA, J., 'Cómo murió García Lorca', in *Nuestra España*, Havana, no. 2, 1939; in *España libre*, Brooklyn, 1 March 1940, p. 2.

BERGAMÍN, JOSÉ, introduction to Lorca's *El poeta en Nueva York* (Mexico, Séneca, 1940; bilingual edition, New York, W. W. Norton, 1940).

*CROW, JOHN A., 'The Death of García Lorca', in *Modern Language Forum*, Los Angeles, XXV (1940), pp. 177–87.

*RÍO, ANGEL DEL, *Federico García Lorca. Vida y obra* (New York, Hispanic Institute in the United States, 1941), pp. 23–4.

OTERO SECO, ANTONIO, 'Así murió Federico García Lorca', in *Iberia*, Bordeaux, 2e Année, no. 2, May 1947.

*CAMACHO MONTOYA, GUILLERMO, 'Por qué y cómo murió García Lorca', in *El Siglo*, Bogotá, 15 November 1947.

*CHÁVEZ CAMACHO, ARMANDO, 'La verdad sobre España', in *El Universal gráfico*, Mexico, 2 January 1948.

*SERRANO SUÑER, RAMÓN, ['Sobre la muerte del poeta García Lorca'], in *El Universal gráfico*, Mexico, 3 May 1948.

*PEMÁN, JOSÉ MARÍA, 'García Lorca', in *ABC*, 5 December 1948.

†*BRENAN, GERALD, *The Face of Spain* (London, Turnstile Press, 1950; Penguin Books, 1965), Chapter VI.

†*BRENAN, GERALD, 'La vérité sur la mort de Lorca', in *Les Nouvelles Littéraires*, Paris, 31 May 1951.

†*COUFFON, CLAUDE, 'Ce que fut la mort de Federico García Lorca', in *Le Figaro Littéraire*, Paris, no. 278, 18 August 1951.

†*COUFFON, CLAUDE, *El crimen fue en Granada* (University of Quito, Ecuador, 1953).

*GARCÍA SERRANO, RAFAEL, *Bailando hacia la Cruz del Sur* (Madrid, Gráficas Cies, 1953), pp. 330–1.

— 'La mort de Lorca', in *L'Express*, Paris, 24 August 1956, p. 17. First publication of extracts from Lorca's death certificate.

†*SCHONBERG, JEAN-LOUIS, 'Enfin, la vérité sur la mort de Lorca. Un assassinat, certes, mais dont la politique n'a pas été la mobile', in *Le Figaro Littéraire*, Paris, no. 545, 29 September 1956.

†*SCHONBERG, JEAN-LOUIS, and COUFFON, CLAUDE, ['Enfin, la vérité sur la mort de Lorca: une lettre de M. Claude Couffon et la réponse de M. J.-L. Schonberg'], in *Le Figaro Littéraire*, 13 October 1956.

*— '*Le Figaro Littéraire* confiesa: "¡En fin, la verdad sobre la muerte de García Lorca!" "No fue la política el móvil"', in *La estafeta literaria*, Madrid, 13 October 1956, p. 1.

†CHABROL, JEAN-PIERRE, 'Grenade a retrouvé les assassins de Lorca', in *Les Lettres Françaises*, Paris, 18 October 1956.

*RIDRUEJO, DIONISIO, Letter to the Minister of Tourism and Information in Madrid, Gabriel Arias Salgado, 22 October 1956, reproduced by Fernando Vázquez Ocaña, *García Lorca. Vida, cántico y muerte* (Mexico, Grijalbo, 1957), pp. 381–2.

†*SCHONBERG, JEAN-LOUIS, *Federico García Lorca. L'homme— L'oeuvre* (Paris, Plon, 1956) Chapter VI.

*M. A., 'A morte de García Lorca', in *Brotéria*, Lisbon, LXIII, November 1956, pp. 480–1.

†*RIVAS CHERIF, CIPRIANO, 'Poesía y drama del gran Federico. La muerte y pasión de García Lorca', in *Excelsior*, Mexico, 6, 13 and 27 January 1957. The first two articles reproduce a conversation with Luis Rosales.

†ALBE [R. JOOSTENS], *Andalusisch Dagboek* (Herk-de-Stad, Belgium, Drukkerij-Uitgeverij Brems, no date but probably 1958).

†*MORA GUARNIDO, JOSÉ, *Federico García Lorca. Testimonio para una biografía* (Buenos Aires, Losada, 1958), Chapter XVIII.

†*COBELLI, ENZO, *García Lorca* (Mantua, Editrice La Gonzaghiana, 2nd edition, May 1954), pp. 64–81.

†*SCHONBERG, JEAN-LOUIS, *Federico García Lorca. El hombre-La obra* (Mexico, Compañía General de Ediciones, 1959), Ch. VI.

†*PIERINI, FRANCO, 'Incontro a Spoleto con la sorella di Federico. Quella notte a Granada. Conchita García Lorca ha raccontato per la prima volta ció che avvenne quando alla famiglia vennero a dire: "lo hanno portato via"', in *L'Europeo,* 17 July 1960.

*WERRIE, PAUL, 'Lettre d'Espagne: García Lorca a reparu sur scène à Madrid', in *Ecrits de Paris,* February 1961, pp. 91–95.

— 'Dramma in Andalusia: Ecco la morte di García Lorca', in *Epoca,* Milan, 2 July 1961.

†LORENZ, GÜNTER, *Federico García Lorca* (Karlsruhe, Stahlberg, 1961), pp. 133–68.

*THOMAS, HUGH, *The Spanish Civil War* (London, Eyre and Spottis-woode, 1961), pp. 169–70.

†*COUFFON, CLAUDE, 'Le crime a eu lieu à Grenade . . .', included in *A Grenade, sur les pas de García Lorca* (Paris, Seghers, 1962), pp. 59–123. The definitive version of Couffon's earlier article. There is a recent Spanish-language edition of this book: Claude Couffon, *Granada y García Lorca,* translated by Bernard Kordon (Buenos Aires, Losada, 1967).

BELAMICH, ANDRÉ, 'Sur la mort de Lorca et ses causes', in *Lorca* (Paris, Gallimard, 1962), pp. 254–58.

†*MARTÍNEZ NADAL, RAFAEL, 'El último día de Federico García Lorca en Madrid', in *Residencia. Revista de la Residencia de Estudiantes,* com-memorative issue published in Mexico, December 1963. Martínez Nadal has reprinted the article in *'El público': amor, teatro y caballos en la obra de Federico García Lorca* (Oxford, The Dolphin Book Co. Ltd., 1970), pp. 9–15.

SOUTHWORTH, HERBERT R., *Le mythe de la Croisade de Franco* (Paris, Ruedo ibérico, 1964), pp. 119–22 and 130–31.

*SAINT-PAULIEN, 'Sur la vie et la mort de Federico García Lorca', in *Cahiers des Amis de Robert Brasillach,* Lausanne, no. 10, Noël 1964, pp. 7–10. Reproduced with title 'Comparer la mort de García Lorca à celle de Brasillach constitue un blasphème' (Saint-Paulien), in *Rivarol,* Paris, 14 January 1965.

*— 'Nuestro entrañable Federico García Lorca, el poeta en Nueva York . . .', in *La estafeta literaria,* Madrid, no. 314, 27 March 1965, p. 36.

*GARCÍA SERRANO, RAFAEL, 'Nota para Madame Auclair', in *ABC,* Madrid, 7 May 1965.

†*CELAYA, GABRIEL, 'Un recuerdo de Federico García Lorca', in *Realidad. Revista de cultura y política,* Rome, no. 9, April 1966.

†*RODRÍGUEZ ESPINOSA, ANTONIO, 'Souvenirs d'un vieil ami', fragments from the memoirs of Lorca's first school-teacher, translated by

Marie Laffranque and published in her *Federico García Lorca* (Paris, Seghers Collection 'Théâtre de tous les temps', 1966), pp. 107-10.

†LAFFRANQUE, MARIE, 'Lorca, trienta años después. 1936–1966', in *Le Socialiste*, Paris, 19 August 1966.

*— *Crónica de la guerra española. No apta para irreconciliables* (Buenos Aires, Editorial Codex, no. 10, October 1966), pp. 224–5, 227, 237–8.

*NEVILLE, EDGAR, 'La obra de Federico, bien nacional', in *ABC*, Madrid, 6 November 1966, p. 2.

*SCHONBERG, JEAN-LOUIS, *A la recherche de Lorca* (Neuchâtel, A la Baconnière, 1966), Ch. VI.

PAYNE, STANLEY, *Politics and the Military in Modern Spain* (Stanford University Press and Oxford, 1967), pp. 416–17.

*AUCLAIR, MARCELLE, *Enfances et mort de Garcia Lorca* (Paris, Seuil, 1968), pp. 359–421 and appendices.

†*GIBSON, IAN, *La represión nacionalista de Granada en 1936 y la muerte de Federico García Lorca* (Paris, Ruedo ibérico, 1971).

GARCÍA LORCA, FRANCISCO, interview with Max Aub reproduced by the latter in his *La gallina ciega* (Mexico, Joaquín Mortiz, December 1971), pp. 243–6.

†ROSALES, LUIS, interview with René Arteaga entitled 'Eran 50 o 60 'Patriotas' los que fueron por García Lorca', in *Excelsior*, Mexico, 13 January 1972.

*APOSTÚA, LUIS, 'Jornada española', in *Ya*, Madrid, 24 March 1972, p. 5.

*GIBELLO, ANTONIO, 'García Lorca y Luis Apostúa', in *El Alcázar*, Madrid, 24 March 1972, p. 2.

*— '¿Qué pretenden?', in *Arriba*, Madrid, 25 March 1972, p. 3.

*APOSTÚA, LUIS, 'Jornada española', in *Ya*, 25 March 1972, p. 5.

*— 'Esto pretendemos', in *Ya*, 26 March 1972.

*GIBELLO, ANTONIO, 'La verdad ocultada', in *El Alcázar*, 27 March 1972, p. 3.

*ROMERO, EMILIO, 'La Guinda', in *Pueblo*, Madrid, 27 March 1972.

†*ROSALES, LUIS, ['Carta de Luis Rosales'], in *ABC*, Madrid, 29 March 1972, p. 14.

†GIBSON, IAN, 'The Murder of a Genius', in *The Guardian*, London, 17 April 1972.

GRANELL, E. F., 'Lorca, víctima marcada por la Falange', in *España libre*, New York, March–April 1972.

*VILA-SAN-JUAN, JOSÉ LUIS, '¿Quién mató a Federico García Lorca?', Chapter Six of *¿Así fue? Enigmas de la guerra civil española* (Barcelona, Nauta, 1971, appeared April 1972), pp. 104–18. The chapter was reproduced in *Sábado gráfico*, Madrid, no. 790, 22 July 1972, pp. 67–71.

†*ROSALES, LUIS, interview with Manolo Alcalá entitled 'Luis Rosales recuerda los últimos días de Federico García Lorca', in *Informaciones*, Madrid, 17 August 1972, pp. 12–13.

†ROSALES, LUIS, interview with Tico Medina entitled 'Introducción a la muerte de Federico García Lorca', in *ABC*, Madrid, 20 August 1972.

*PEMÁN, JOSÉ MARÍA, 'Las razones de la sinrazón', in *ABC*, Madrid, 23 September 1972.

*—, 'En torno a la muerte de García Lorca', in *Sábado gráfico*, Madrid, 21 October 1972.

Index

NOTE: In Spanish surnames the father's name is followed by that of the mother. Often the mother's name is dropped but if the patronym is more common than the mother's name, as is the case with Federico Garcia Lorca, the tendency is to use the latter. Most surnames in this index, however, are listed under the patronym, i.e. Luis Rosales Camacho will be found under 'R', as Rosales Camacho, Luis.